the Pastry Queen

the Pastry Queen

Rebecca Rather

with alison oresman

photography by Laurie Smith

royally good recipes from the
Texas Hill Country's
Rather Sweet
Bakery & Café

TEN SPEED PRESS
Berkeley | Toronto

Ten Speed Press
Box 7123
Berkeley, California 94707
www.tenspeed.com

Distributed in Australia by Simon & Schuster
Australia, in Canada by Ten Speed Press Canada,
in New Zealand by Southern Publishers Group, in
South Africa by Real Books, and in the United
Kingdom and Europe by Publishers Group UK.

Cover and book design by Toni Tajima

Library of Congress Cataloging-in-Publication
Data on file with publisher

ISBN-10: 1-58008-562-8
ISBN-13: 978-1-58008-562-5

Printed in China

5 6 7 8 9 10 — 10 09 08 07 06

To my mother, for telling me I could do anything;
my father, for instilling in me a strong work ethic;
and my beautiful daughter, Frances, for putting up with
years of living under and around my pastry table.

—R.R.

To Warren, for his unwavering support and
his good-natured acceptance of the extra ten pounds
gained in the line of duty as principal taste tester.
To Danny and Callie, for being their lovable selves.

—A.O.

★ Contents ★

Acknowledgments xi

BREAKFAST EATS, MUFFINS, AND SCONES 6

Jailhouse Potato-Cinnamon Rolls **8**

Fresh Ginger-Pear Quick Bread **11**

Eddie's Autumn Pumpkin Bread with Pecan Streusel Topping **12**

Jonnie's Breakfast Granola **13**

Kolaches **15**

Mother's Day Pancakes **18**

Individual Baked Omelets **19**

Crème Brûlée French Toast **20**

Banana Bran Muffins **21**

Peach Jam Scones **22**

Chocolate Chip Scones **23**

Apple-Smoked Bacon and Cheddar Scones **24**

Essence of Orange Muffins **27**

Whole Lemon Muffins **28**

PIES AND TARTS 30

Texas Big Hairs Lemon-Lime Meringue Tarts **32**

Texas Big Hairs Chocolate-Hazelnut Meringue Tarts **36**

Bourbon Pumpkin Tart with Struesel Topping **38**

Fredericksburg Peach Cream Cheese Tart **40**

Frangelico-Hazelnut Fruit Tart **42**

Black-and-White Cranberry Tarts **43**

Buttermilk Pecan Pie **45**

Fourth of July Fried Pies **47**

Aunt Mollie's Coconut Cream Pie **50**

Chef Mark's Southern Comfort Apple Pie **53**

Silken Chocolate-Walnut Tart **55**

Grasshopper Pie **56**

EVERYDAY DESSERTS AND CANDIES 58

Emergency Fruit Crostatas **61**

Petite Pavlovas with Lemon Cream and Fresh Fruit **64**

Hill Country Peach Cobbler **65**

Individual Pear-Maple Cobblers **66**

Mexican Chocolate Fudge-Pecan Cake **67**

Mahogany Cake **70**

Orange-Date Bundt Cake **72**

Totally Rummy Pound Cake **74**

Glazed Lemon-Cranberry Loaf Cake **76**

Oatmeal Crisps **77**

Cappuccino Cheesecakes **78**

Mrs. Chisholm's Divinity **79**

Coconut Cream Flan **80**

Texas Pralines **81**

DESSERTS FOR SPECIAL OCCASIONS AND HOLIDAYS 82

American Beauty Cake **84**

Tuxedo Cake **86**

Larger-than-Life Praline Cheesecake **89**

Bananas Foster Shortcakes **90**

Strawberry Ricotta Cake **92**

Peach Queen Cake with Dulce de Leche Buttercream Frosting **94**

Cream-Filled Pumpkin Roll **97**

Mini Apple-Cinnamon Loaves with Calvados Glaze **99**

Espresso Crème Brûlée **100**

Toffee Bar Brownie Torte **102**

Tiramisù with Homemade Ladyfingers **104**

Dulce de Leche–Arborio Rice Pudding **106**

Muchas Leches Cake with Sugared Almonds **109**

Almond Bliss German Chocolate Cake **112**

Seventh Heaven Chocolate Truffle Cake **114**

White Chocolate–Snickers Mousse **118**

White-on-White Buttermilk Cake with Jack Daniel's Buttercream **120**

Tropical Carrot Cake with Coconut–Cream Cheese Frosting **122**

COOKIES, BROWNIES, AND BARS 124

My Favorite Chocolate Chip Cookies **127**

Triple-Threat Chocolate Chip Cookies **128**

Sugar Saucers **130**

Chock-Full-of-Nuts Cookies **132**

Café Chocolate-Cherry Bites **133**

Caramel-Filled Brownies **135**

Turbo-Charged Brownies with Praline Topping **137**

Double-Ginger Chews **140**

Ruby-Flecked Florentines **141**

Dulce de Leche Macaroons **142**

Snow-Tipped Sand Tarts **143**

Texas Pecan Pie Bars **145**

Blackberry Pie Bars **146**

Lemon-Champagne Bars with
   Strawberry Brûlée Topping **147**

Bunches of Biscotti **148**

LUNCHES AND LIGHT DINNERS 150

Beer Bread **153**

Rocket Rolls **154**

Nuevo Texas Waldorf Salad **156**

Rather Rich Corn Muffins **157**

Apple-Almond Chicken Salad with
   Homemade Mayonnaise **158**

Field Greens with Spiced Pecans,
   Goat Cheese, and Balsamic
   Vinaigrette **160**

Chicken Satay with Yogurt-Cucumber
   Dipping Sauce **162**

Caesar Salad Pizzas **163**

Wild Rice and Chickpea Salad **167**

Wild Mushroom Soup **168**

Curried Butternut Squash Soup **169**

Texas Tortilla Soup **170**

Gulf Coast Shrimp Quesadillas **172**

Brie and Brisket Quesadillas **174**

Rather Sweet Bread and Cheese
   Board **177**

Green Chile Crab Cakes with Tomatillo
   Salsa **178**

All-Sold-Out Chicken Pot Pies **180**

Prosciutto Tostadas with Shrimp and
   Parsley **183**

King Ranch Casserole **184**

Ground Beef Gorditas **186**

Savory Crab and Shrimp
   Cheesecake **188**

TREATS KIDS LOVE 190

Sticky-Fingers Bars **193**

Ginger People **194**

Franny's Fave Peanut Butter–
   Banana Cream Pie with Hot Fudge
   Sauce **196**

Peanut Buttercups with Peanut-
   Penuche Icing **200**

PB&J Cookies with Honey-Roasted
   Peanuts **203**

Mars Pies **204**

Pretty-in-Pink Shortbread Pigs **206**

Maple-Glazed Oatmeal Cookies **209**

Jubilation Granola Chews **210**

Pumpkin Yumkins **211**

DRINKS 212

Watermelon Lemonade **214**

Frothy Vanilla Milk **215**

Tommye Wood's Milk (Sure Packs a)
   Punch **216**

Rather Sweet Sangria **217**

Hill Country Guanabana
   Margaritas **218**

No Bull Bloody Marys **219**

Index 220

Acknowledgments

Most mornings I smell like an Apple-Smoked Bacon and Cheddar Scone as I drive my daughter Frances to school. I'm often at the bakery for a few hours before her classes start, and lately, she has taken to spraying me with perfume to kill the smell. My daughter knows better than anyone that running a bakery is all-consuming. She knows that getting away isn't easy, either—the smells endure long after you've closed the bakery door. I want to thank her for her patience with me as I worked to raise her and run a business at the same time. Being a single mother isn't always easy, and neither is being the daughter of one. Frances has helped me out of more last-minute jams than I can count, including delivering countless loaves of bread to restaurants, pitching in to produce seven hundred fried pies for a local festival, and working at the bakery's counter. I love you, Franny.

When I first told my friend and colleague Dan Kamp that I was planning to open a new bakery in Fredericksburg, he said, "I believe in you. You can do this, but you can't do it alone. You need help with the business side. I know we can make this work together." Three years later, we are, and he was right. I couldn't have done it without him. Thank you to my wonderful staff: Marcella, my first pastry person; Beatrice; and Thomas—they do breakfast, they do it all. Nancy and Wanda run the dining room with efficiency and charm. My eleven-year-old sidekick, Graham Comstock, is a big help in the kitchen and has already mastered the art of making a fine lemon tart. And I can never forget all the teens who over the years have handled the crowds at the bakery counter while keeping their cool and maintaining their sense of humor.

I want to thank the people of Fredericksburg for supporting us, too—from our loyal customers, many of whom have become my friends, to the shopkeepers who send customers our way. A few special Fredericksburg friends deserve particular mention for supporting me as a businesswoman and a friend: Jan Alexander, Lauren Cone, Lane Hutchins, Kim Robertson, and Deann Sears. Thanks, too, to my Austin friends Melanie Adler and Kristen Ohmstede. My friend, writer and chef Paula Disbrowe, gets extra thanks for always being there for me.

Thanks to *Texas Monthly* senior food editor Pat Sharpe, and to Virginia Wood at the *Austin Chronicle*. They've always believed in me and backed it up with the written word.

My publicist Pam Blanton's enthusiasm and great ideas have helped me many times over the years. And thanks to my agent Doe Coover for taking on a first timer and getting me my first book contract. A special thanks to my friend and colleague Paige Conn, who took time out of her busy life as a teacher and mother to test almost every recipe in the book. Her input was invaluable.

It was a joy to work with talented food photographer Laurie Smith, who managed to make my food look great while simultaneously making the hard work of the photo shoot seem fun. My friend Barbara Parrish used her impeccable taste to assemble a beautiful array of props from her own home and nearby kitchen and antique stores for the photo shoot. Her expert eye and organizational skills contributed greatly to the finished product. Working with Lauren Bade, The Homestead, and Der Küchen Laden was a pleasure, too.

Ten Speed associate art director and designer Toni Tajima has perfectly captured my style and life's work in these pages.

This book never would have happened without "my writer," Alison Oresman, who spearheaded this project from start to finish. We met on horseback at a cattle drive and cowboy cookout arranged for a culinary professionals' conference. When she told me she was a writer, I said I'd always wanted to write a book, and that I already had a name and a table of contents in mind. "I'm looking for a new project," she said. Within weeks she had flown from her Washington State home to my Austin bakery to collect recipes. Within a few months she had found our agent. When I moved the business from Austin to Fredericksburg, she rewrote the book proposal with the new bakery in mind. We spent hours on the phone, discussing recipes, and often I dictated recipes to her as I made them. Many times I gave her recipes scaled for a large bakery. She scaled them down and tested them all, making sure they were accessible for home cooks. Getting the book out has been a longer process than either of us expected. We always knew we'd come away with a great book, but I don't think we realized we'd build such an enduring friendship. I'm eternally grateful for both.

—R.R.

I love to make dessert because I love to eat dessert. When I met Rebecca and learned she needed help writing a dessert cookbook, I couldn't believe my luck. A chance to make dessert as part of my professional life sounded fabulous. Four years later, people ask me, "Aren't you tired of making dessert?" I am not. I love to sample the dough; I love the smell of something, anything sweet baking in the oven; and I love the reception I get when I show up with dessert in hand.

So the biggest thank you goes to Rebecca, for giving me the chance to do something for a living that I would happily do for free. Not only has it been fun, it has been educational. (My parents would approve.) Few amateur bakers have the opportunity to work so closely with a professional. Rebecca taught me to lose my fear of yeast dough, to loosen up in the kitchen, and to change and refine recipes without trepidation. She has shared her secrets with generosity and humor.

Thanks to my Hilltop Community neighbors in Bellevue—the finest dessert guinea pigs anywhere—for their honest input and unfaltering support. I promise I will keep bringing desserts to summertime potlucks.

Thanks to Doe Coover for her expert guidance, for her razor-sharp editing pen, and for championing the book until it sold.

Thanks to Ten Speed editor Lorena Jones, who brought a steady hand, excellent judgment, and a winning combination of compassion and toughness to the project.

Thanks to my friends Emily Anderson, Marcia Crosetto, Jane Dudley, Marsha MacInnis, Norma Rosenthal, Kristen Webb, and Colleen Willoughby for listening to me talk endlessly about the book without once telling me to shut up. (Extra kudos to Kristen, Emily, Norma, and my mother for helping me to test recipes.) Thanks to my friends at the Washington Women's Foundation for continually asking how the book was going, no matter how long the process seemed to drag out. And Samadhi Yoga's Kathleen Hunt and my felow 9AM–class yoginis helped me stay centered throughout the writing process.

I loved working with tester Paige Conn, whose precision and ideas made me feel like she was just around the corner instead of halfway across the country.

A special thanks to Marcia Houdek-Jimenez for being so good at what she does. I couldn't have done it without her. And thanks to everyone at Rather Sweet in Fredericksburg for putting up with my endless phone calls and numerous visits.

Thanks to my mom, Patricia Oresman, for teaching me how to bake a cake at a young age and for coming all the way from New York City for a weeklong baking marathon during the last stages of writing this book. And thanks to my dad, Donald Oresman, for contributing the majority of books to what has to be one of the most extensive private cookbook collections this side of the Mississippi.

Finally, lots of love and appreciation for my husband Warren, whose unflagging support allows me to achieve the impossible. More love to my daughter, Callie, who has helped with editing and record-keeping, and to my son, Danny, who is a discerning dessert critic.

—A.O.

Introduction

New customers poke their heads through the door of my Fredericksburg, Texas, bakery and ask, "Where's the Pastry Queen? I want to meet the Pastry Queen." They're probably surprised when I come out in my red high-top sneakers and baggy chef's pants. What do they expect, Texas-style royalty? You know the stereotype: a makeup-laden, frosted blonde with gigantic hair. (Instead, they get me—tall, auburn, and sassy with just enough of a drawl to brand me as a born-and-bred Texas girl.) And just for the record, the biggest hair anyone ever will see in my bakery sits under the counter, not behind it—on my Texas Big Hairs Lemon-Lime Meringue Tarts (page 32), topped with a wild, spiky mass of meringue.

So why the Pastry Queen? It started years ago when a bunch of female pastry chefs started going out for monthly dinners. We always had a good time, though truthfully, sometimes we got a little rowdy. Virginia Wood, longtime food columnist for the *Austin Chronicle*, reported on our monthly get-togethers and dubbed us the Pastry Queens. One by one, the women in the group dropped out of the baking business until finally, I was the only one left. The dinners were forgotten, but the name lived on. Virginia referred to me as the Pastry Queen whenever she mentioned me in print. The name caught on. My onetime business partner started using it, too. In 1999, when we opened our business, Rather Sweet Bakery, in Austin, he had THE PASTRY QUEEN printed in red on the front window with a little spiked crown hovering above it. I've since moved my bakery to a larger space in Fredericksburg, a small tourist town about seventy-five miles west of Austin. Naturally, the Pastry Queen's crown moved with me to my new place, Rather Sweet Bakery and Café.

I certainly don't feel like a queen, or even a princess—especially when I'm scrubbing the floor of my bakery at 10:00 P.M. Owning a business means getting up at 4:00 A.M. to start the focaccia for lunchtime sandwiches or staying long after closing to get a jump on the breakfast orders I fill for several local bed-and-breakfasts. It means counting the day's receipts and worrying about tomorrow's deliveries, making sure the early morning shift is covered when my counter help calls in sick, and figuring out how to fix the Hobart mixer when it jams. Then there's the food! I do everything from scratch: I make my own mayonnaise, salsa, and even the fruit fillings for my pastries. Every night I make a pot of homemade chicken stock for the next day's soup and conjure up ideas for my ever-changing luncheon special.

I'm always on the lookout for ways to improve. I change recipes—even my own—with the wave of a spatula, if I think it will make them better. Sometimes I get cantankerous and think, *No recipe is going to tell me what to do.* If there's one rule I follow, it's this: don't be afraid to change. I love to experiment. Creating new recipes means taking risks, trying things out.

At Rather Sweet, we do more than dessert. We serve both breakfast and lunch and, on weekends, dinner. Bleary-eyed physicians push through the door at 7:00 A.M. and peer into our glass cases stuffed with rows of gooey cinnamon rolls, oversize scones, and fat muffins. Sometimes, depending on my mood, I make delicate Whole Lemon Muffins or Essence of Orange Muffins glazed with citrus icing. Our hearty Apple-Smoked Bacon and Cheddar Scones sell out most days (see pages 28, 27, and 24).

I always have a breakfast special and a couple of trays of kolaches (page 15). Kolaches are big with Texans, and we make them in both sweet and savory versions. The center of each pillowy, white yeast-bread square is filled with sausage, pineapple, or fresh peaches. Still, some of my customers have eyes only for Texas-size Jailhouse Potato-Cinnamon Rolls (page 8) slathered with creamy white icing and fragrant with cinnamon. Once I saw a fight erupt over the last one in the case.

At lunchtime we crank up the music—maybe it's the Gypsy Kings or Asleep at the Wheel—and start cranking out sandwiches made with our own focaccia or bullet-shaped Rocket Rolls (page 150). Brushed before baking with olive oil to give them shiny tops, Rocket Rolls are lightly sweetened egg bread similar to challah. My lunchtime specials range from All-Sold-Out Chicken Pot Pies (page 176) with a rich and flaky cream cheese crust to Brie and Brisket Quesadillas with fruity barbecue sauce (page 170).

For dessert, there are larger-than-life cookies—what else would we eat in Texas?—and a changing array of bars, cakes, pies, and tarts. Some of my favorites are Sticky-Fingers Bars (page 189), made with Snickers, chopped peanuts, and a layer of bittersweet chocolate; Tropical Carrot Cake with Whipped Coconut–Cream Cheese Frosting (page 114); Black-and-White Cranberry Tarts (page 43), rich chocolate cookie crusts filled with white chocolate, cream, and tangy cranberries; and Turbo-Charged Brownies with Praline Topping (page 134), fudgy, coffee-spiked brownies covered with toasted pecans and caramelized sugar.

In *The Pastry Queen* you won't find a lot of fussy recipes that take hours to construct and decorate. My pastries aren't styled. They are free-form. In fact, I don't like anything that's too perfect. My philosophy is, it's homemade, why hide it? So I shape my spiky-topped meringue lemon-lime tarts with my hands, using my fingers to pull the meringue into a mass of pointy peaks. My Emergency Fruit Crostatas (page 61) are rustic-looking tarts made with dough that I push into shape and top with fruit. To keep the fruit from sliding out, I fold up the sides of the pastry along the edges. (No two are alike.)

Many wonderful books have been written about the technicalities of baking, but mine is informal by design. Baking for me is about having fun and being creative. I don't believe baking is that complicated or has to be that precise, and I don't go strictly by the book. That's why I've written my own. I take recipes and make them mine, and that's what I encourage you to do, too. Make desserts with flavors you like. If you adore hazelnuts, use them, even if the recipe calls for pecans. Get comfortable experimenting with flavors. Play with recipes. I do.

Many of my recipes have been created for the restaurants and catering companies that I've worked for during my fifteen-year career as a pastry chef. Now that I have my own bakery, my customers inspire me. The bed-and-breakfast crowd—there are more B and Bs per capita in Fredericksburg than in any other Texas town—is partial to my breakfast egg muffins—Egg Kolaches with a soft white-bread layer on the bottom and an omelet baked on top. They're like eating a piece of bread along with your eggs. No plate necessary.

My place in Fredericksburg is bigger and more elegant than my first bakery in Austin, where I worked in an open kitchen in the back. Here, there's a courtyard in front, an outdoor fountain, and a covered porch with al fresco seating. My pastry counter stands in a separate room, which is ideal for those who want to grab a treat and go; and there's an adjoining dining room for those who want to sit for a leisurely meal or snack. In my Fredericksburg digs, if you want to see my kitchen, you'll need an invitation!

While my Austin place felt like the *Cheers* of bakeries, with a loyal neighborhood following, my bakery in Fredericksburg—a picturesque town of more than nine thousand in the Texas Hill Country—is more like Mayberry. My customers are part of my extended family.

During one Christmas crunch, VelAnne Howle, who was at the time the mayor of nearby Luckenbach (population 4), saw we were busy and jumped right in. She helped me whip up a batch of Apple-Almond Chicken Salad with Homemade Mayonnaise (page 154). She must have figured her black Stetson was some sort of Texas toque, because she never took it off.

You won't catch me sporting a Stetson at work, but there's no question my baking style has been influenced by my Texas upbringing. I love Texas and the way Texans think. Texas-style means making it better, making it bigger, making it over-the-top. I say: if you are going to make dessert and you are going to eat it, make it as high as it can be, use the best chocolate and the juiciest fruit. I don't do low-fat desserts. If I am going to eat dessert, I want it to be really, really sinful; I want it to be great.

I believe in old-fashioned, from-scratch baking, probably because that's what I learned from my family. My grandmother's counters were lined with pies and cakes—she was a big woman—and one of my aunts baked all of her own bread. My father hunted and cooked whatever he bagged, and my mother was a fine home cook.

I started baking for friends when I was a young girl, specializing in birthday cakes and brownies. When my mother became ill with kidney disease, cooking became a necessity. I took over as family chef.

Baking helped me with my studies, too. I made Mexican Chocolate Fudge–Pecan Cake (page 67) for my high school math teacher because I was in danger of failing his class. Miraculously, I passed. Now I make miniature versions of the same cake for my own bakery. It's a chocolate Bundt cake flavored with Mexican vanilla and a touch of cinnamon, and topped with toasted pecans. A bittersweet chocolate glaze covers the whole dessert.

I baked my way through high school and college and compiled an informal cookbook of my favorite recipes. I always loved baking, but I thought I had to get a real job, so I modeled and ran a clothing store. Then I went into real estate. My open houses were often packed. Now I suspect it was because I always brought homemade desserts. Soon I was baking goodies for many company open houses.

I married and moved to River Oaks, a tony Houston neighborhood. I gave cinnamon rolls to friends for Christmas, and before long they were ordering them by the dozen. My neighbors began asking for wedding cakes.

Finally it hit me: I could make money *and* do something I enjoyed. My friend Mariana Lane and I started a catering company and ran it out of our home kitchens. We did parties for friends and neighbors. We each had a baby. We carried our babies on our hips and cooked. Orders for birthday cakes came pouring in after we showed off a huge carousel cake with marzipan animals that I made for my daughter's birthday. Business boomed. I burned out two Thermador ovens and had to replace all the burners on my stove. My husband was not amused.

I decided to get a real job in catering and worked for two Houston companies in succession. Still, I was pretty green. If my boss used a culinary term I didn't understand, I'd head to the library or bookstore to look it up.

I left my job at the Houston catering company about the same time my divorce was final. I moved into a tiny apartment with my little girl, Frances, and baked for a nearby restaurant in exchange for rent. Later, I got a job as executive pastry chef for one of Houston's top restaurateurs, Tony Vallone. Tony gave me my first chef's jacket. I began to feel like a professional. It was a big responsibility, though, wearing that jacket with my name embroidered on it. I worked for Tony for four years and later was hired to develop and oversee a new line of cafés called Bread Alone for the Austin-based Schlotzsky's, Inc.

Although I've loved every job I've had, I'm happiest now that I have my own bakery. I don't have all the fancy equipment I had at my corporate job. I use many of the same things home bakers have in their own kitchens. (I like to say that everything in my bakery is old except the kids working the front counter.) My background as a self-taught baker gives me a special empathy for home cooks. I know how to keep things clear and simple. Many of my recipes can be made in stages. Like most home cooks, I'm always pressed for time. My knives may not always be sharpened. I have a simple metal table instead of the fabulous marble counter I had at my corporate job.

I buy paint scrapers (to use as bench scrapers for cutting dough, scraping up flour from countertops, and so on) at the hardware store, because paint scrapers are a lot cheaper than the bench scrapers sold at the fancy cookware stores. Don't have a kitchen torch? Use a workshop propane torch to caramelize sugar and brown meringue. Now that I'm running my own business, I find that necessity is the mother of improvisation.

If I make a mistake, I fix it. Almost anything can be saved with whipped cream and powdered sugar. When I was executive pastry chef for Tony Vallone's eponymous Houston-based restaurant, I made a soufflé cake for a group of VIP women. It came out of the oven as flat as a two-by-four. First I panicked, then I topped the fallen cake with whipped cream and rolled it up—and the result became one of the best-selling desserts at the restaurant.

I take a hands-in approach to baking: I love getting my hands in the dough. I like the feel of it. Maybe that's because I wasn't allowed to play in the dirt when I was a child.

When I worked for a large corporation, I could use only so many strawberries per tart, or so many ounces of chocolate. Now that I own my own bakery, I add as many strawberries as I think will look and taste good. As a home cook, you are in charge as well: add more raisins, add more chocolate. Don't skimp.

It's incredible that you can take flour, sugar, water, and eggs and make something that's unbelievably good. I'm living proof that baking is easier than it seems. I'm a self-taught baker and I've made desserts for some of the pickiest celebrities, worked at fancy restaurants, and run bakeries owned by a large corporation. If I can do it, so can you.

Let me know how it all works out. You can email me (pastry_queen@yahoo.com) or my cowriter, Alison Oresman (alison oresman@comcast.net), with questions or comments at any time. We'll get back to you as soon as we can.

BREAKFAST EATS,
Muffins, AND Scones

BREAKFAST AT RATHER SWEET belongs to our regulars. Many gather in groups, and each has a distinct character.

The men's group shows up at 8:00 A.M. There's Rand, a chocolate importer; Bob, owner of a nearby outfitting company; and Bruce, owner of the local feed store. Rand orders kolaches, our fluffy, fruit- or meat-filled rolls, and heads back to my kitchen for a handful of bittersweet chocolate disks to drop into his coffee. Bruce eats a bran muffin and orders a few to take home. And Bob, who is on a low-carb diet, orders bacon and eggs. (He's already lost thirty pounds.) They sit outside by the front door and talk about everything from turkeys—Bruce raises them—to teenagers. I'm sure they discuss everyone who comes in and out of the bakery. They're big gossips.

Joanie, Meagan, and Pam, once a group of four, are mourning the loss of their friend Emily, who recently passed away. They drink green tea, munch on Peach Jam Scones, and eat breakfast tacos. They have intense conversations. I don't like to interrupt.

One of my regulars, Jim, owns a top bed-and-breakfast here. He pops in through the back door to grab a box of baked goodies. His guests find our pastries outside their bedroom doors each morning.

My longtime customers know where everything is. Half of them know how to work the cash register. If things get busy, they'll ring up their food and continue helping anyone else standing in line. If they're short on cash, they sign IOUs. They always pay us back.

I like it that people feel comfortable here. The setting is so beautiful. Outdoor seating in the flower-filled courtyard is open year-round, except in the dead of winter.

I change the breakfast menu seasonally. With fall's approach, I'll make Fresh Ginger-Pear Quick Bread and pumpkin bread again. Spring brings Whole Lemon Muffins. But some things never will leave our menu. I'd be burned at the stake if I stopped making kolaches. Apple-Smoked Bacon and Cheddar Scones are a must-have. Once, when I didn't get around to making cinnamon rolls for two days running, one of my customers bitterly complained that he was losing weight.

Without regulars, Rather Sweet would be out of business. A scary thought, because it's not just a business anymore, it's a community—one that I and everyone who works here have grown to love beyond measure.

Jailhouse Potato-Cinnamon Rolls

Years ago, a close relative sent me a newspaper recipe clipping for potato dinner rolls that were popular with the inmates at Jefferson County Jail. I transformed the recipe into these potato-cinnamon rolls and named them accordingly.

YIELD: 24 LARGE ROLLS

CINNAMON ROLLS

2 medium russet potatoes

1 ounce active dry yeast (4 packets)

³/4 cup plus 1 teaspoon sugar

1 cup (2 sticks) unsalted butter, melted

3 large eggs

2 teaspoons salt

9 cups unbleached flour

FILLING

4 cups pecans

4 cups firmly packed golden brown sugar

2 tablespoons ground cinnamon

1 cup (2 sticks) unsalted butter, melted

ICING

2¹/2 cups powdered sugar

¹/4 cup milk

¹/2 teaspoon vanilla extract

To MAKE THE ROLLS: Fill a large saucepan three-quarters full with water and set on high heat to boil. Peel and quarter the potatoes. Add the potatoes to the water and bring to a second boil. Decrease the heat to medium until the potatoes are simmering. Cook the potatoes until tender when pierced with a fork, about 10 to 15 minutes. Remove the potatoes, reserving 3 cups of the cooking water. Set the potato water aside to cool, until it registers 110° to 115°F on a candy thermometer.

In a large bowl, mash the potatoes—you will have 1¹/2 to 2 cups worth—by hand or using a mixer on medium speed.

In a medium bowl, mix the reserved cooled potato water, yeast, and the 1 teaspoon of sugar. Stir until the yeast has dissolved. Let the mixture rest until foamy, about 5 minutes. In a large bowl, whisk together the potatoes, ³/4 cup sugar, melted butter, eggs, salt, and yeast–potato water. Add the flour in 3-cup increments and stir with a spoon until the flour is incorporated. Place the dough in a large greased bowl. Cover with a damp cloth and leave in a warm place until

(continued)

8

thc dough doubles in size, about 1 to 1½ hours.

Leaving the dough in the bowl, punch it down until it deflates (1 or 2 punches with your fist will do). Cover the bowl with plastic wrap. At this point the dough can be refrigerated until the next day.

To MAKE THE FILLING: Preheat the oven to 350°F. Arrange the pecans on a baking sheet in a single layer and toast them in the oven for 7 to 9 minutes, until golden brown and aromatic. Coarsely chop the pecans.

Combine the brown sugar and cinnamon in a medium bowl.

Remove the dough from the bowl and divide it in half. On a clean, floured surface, roll each half into a ¼-inch-thick rectangle. Spread each rectangle with half of the melted butter. Cover each buttered rectangle with half of the brown sugar mixture. Sprinkle the dough with an even layer of pecans.

Generously grease two 9 by 13-inch disposable pans with butter. Carefully roll up each rectangle, starting on 1 long side of the dough. Using a very sharp serrated knife, cut each roll crosswise in 2-inch slices. Place the slices, cut side down, in the pans, spacing the rolls about 1 inch apart so they have room to expand. Make sure the end flap of each roll is set snugly against a side of the pan, so it does not unravel while rising. Put 8 rolls in each pan. (At this point the rolls can be tightly covered in a layer of plastic wrap and a layer of foil and frozen up to 3 weeks. Defrost the rolls in the refrigerator overnight or for 1 hour at room temperature

and continue following the directions from this point.) Set the rolls in a warm, draft-free place and let them rise until they get puffy, 45 minutes to 1 hour.

Preheat the oven to 375°F. Bake the rolls for 20 to 25 minutes, or until light brown.

To MAKE THE ICING: Combine the powdered sugar, milk, and vanilla in a medium bowl. Spread the icing on top of the rolls while they are still warm. Serve warm or at room temperature.

Rather Sweet Variation

For orange-potato rolls, prepare the dough as directed. For the filling, substitute 4 cups granulated sugar for the brown sugar, omit the cinnamon, and stir in 2 tablespoons grated orange zest. For the icing, substitute ¼ cup freshly squeezed orange juice for the milk, and substitute 1 tablespoon grated orange zest for the vanilla.

Tip: Is it dead or alive? Mixing the yeast with water and sugar and waiting a few minutes to see if it will foam tells you whether the yeast is viable. If it doesn't foam, the yeast is dead and your rolls won't rise. Throw the mixture away and start again with a new batch of yeast. By "proofing," or testing, the yeast's viability, you avoid wasting a whole batch of dough and a whole lot of time.

Fresh Ginger-Pear Quick Bread

Jonnie Stansbury—friend, mentor, and all-around great person—gave me this recipe. She used to own Blair House, a beautiful inn in Wimberley, Texas, just outside of Austin. I'd periodically go there to help her teach cooking classes, a regular offering for her guests. For me, it was a great escape and a great learning experience. She is one of the most knowledgeable chefs I know. This is a rich, dense bread with a deliciously pronounced ginger flavor. Make sure it is completely cool before cutting or it will crumble.

YIELD: 1 LOAF

2 large ripe pears

3 tablespoons 1/8-inch cubes peeled fresh ginger

1/3 cup buttermilk

1 1/2 teaspoons vanilla extract

Zest of 1 lemon, preferably organic

Zest of 1 orange, preferably organic

2 cups all purpose flour

1 teaspoon baking powder

1/2 teaspoon baking soda

1/4 teaspoon salt

1/2 cup (1 stick) unsalted butter, at room temperature

1 cup sugar

2 large eggs, lightly beaten

Preheat the oven to 350°F. Grease a 9 by 5-inch loaf pan with butter, then sprinkle it with all purpose flour. Turn the loaf pan upside down and tap out the excess flour.

Peel, core, and cut the pears into ¼-inch cubes. Stir the pears and ginger together in a medium bowl.

Pour the buttermilk into a measuring cup; stir in the vanilla and all the zest.

In a medium bowl, stir together the flour, baking powder, baking soda, and salt.

Using a mixer fitted with a paddle attachment, beat the butter and sugar in a large bowl on medium-high speed. Add the eggs, one at a time, beating for 20 seconds between each addition. Add the flour mixture alternately with buttermilk mixture, beating on low speed just until combined after each addition. Fold in the ginger-pear mixture.

Pour the batter into the loaf pan and bake about 55 minutes, until a skewer inserted into the middle of the loaf comes out clean. Cool the bread in the pan for 5 minutes. Invert the bread onto a baking rack. Cool the bread completely before covering it tightly with plastic wrap for storage. The bread will keep up to 3 days at room temperature, or up to 3 weeks if frozen. Thaw the bread completely at room temperature and reheat it slowly in a 300°F oven about 15 minutes.

Eddie's Autumn Pumpkin Bread with Pecan Streusel Topping

Steve, a friend and colleague from my Schlotzsky's Bread Alone days, gave me this recipe. He got it from his partner, Eddie, who said it was his favorite recipe. We made it a lot at Bread Alone. I told Eddie that someday I'd write a book and include his recipe. Sadly, he has since died, but every time I make this bread I think of him. This one is for you, Eddie.

A deliciously moist quick bread, this can be baked in loaf or muffin pans. It keeps exceptionally well, making it a perfect traveler for out-of-town Thanksgivings. I always make two loaves and freeze one for an emergency.

YIELD: 2 LOAVES OR 36 MUFFINS

BREAD

- 1½ cups pecan pieces
- 1 cup vegetable oil, such as canola or safflower
- 3 cups sugar
- 4 large eggs
- 1 (15-ounce) can pure pumpkin
- 1 cup water
- 3 cups all purpose flour
- 2 teaspoons baking soda
- 1½ teaspoons ground nutmeg
- 1½ teaspoons ground allspice
- 1½ teaspoons ground cinnamon
- 1½ teaspoons ground cloves
- ½ teaspoon salt

TOPPING

- ½ cup firmly packed golden brown sugar
- ¼ cup (½ stick) unsalted butter, melted and slightly cooled
- 2 teaspoons ground cinnamon
- ½ cup toasted pecan pieces (above)

To MAKE THE BREAD: Preheat the oven to 350°F. Arrange the pecans on a baking sheet in a single layer and toast them in the oven for 7 to 9 minutes, until golden brown and aromatic. Reserve ½ cup of the toasted pecans for the topping.

Grease two 9 by 5-inch loaf pans or 36 standard-size muffin cups with butter or cooking spray.

Whisk the oil and sugar in a large bowl. Add the eggs, pumpkin, and water and whisk until combined. Stir in the flour, baking soda, spices, and salt. Gently stir in 1 cup of the pecan pieces. Pour half of the batter into each loaf pan. For muffins, fill the muffin pans almost to the top with batter.

To MAKE THE TOPPING: Stir the sugar, butter, cinnamon, and the reserved ½ cup of pecan pieces in a medium bowl. Sprinkle the topping liberally over the loaves or the muffins before baking.

Bake the loaves for 1 hour, or until a toothpick inserted into the center comes out clean. Bake the muffins for 30 to 35 minutes.

Tip: Pumpkin is a nutritional powerhouse on its own, but if you want to increase the health quotient here, substitute a cup of whole wheat pastry flour for 1 cup of the all purpose flour.

Jonnie's Breakfast Granola

There's a special place on my pastry counter for beribboned cellophane bags of this granola, a favorite of mine and a multitude of my customers. Some people buy it for gifts, others eat it on the premises with milk and fresh fruit, and customers on the go take it in paper cups with plain yogurt. My friend DeAnn will fuss at me if I don't have it. And I absolutely have to have it for the Wednesday ladies' walking group.

The recipe came from my good friend and mentor, Jonnie Stansbury. Almost any dried fruit works well in this recipe, but my favorites are dried cherries and apricots. Sometimes I feel the need to add dried figs, too. Remember not to add the dried fruit until after the granola has been baked.

YIELD: ABOUT 14 CUPS

3/4 cup vegetable oil, such as canola or safflower

1/2 cup honey

1 cup firmly packed golden brown sugar

1 tablespoon vanilla extract

1/2 teaspoon salt

8 cups old-fashioned rolled oats

1/2 cup sunflower seeds (optional)

1/2 cup sweetened flaked coconut

1 cup sliced almonds

1 cup chopped dried apricots

1 cup dried cherries or cranberries

Preheat the oven to 325°F. In a large saucepan set over medium heat, combine the oil, honey, brown sugar, vanilla, and salt. Stir until the sugar dissolves, about 3 minutes. In a large bowl, combine the oats, sunflower seeds, coconut, and almonds. Pour the warm oil and honey mixture into the oat mixture and stir until combined.

Spread the mixture evenly on two 12 by 17-inch rimmed baking sheets. Bake for 20 minutes, stirring several times, until the granola is a deep golden brown. Cool completely before adding the dried fruit. Store in an airtight container up to 3 weeks.

Kolaches

Soft, sweet, and utterly addictive, kolache yeast buns are big all over Texas. Some say the recipe is Polish; others claim it originated with the Czechs. I've seen it spelled in at least three different ways, but around here at least there seems to be consensus on its pronunciation: koh-LAH-chee.

I started with a recipe given to me by my customer Charlie Stenicka and tweaked it with a little more sugar and a little more yeast until I got it where I wanted it. Kolaches can be flavored in myriad ways with both sweet and savory fillings. My breakfast kolaches are pressed into muffin tins, filled with an omelet mixture, and baked. It's Rather Sweet's answer to that ubiquitous portable breakfast, the Egg McMuffin. Of course, I think ours (see the egg kolache variation on page 19) beats theirs by a mile.

YIELD: 16 TO 18 BUNS

DOUGH

 2 cups milk

 1 (¼-ounce) package active dry yeast

 ½ cup lukewarm water (110° to 115°F)

 ½ cup (1 stick) unsalted butter

 2 large eggs

 1¼ cups sugar

 2 teaspoons salt

 8½ cups all purpose flour

POPPY SEED FILLING

 2 ounces poppy seeds

 ½ cup milk

 ¼ cup sugar

 1 tablespoon Lyle's Golden Syrup (see **Tip** on page 17) or light corn syrup

 1 teaspoon vanilla extract

 ⅛ teaspoon salt

STREUSEL TOPPING

 ½ cup all purpose flour

 ½ cup sugar

 3 tablespoons chilled unsalted butter, cut into small pieces

To make the dough: Warm the milk in a medium saucepan set over medium heat until it begins to steam and form a skin; do not boil. Cool for 10 to 15 minutes until it registers 110° to 115°F on a candy thermometer. Dissolve the yeast in the lukewarm water and let sit until foamy, about 5 minutes. Melt the butter in a microwave or a small saucepan over medium-low heat. Remove from the heat and let cool for 5 minutes.

In a large bowl, whisk together the eggs, sugar, salt, and melted butter. Add the cooled milk and the yeast mixture. Gradually add the flour to the batter, 2 cups at a time. Use your hands or a wooden spoon to mix the flour with the wet ingredients. Keep adding the flour until it is completely incorporated and the dough begins to hold together. Use a light touch; don't pound or overwork the dough or you'll get tough kolaches. The dough will be sticky, moist, and light.

(continued)

Lightly grease a large bowl with vegetable oil. Transfer the dough to the bowl, cover loosely with plastic wrap, and let it rise in a warm, draft-free place until doubled in size, 1 to 2 hours (a dent should remain when the dough is touched lightly). Leaving the dough in the bowl, punch it down until it deflates (1 or 2 punches with your fist will do). Cover the bowl with plastic wrap, and refrigerate for at least 4 hours, or overnight.

To MAKE THE POPPY SEED FILLING: Combine the poppy seeds and milk in a medium saucepan. Cook at medium-low heat for 30 minutes, stirring frequently; do not let the mixture simmer or boil. Add the sugar, syrup, vanilla, and salt; cook on medium-low heat until slightly thickened, about 5 minutes. Let the mixture cool for 5 minutes before filling the kolaches.

Grease a 12 by 17-inch baking sheet with butter or cooking spray. With lightly oiled fingertips, shape the dough into 2½-inch-diameter balls, about the size of small limes. Arrange the balls evenly on the baking pan, 3 across and 6 down.

To fill the kolaches, use your thumb or finger to make a generous indentation in the middle of each dough ball, being sure not to pierce the bottom of the dough. Mound about 1 heaping teaspoonful of poppy seed filling in the indentation. Cover the rolls with a clean tea towel and let the rolls rise in a warm, draft-free place until almost doubled in size, about 1 hour.

Preheat the oven to 375°F.

To MAKE THE STREUSEL TOPPING: Use your hands or a food processor fitted with a metal blade to mix the flour, sugar, and butter until crumbly. Scatter the topping over the kolaches just before baking.

Bake the kolaches until lightly browned on top, 25 to 30 minutes.

Cool the kolaches for 20 minutes before serving. Serve warm or at room temperature.

Rather Sweet Variations

For sausage kolaches, follow the directions above to make the dough. Press it into 5-inch circles. Place 1 tablespoon grated Cheddar in the center of each circle. Roll a medium-size Texas smoked sausage in each round, pigs-in-blankets style. Set on baking sheets, seam side down. Let the rolls rise in a warm place for about 1 hour. Bake as directed above.

For cheese-filled kolaches, combine one 14-ounce carton dry-curd cottage cheese with ¼ cup sugar, the grated zest of 1 lemon, 1 teaspoon vanilla extract, and 2 egg yolks. Make the kolaches as directed above, substituting the cheese filling for the poppy seed filling.

For pineapple-filled kolaches, combine 1 (8-ounce) can crushed pineapple in its own juice with 1 tablespoon cornstarch in a small saucepan. Cook over medium heat until the sauce thickens, about 3 to 5 minutes. Stir in 2 tablespoons unsalted butter. Make the kolaches as directed above, substituting the pineapple filling for the poppy seed filling.

For peach-filled kolaches, combine 2 cups pitted, chopped peaches with 1 cup good-quality peach jam, such as our local Fischer & Wieser, in a medium bowl. Make the kolaches as directed above, substituting 2 tablespoons of the peach mixture for the poppy seed filling.

For egg kolaches, preheat the oven to 375°F. Grease a Texas-size muffin pan (each muffin cup is about 3½ inches in diameter at the top and 2 inches deep) with butter or cooking spray. Pinch off golf ball–size pieces of dough and flatten them into ¼-inch-thick disks large enough to line the bottom of each muffin cup. (Unlike the previous recipes, the dough does not need a second rising once it is pressed into the muffin cups.) Fill each dough-lined muffin cup almost to the top with the Individual Baked Omelets mixture (see page 19). Bake for 20 to 30 minutes, until the egg mixture is set. Makes 6 egg kolaches. Extra kolache dough can be kept in the refrigerator, well wrapped, up to 3 days.

Tip: Lyle's Golden Syrup, imported from Britain, is a pure cane sugar syrup with a mild caramel flavor. It is widely available in grocery stores.

17

Mother's Day Pancakes

My childhood friend Kay Oxford gave me this recipe. (I'm not sure where it came from because Kay's mother, who was also my godmother, scribbled it on a torn piece of brown grocery sack.) Kay and I thought this was the best pancake recipe ever, and I haven't changed my opinion since. My mother was ill through much of my childhood, and I loved fixing her breakfast. I'd make pancakes and bring them to her on a tray with bacon, freshly squeezed orange juice, and a small vase of fresh flowers. I would sit on the end of the bed and watch while she ate.

I make the same pancakes at Rather Sweet, but they aren't the ladylike pancakes I made for Mom. They are generous—five inches across. They come out high and fluffy, and we serve them with warmed maple syrup and fat pats of butter.

YIELD: 15 LARGE PANCAKES

2 large eggs

3 1/2 to 4 cups buttermilk

1 teaspoon baking soda

3 cups all purpose flour

2 teaspoons baking powder

1 teaspoon salt

2 teaspoons sugar

1/4 cup (1/2 stick) unsalted butter, melted

1 teaspoon vanilla extract (optional)

1 tablespoon butter, for frying

Whisk together the eggs and buttermilk in a large bowl. Add the baking soda and whisk until combined. Add the flour, baking powder, salt, and sugar; whisk until just incorporated. Stir in the melted butter and vanilla. Pour the batter into a pitcher. (The batter will keep for 2 to 3 days, covered and refrigerated.)

Set a griddle or frying pan on the stove over medium heat. Add some of the butter for frying; when it begins to foam, pour some of the batter into the pan to make pancakes of whatever size you wish. When bubbles form on top of the pancakes, flip them and cook until the bottoms are golden brown. Serve immediately.

Rather Sweet Variation

Cut 2 ripe bananas into 1/4-inch slices and stir them into the batter. Cook as directed above. To make chocolate-banana pancakes, stir in 1/2 cup mini chocolate chips with the bananas. Your kids will love them.

Tip: I've given a range for the amount of buttermilk in this recipe. If you like thick pancakes, use less buttermilk; for thinner pancakes, use more.

Individual Baked Omelets

Morning best sellers at Rather Sweet, these savory omelets pack a lot of flavor into a deceptively small package. I usually make them with thickly sliced apple-smoked bacon, potato, onion, and bell pepper, but almost any vegetable or meat can be diced or sliced and sautéed before being added to the omelets. Some of my favorite additions include mushrooms, zucchini, green onions, precooked crumbled sausage, and diced ham. Equally good hot out of the oven or served at room temperature, they make a satisfying grab-and-dash breakfast.

YIELD: 6 OMELETS

2 tablespoons unsalted butter

1 medium russet or red-skinned potato, peeled and cut in 1/2-inch dice

1 small yellow onion, diced

1 teaspoon salt

1/2 red bell pepper, seeded and diced

4 slices bacon, cooked and chopped into small pieces

1 fresh tomato, seeded and finely chopped

6 large eggs

1/2 cup heavy whipping cream or half-and-half

1/4 teaspoon freshly ground black pepper

Dash of hot pepper sauce, such as Tabasco (optional)

Preheat the oven to 350°F. Generously butter 6 Texas-size (3½ inches in diameter and 2 inches deep) muffin cups or line them with muffin wrappers. Melt the butter in a medium skillet set over medium heat. Add the potato, onion, and ½ teaspoon of the salt; sauté for about 5 minutes, stirring occasionally. Add the red pepper and sauté for 15 minutes longer, continuing to stir occasionally. Taste to make sure the potato is cooked through; if not, cook for a few minutes longer, until the potato is fully cooked but not mushy. Remove the vegetable mixture from the heat and stir in the bacon and tomato.

Whisk the eggs, cream, remaining ½ teaspoon salt, the pepper, and hot sauce together in a large bowl. Stir in the vegetable mixture. Pour the egg mixture evenly into the muffin cups. (The egg mixture may almost reach the top, which is okay.) Bake for 20 to 30 minutes. Lightly shake the pan; if the omelets look or feel runny in the middle, bake for 5 minutes longer, until firm. Serve warm.

Tip: To cut down on the sautéing time, you may cover the diced potatoes with water in a medium saucepan and heat at a low boil for 5 minutes while you chop the other veggies for the omelet. Drain the potatoes thoroughly and sauté with the rest of the vegetables.

Crème Brûlée French Toast

Challah, a traditional Jewish egg bread, makes this luscious brunch dish very rich. I like to prepare the casserole ahead and refrigerate it the night before it's served. In the morning, I just bake it, caramelize the sugar on top, and bring it on out.

YIELD: 8 TO 10 SERVINGS

1 large loaf of challah bread

8 large egg yolks

4 cups heavy whipping cream or
    half-and-half

3/4 cup plus 3 to 4 tablespoons sugar

1/4 teaspoon salt

1/4 cup vanilla extract

2 tablespoons unsalted butter, melted

Grease a 2½-quart oven-safe casserole or soufflé dish. Slice the challah into ½-inch slices, then into cubes. In a large bowl, whisk together the egg yolks, cream, ¾ cup sugar, salt, vanilla, and butter. Put a quarter of the bread cubes in the casserole dish. Pour in enough of the cream mixture to cover the bread. Using a spoon, press the cream mixture into the bread so that it is thoroughly soaked. Continue layering in the same way until all the bread is soaked with the cream mixture. Cover the casserole tightly with aluminum foil and refrigerate at least 1 hour, or overnight.

Preheat the oven to 325°F. Put the casserole in a larger baking pan and set it in the oven. Pour enough boiling water into the larger pan to reach halfway up the sides of the casserole. Bake for 1½ hours, until the top is light brown and set.

Remove the casserole from the oven and sprinkle the 3 to 4 tablespoons sugar over the top in an even layer. Use a broiler set on high (set the casserole just a few inches from the heat source) or a kitchen torch to cook the topping until the sugar becomes brown and liquefies. (It will harden as it cools.) Serve warm or at room temperature.

Rather Sweet Variation

For individual Crème Brûlée French Toast, layer the bread and cream mixture in 8 to 10 individual greased ramekins. Bake as directed for 1 hour and caramelize the sugar topping.

Banana Bran Muffins

Most commercially made bran muffins turn to sawdust in your mouth and, as far as I can tell, are eaten for health, not pleasure. This is the only lower-fat muffin to be had in my bakery, but it doesn't taste like one. A customer of mine buys several for his wife daily and reports that she becomes exceedingly cranky if she doesn't get her daily muffin fix.

YIELD: 6 TEXAS-SIZE MUFFINS

2 cups high-fiber cereal made with wheat bran, such as **All-Bran**

1 cup skim or low-fat milk

1 large egg

1 large egg white or 3 tablespoons egg substitute

1/2 cup firmly packed golden brown sugar

1/4 cup honey

1/4 cup canola oil

1 ripe to overripe banana, mashed

2 teaspoons vanilla extract

2/3 cup whole wheat pastry flour

2/3 cup all purpose flour

1/2 teaspoon salt

1 tablespoon baking powder

Additional high-fiber cereal, for sprinkling on muffins

Preheat the oven to 375°F. Grease 8 Texas-size (3½ inches in diameter and 2 inches deep) muffin cups with butter or cooking spray or line them with muffin wrappers. Stir together the bran cereal and milk in a large bowl; let the cereal soak for at least 5 minutes. In a separate medium bowl, whisk the egg and egg white until slightly frothy. Stir in the brown sugar, honey, canola oil, banana, and vanilla. Pour the liquid mixture into the bran mixture and stir until combined. Combine the whole wheat and all-purpose flours, salt, and baking powder in a medium bowl. Pour the flour mixture into the bran mixture and stir until the flour is no longer visible, about 15 strokes. Spoon the batter into the muffin pan, filling the cups almost to the top. Decorate the muffin tops with a sprinkling of high-fiber cereal.

Bake for 25 minutes, or until the muffins are golden brown and a toothpick inserted into the middle comes out clean. Serve warm or at room temperature.

Tip: Overripe bananas, with their characteristic deep brown skins, never seem to be on hand when you need them. At other times, you guiltily throw them out once they've turned from golden yellow to an unappetizing brown. But wait! Don't toss them out, toss them into the freezer. Their leathery brown skins act as a protective covering, allowing you to freeze them uncovered for weeks, ready to be defrosted for 30 to 60 seconds in the microwave and used whenever you need them.

Peach Jam Scones

I miss my three roosters, and I'm certain they miss my peach jam scones. The trio started out as a neighbor's Easter chicks, but quickly grew into gorgeous white roosters. They slept in a tree behind the bakery and used to greet me in the early morning hours with wild crowing. They'd flap down to the bakery's back steps and I'd feed them leftover scones and bread. They were particularly partial to peach scones. They were fat and happy and followed me all over the grounds around the bakery. I treated them like pets and they quickly adapted to their new-found roles. They always came when I called. Sadly, they were not as friendly to others. They bothered people at the nearby B and B and had to be relocated to a farm.

YIELD: 8 LARGE SCONES

6 cups all purpose flour

1¼ cups sugar

¼ cup baking powder

¼ teaspoon salt

1½ cups (3 sticks) chilled unsalted butter

1½ to 2 cups buttermilk

½ cup peach jam

3 fresh peaches, peeled and sliced, or
   1 (8-ounce) package frozen peaches,
   defrosted and drained

Preheat the oven to 425°F. In the bowl of a food processor fitted with a metal blade, process the flour, 1 cup of the sugar, the baking powder, and salt for about 30 seconds. Cut the butter into ½-inch cubes and add it to the flour mixture. Pulse about 15 times, until the butter-flour mixture is crumbly. With the processor running, slowly pour 1½ cups buttermilk through the feed tube. Stop the processor as soon as the buttermilk has been added. If the dough has begun to stick together in a ball, remove it. If not, add more buttermilk, 1 tablespoon at a time, and pulse until the dough begins to clump up and form a ball.

Place the dough on a lightly floured flat surface. Use your hands to pat the dough into a ¼-inch-thick rectangle, about 12 by 10 inches. Spread a thin layer of jam lengthwise over half the dough and arrange the peach slices in a single layer on top of the jam. Fold the plain dough over the peaches to make a 12 by 5-inch rectangle with the jam and peaches folded inside. Cut the dough into 8 triangles and sprinkle the top of the scones with the remaining ¼ cup sugar.

Bake on an ungreased baking sheet for 10 to 15 minutes, until the scones are a light golden brown. Serve warm or at room temperature.

Chocolate Chip Scones

The most decadent midmorning snack I can imagine—these scones with a cup of dark roast coffee, served black. One day I tested two versions of the same recipe: one made with butter only, the second with a combination of butter and heavy cream. I brought them out to four of my regular midmorning customers. The butter-cream batch won hands down. I haven't served them any other way since.

YIELD: 8 LARGE SCONES

1 cup pecans

3 cups all purpose flour

1 cup sugar

1/2 teaspoon salt

1 tablespoon baking powder

10 tablespoons chilled unsalted butter

1 teaspoon vanilla extract

1 1/2 to 2 cups heavy whipping cream

1 cup semisweet or bittersweet chocolate chips

Preheat the oven to 350°F. Arrange the pecans on a baking sheet in a single layer and toast them in the oven for 7 to 9 minutes, until golden brown and aromatic. Coarsely chop the pecans.

Increase the oven temperature to 425°F.

Process the flour, sugar, salt, and baking powder for about 30 seconds in the bowl of a food processor fitted with a metal blade. Cut the butter into 1/2-inch cubes and add to the flour mixture. Pulse about 15 times, until the butter-flour mixture is crumbly. Stir the vanilla into the cream.

With the food processor running, slowly pour 1 1/2 cups of the cream through the feed tube. Stop the processor as soon as the cream has been added. If the dough has begun to stick together in a ball, remove it. If not, add more cream, 1 tablespoon at a time, and pulse until the dough it begins to clump up and form a ball.

Place the dough on a lightly floured flat surface and knead in the chocolate chips and pecans, handling the dough as little as possible. Form the dough into a 3/4-inch-thick round. Cut into 8 wedges and bake on an ungreased baking sheet about 10 minutes, until the scones are a light golden brown. Serve warm or at room temperature.

Tip: Scones are best eaten warm out of the oven. They are still good at room temperature for the rest of the day if they've been well wrapped after cooling. Second-day scones, alas, are definitely second-best. They're edible, but nowhere near as good as they were the day before.

Apple-Smoked Bacon and Cheddar Scones

My best-selling scone ever, this is a variation of a recipe I learned when I trained with noted bread maker Daniel Leader, owner of Bread Alone in Boiceville, New York, which is famous for its hearth-baked, European-style bread. Apple-smoked bacon gives these simple scones a distinctive flavor, but bacon of any stripe will work. Cheddar is my favorite, but if I'm out of it, I substitute any cheese I have on hand—Swiss, Monterey Jack, or Havarti. These hearty scones serve as portable breakfasts for several of my morning customers. For an even richer scone, substitute heavy cream for half of the buttermilk.

YIELD: 8 TO 10 SCONES

3 cups all purpose flour

1 tablespoon baking powder

1 teaspoon salt

2 teaspoons freshly ground black pepper

1/2 cup (1 stick) chilled unsalted butter, cut into small cubes

1 1/2 cups grated Cheddar cheese

4 green onions, thinly sliced

10 slices bacon, cooked and chopped into 1-inch pieces

3/4 to 1 1/2 cups buttermilk

1 large egg

2 tablespoons water

Preheat the oven to 400°F. Using a mixer fitted with a paddle attachment, combine the flour, baking powder, salt, and black pepper in a large bowl on low speed. With the mixer running, gradually add the cubes of butter until the mixture is crumbly and studded with flour-butter bits about the size of small peas. Add the grated cheese and mix just until blended. (This can also be done by hand: In a large bowl, stir together the flour, baking powder, salt, and pepper. Gradually cut in the butter with a pastry blender or two knives until the mixture resembles small peas. Stir in the cheese.)

Add the green onions, bacon, and 3/4 cup of the buttermilk to the flour and cheese mixture. Mix by hand just until all the ingredients are incorporated. If the dough is too dry to hold together, use the remaining buttermilk, adding 1 tablespoon at a time, until the dough is pliable and can be formed into a ball. Stir as lightly and as little as possible

(continued)

to ensure a light-textured scone. Remove the dough from the bowl and place it on a lightly floured flat surface. Pat the dough into a ball. Using a well-floured rolling pin, flatten the dough into a circle about 8 inches wide and ½ inch thick. Cut the dough into 8 to 10 equal wedges, depending on the size scone you prefer.

Whisk the egg and water in a small mixing bowl to combine. Brush each wedge with the egg wash. Place the scones on an ungreased baking sheet and bake for 18 to 20 minutes, or until golden brown and no longer sticky in the middle. Serve warm.

Rather Sweet Variation

My customers demand a peppery bacon-Cheddar scone. If you're a freshly ground pepper aficionado, too, add at least 1 more teaspoon to the recipe. (I often use a total of 1 tablespoon of pepper and I prefer it coarsely ground.) To give these a Texas twist, I add 2 chopped and seeded fresh jalapeño peppers.

Essence of Orange Muffins

These delicate, cakey muffins are not too sweet. They are best when warm and fresh, but can be cooled and then frozen up to two weeks. Defrost them at room temperature. Just before you are ready to eat them, warm them in a 325°F oven for 5 to 7 minutes. No need to butter these, they are rich and delicious au naturel. This is one of my favorite master muffin recipes. These muffins are fabulous plain, but I often add a cup of whatever fruit is in season. In the fall, I add fresh cranberries; in late spring it's raspberries or peaches. I make a batch of muffins with blueberries almost daily year-round. Dried fruit works well, too. Dried cranberries and cherries are two of my favorites.

YIELD: ABOUT 8 TEXAS-SIZE MUFFINS

MUFFINS

- 1 cup milk
- 1/2 cup freshly squeezed orange juice
- 1/2 cup sour cream
- 2 large eggs
- 1 cup (2 sticks) unsalted butter, melted and slightly cooled
- 3 1/2 cups all purpose flour
- 1 cup sugar
- 1 1/2 tablespoons baking powder
- 1/2 teaspoon salt
- Zest of 1 orange, preferably organic

ORANGE GLAZE

- 1/4 cup freshly squeezed orange juice
- 1 1/2 cups powdered sugar
- 1 teaspoon grated orange zest, preferably organic

To MAKE THE MUFFINS: Preheat the oven to 350°F. Grease 8 Texas-size (3 1/2 inches in diameter and 2 inches deep) muffin cups with butter or cooking spray or line them with muffin wrappers. Whisk together the milk, orange juice, sour cream, eggs, and butter in a medium mixing bowl. Combine the flour, sugar, baking powder, and salt in a large bowl. Pour the milk mixture into the dry ingredients and stir just until the flour is incorporated. Gently fold the orange zest into the batter.

Spoon the batter into the muffin pan, filling each cup just to the top. Bake the muffins for about 25 minutes, until they are golden brown around the edges and a toothpick inserted into the center comes out clean. Cool the muffins in the pans for about 5 minutes, then transfer them to a cooling rack and glaze. (This would be a great time to eat them, too.)

To MAKE THE GLAZE: Combine the orange juice, powdered sugar, and zest in a medium bowl. Spread the mixture on top of each muffin. Serve warm or at room temperature.

Tip: Although the original recipe calls for whole milk, I have had good results using skim or low-fat milk. Use whatever you have on hand.

Whole Lemon Muffins

It's hard to believe that an entire ground fresh lemon—skin, pith, and all—goes into this recipe, but it gives these nutty muffins a deep lemon flavor. A generous helping of plain yogurt combines with the lemon to make a muffin that is both tangy and sweet, and as far as many of my customers are concerned, utterly irresistible.

YIELD: 12 TEXAS-SIZE MUFFINS

MUFFINS

- 1 medium lemon, preferably organic
- 1 cup walnuts or pecans
- 1 cup (2 sticks) unsalted butter, at room temperature
- 1½ cups sugar
- 3 large eggs
- 2 teaspoons vanilla extract
- 2¾ cups all purpose flour
- 1 teaspoon baking soda
- 1 tablespoon baking powder
- 1 teaspoon salt
- 1⅔ cups (16 ounces) plain whole-milk yogurt

GLAZE

- 1 cup powdered sugar
- Freshly squeezed juice of 2 small lemons
- ½ teaspoon vanilla extract

To MAKE THE MUFFINS: Preheat the oven to 350°F. Grease 8 Texas-size (3½ inches in diameter and 2 inches deep) muffin cups with butter or cooking spray or line them with muffin wrappers.

Wash and dry the lemon, cut it into quarters, and remove the seeds. Process the quartered lemon (skin, pith, and all) in a food processor fitted with a metal blade for 1 minute or more, until it is completely ground up. Scrape the lemon into a medium bowl. Without washing the food processor, add the walnuts and pulse 10 to 12 times. (The nuts will clean the processor bowl.) Add the walnuts to the processed lemon and stir to combine. Set the lemon-nut mixture aside to be used later.

Using a mixer fitted with a paddle attachment, cream the butter in a large bowl on medium-high speed about 1 minute. Scrape down the sides of the bowl. Add the sugar and mix on medium-high until light and fluffy, about 2 minutes. Scrape down the bowl. Add the eggs all at once and beat on medium speed about 1 minute. Add the vanilla and beat on medium for about 30 seconds, until well incorporated. In a medium bowl, stir together the flour, baking soda, baking powder, and salt. Add one-third of the flour mixture to the batter and beat on medium-low speed just until it is incorporated. Add half of the yogurt and beat on medium speed until it is just incorporated. Continue to add the flour mixture and yogurt alternately, beating just long enough to incorporate. (End with the dry ingredients.)

Gently stir in the lemon-nut mixture. Spoon the batter into the muffin pans, filling each cup just to the top. Bake for 30 to 35 minutes, until they are slightly browned and a toothpick inserted into the middle of a muffin comes out clean. Let the muffins cool in their pans about 5 minutes. Remove the muffins from the pans.

To MAKE THE GLAZE: Combine the sugar, lemon juice, and vanilla in a medium bowl. Drizzle the glaze over the warm muffins. The glaze will harden in about 15 minutes.

These are at their very best served warm, but if wrapped tightly in plastic wrap once completely cool they will still taste great for about 3 days. They can be frozen up to 3 weeks.

Tip: Most standard muffin recipes will tell you to fill muffin cups two-thirds of the way to the top. This makes a neat, perfectly rounded muffin. I like to fill mine just to the top of the pan. As the muffins bake, they rise and spill over the edges of the muffin cups to create delectable crunchy edges. (Don't worry; the batter will not spill over the muffin pan, creating a mess on the bottom of your oven. This method will not work with cupcake batter, which rises more and likely *will* end up dripping onto your oven floor.)

PIES and Tarts

PIES AND TARTS remind me of my grandma and all the pies she always had lining her kitchen counter. She loved meringue and was always making numerous varieties of meringue pies. I suppose it's no coincidence that my signature dessert has turned out to be Texas Big Hairs Lemon-Lime Meringue Tarts. Although their oversize meringue tops might be a little too wildly spiky to suit Grandma's old-fashioned sensibilities, I'm certain they would have impressed her, and I'm even more certain she would have devoured hers with gusto.

I never did get any of my grandmother's pie recipes, but I've included some of my nostalgic favorites from childhood: my great-aunt Mollie's Coconut Cream Pie and my own version of Grasshopper Pie, which I grew to love during childhood visits to a Houston department store's restaurant.

At Rather Sweet, the holidays always bring a crush of special orders for pies. I lost count of the number of times I made Silken Chocolate-Walnut Tart last season. Another holiday favorite is the Bourbon Pumpkin Tart with Streusel Topping. Gloria Hall and her husband, Ken—a locally famous high school and college football player who set state records, some of which remain unbroken—always ask to get a call when I make my Texas Big Hairs tarts. I delivered a batch to them on New Year's Eve.

On Independence Day I make Fourth of July Fried Pies, fruit-filled pastries that are deep-fried. One year I made seven hundred of them for a local festival called Night in Old Fredericksburg, held outdoors in the town square. We made them the night before, and the next day, I came down with the flu. My daughter, Frances, and her friend Ashley, along with my business partner, Dan, stood for hours frying them while I sat dazed in a nearby lawn chair. It was a blazing-hot day. We sold all seven hundred pies. We now refer to the ordeal as the Nightmare in Old Fredericksburg. Next year, maybe we'll bring cookies.

Texas Big Hairs
Lemon-Lime Meringue Tarts

These tangy tarts are so-named because their spiky meringue tops remind me of certain local hairstyles. To complete the tarts' signature look, I use a kitchen torch to give the meringue a golden brown glow. One year, I made 250 of these for a Women Chefs and Restaurateurs conference in San Francisco.

As we took off on our flight to California, my partner shot me a wild-eyed look and said, "You don't have that darn torch with you...do you?" She was worried that the torch's propane gas canister would burst and blow up the plane. I let her squirm a little before I answered, "Guess we'll have to pick one up in San Francisco."

Don't worry if you don't have a torch; these can be browned quickly under the broiler. If you want to skip the meringue altogether, the tarts taste fine without it. Be sure to start this dessert with plenty of advance time: the lemon-lime curd must be chilled for at least four hours before the meringue topping is added. I use disposable foil pans with a 1-cup capacity that measure 4 3/8 inches in diameter by 1 3/16 inches high for all of my individual tart and pie recipes. They are available at many grocery stores.

I can't deny my Texas roots, and as a result, I can't resist making BIG baked goods. My signature tarts are no exception. I haven't reduced their size here, because I love how their generous size adds to the drama of their look, and I think you will, too. But unless you're feeding a passel of people with Texas-size appetites, they may prove to be just a bit too much of a good thing. My solution is simple: bring the tarts to the table on a large platter for all to admire. Then, using a serrated knife dipped in a tall glass of warm water, cut them in half and serve.

YIELD: 8 TARTS

CRUST

- 1 1/2 cups pecans or sliced almonds
- 1 cup (2 sticks) unsalted butter, at room temperature, plus about 2 tablespoons for greasing the tart pans
- 1 cup powdered sugar
- 2 teaspoons vanilla extract
- 1 1/2 cups all purpose flour
- 1/4 teaspoon salt

LEMON-LIME CURD

- 10 extra-large eggs yolks (reserve the egg whites for the meringue)
- 1 1/2 cups sugar
- 1/2 cup freshly squeezed lemon juice
- 1/2 cup freshly squeezed lime juice
- Zest of 2 lemons, preferably organic
- 2 tablespoons unsalted butter

MERINGUE

- 10 extra-large egg whites, at room temperature
- 3 cups sugar

To MAKE THE CRUSTS: Preheat the oven to 350°F. Arrange the pecans on a baking sheet in a single layer and toast them in the oven for 7 to 9 minutes, until golden brown and aromatic. (If using almond slices, toast for 5 to 7 minutes.) Coarsely chop the pecans.

With your fingers, butter eight 4⅜-inch, 1-cup capacity disposable foil tartlet pans, using about 2 tablespoons softened unsalted butter total.

Using a mixer fitted with a paddle attachment, cream the butter and sugar in a large bowl on medium-high speed until fluffy, about 3 minutes. Add the vanilla, then gradually add the flour and salt and combine on low speed until incorporated. Add the nuts and mix on low speed just until they are incorporated. Form the dough into

a ball—it will be sticky—and cover it with plastic wrap. Refrigerate at least 30 minutes.

Preheat the oven to 350°F. Remove the dough from the refrigerator, divide into 8 equal portions, and press into the prepared pans, making sure it comes up to the top edge of the pans. If the dough sticks to your hands, dust them with flour as often as necessary.

Bake the crusts about 20 minutes, until golden brown. Remove from the oven and cool at least 30 minutes before filling with lemon-lime curd. (Don't worry if the tart bottoms look wrinkly.) At this point, the crusts can be cooled and stored in airtight containers for up to 2 days.

(continued)

To MAKE THE CURD: Whisk the egg yolks, sugar, lemon juice, lime juice, and zest in the top of a double boiler or in a metal bowl placed over a saucepan filled with 2 inches of simmering water (the simmering water should not touch the bottom of the bowl). Add the butter to the egg yolk mixture and whisk until melted and smooth. Cook about 40 minutes, stirring lightly with a whisk about every 15 minutes. The curd should be thick, resembling the consistency of loose custard. Transfer the warm mixture to a bowl and cover it with plastic wrap, pressing the wrap onto the surface of the curd, sealing it and leaving no air between the wrap and the curd. Refrigerate the curd for at least 4 hours and up to 3 days. For express cooling, freeze it for at least 1 hour.

To MAKE THE MERINGUE: Set a large, perfectly clean metal bowl over a pot of simmering water. Pour in the egg whites and sugar. (If there is a trace of fat in the bowl, the eggs won't reach their proper volume.) Heat the egg whites and sugar while whisking constantly until the sugar melts and there are no visible grains in the meringue. Take a little meringue mixture and rub it between your fingers to make sure all sugar grains have melted. Remove the meringue from over the simmering water and whip it with a mixer fitted with a whisk attachment on low speed for 5 minutes; increase the speed to high and beat 5 minutes longer, until the meringue is stiff and shiny.

Position an oven rack in the center of the oven and preheat the broiler. To assemble the tarts, spoon the chilled lemon-lime curd into the crusts, filling them about three-quarters of the way to the top. Pile the meringue on top of the curd. Style the meringue with your fingers by plucking at it to tease the meringue into jagged spikes. Having a bit of meringue stuck to your fingers will help you form big spikes on the tarts. (For those who do not like the hands-on approach, stroking the meringue with the back of a spoon works almost as well, but is not as much fun.)

Set the tarts on the middle rack of the oven and broil until the meringue topping turns golden brown, about 1 minute. Watch the tarts closely, as they can turn from browned to burned in a matter of seconds. (If you are using a kitchen torch, hold it 2 to 3 inches away from the meringue and move the flame slowly around the meringue until it is browned all over.) The tarts should be served the day they are assembled.

Tip: Zest is the colored, outermost layer of the skin of a citrus fruit. The best zester on the market today is a Microplane, originally created as a woodworking tool and now available at most cookware stores. If you don't have a Microplane, grate the lemons and limes using the smallest holes of a grater. Whatever you use, be sure to stop grating as soon as you reach the bitter white pith underneath the colored part of the fruit. And don't forget to wash the fruit thoroughly before grating or zesting. Zest the fruit whole first, and then squeeze the juice out of it. It is easiest to extract the juice from citrus fruit that is at room temperature.

Texas Big Hairs Chocolate-Hazelnut Meringue Tarts

I've always longed to have one of my desserts featured in Chocolatier *magazine. But when the call came, I faced a dilemma. I wanted them to publish my signature recipe; unfortunately, that recipe, Texas Big Hairs Lemon-Lime Meringue Tarts, doesn't include a drop of chocolate. I stewed for several days before coming up with the solution—a chocolate version of my Big Hairs dessert. I can't believe it took me so long.*

YIELD: 4 TARTS

CRUST

- 1/3 cup hazelnuts
- 1/2 cup (1 stick) unsalted butter, at room temperature, plus 1 tablespoon for greasing the tart pans
- 1/2 cup powdered sugar
- 2 teaspoons Frangelico
- 1/4 teaspoon salt
- 3/4 cup all purpose flour

GANACHE

- 1 cup heavy whipping cream
- 1 tablespoon unsalted butter
- 1/8 teaspoon salt
- 1 vanilla bean, halved lengthwise
- 7 ounces bittersweet chocolate, finely chopped

MERINGUE

- 4 large egg whites, at room temperature
- 3/4 cup sugar

To MAKE THE CRUSTS: Preheat the oven to 350°F. With your fingers, butter four 4³⁄₈-inch, 1-cup capacity disposable foil tartlet pans, using about 1 generous tablespoon softened unsalted butter total.

Arrange the hazelnuts on a baking sheet in a single layer and toast them in the oven for 7 to 9 minutes, until golden brown and aromatic. Immediately gather the nuts in a kitchen towel and rub vigorously to remove the skins. Chop the nuts.

Using a mixer fitted with a paddle attachment, cream the butter and sugar in a large bowl at medium-high speed until fluffy, about 3 minutes. Mix in the Frangelico and salt. Gradually add the flour and combine on low speed until just incorporated. Add the hazelnuts and mix on low speed just until incorporated. Form the dough into a ball, wrap in plastic wrap, and refrigerate for 30 minutes.

Remove the dough from the refrigerator, divide into 4 equal portions, and press into the prepared pans, making the sure the dough comes up to the top edge of the pans.

Bake 12 to 15 minutes, until golden brown. Remove from the oven and cool for 30 minutes on racks. (Don't worry if the tart bottoms look wrinkly.) At this point, the crusts can be cooled and stored in airtight containers for up to 2 days.

To MAKE THE GANACHE: In a heavy-bottomed saucepan, combine the cream, butter, salt, and vanilla bean. Bring to a gentle boil over medium heat. Remove the pan from the heat and take out the vanilla bean halves. Using a paring knife, scrape out the vanilla pod's tiny black beans and add them to the cream mixture. Put the chopped chocolate in a large bowl and pour the hot cream over it. Let stand for 5 minutes, then whisk until smooth. Spoon the ganache into the tart shells, dividing it evenly among them. Refrigerate the tarts at least 30 minutes, or until the ganache is set.

To MAKE THE MERINGUE: Set a large, perfectly clean metal bowl over a pot of simmering water. Pour in the egg whites and sugar. (If there is a trace of fat in the bowl, the eggs won't reach their proper volume.) Heat the egg whites and sugar while whisking constantly until the sugar melts and there are no visible grains in the meringue. Take a little meringue mixture and rub it between your fingers to make sure all sugar grains have melted. Removed the meringue from over the simmering water and whip it with a mixer fitted with a whisk attachment on low speed for 5 minutes; increase the speed to high and beat 5 minutes longer, until the meringue is stiff and shiny.

Position an oven rack in the center of the oven and preheat the broiler. Pile the meringue on top of the tarts, being sure to seal each tart by spreading the meringue to the edge of the pan. Style the meringue with your fingers by plucking at it to tease the meringue into jagged spikes. (For those who do not like the hands-on approach, shape the meringue with the back of a spoon.)

Broil the tarts until the meringue turns golden brown, about 1 minute. Watch the tarts carefully, as they can turn from browned to burned in a matter of seconds. (If you are using a kitchen torch, hold it 2 to 3 inches away from the meringue and move the flame slowly around the meringue until it is browned all over.) The tarts should be served the day they are assembled.

Tip: For this recipe, I get the best results using El Rey 70 percent bittersweet chocolate. Like the lemon-lime tarts, they are large enough to be cut in half to double the servings, if you wish.

Bourbon Pumpkin Tart with Streusel Topping

This is a perfect gift to bring to Grandmother's house on Thanksgiving or Christmas (especially if she enjoys a nip every once in a while). Bourbon adds a delightful depth to the flavor without being overpowering. Easy to make and elegant to look at, this tart will impress the whole family when you show up with it in tow.

YIELD: 8 TO 10 SERVINGS

1 unbaked Lemon Zest Tart Crust, lemon zest omitted (page 40)

PUMPKIN FILLING

1 (15-ounce) can pure pumpkin

3 large eggs

1/2 cup granulated sugar

1/4 cup firmly packed dark brown sugar

1/4 teaspoon salt

1 teaspoon ground cinnamon

1 teaspoon ground ginger

1/2 teaspoon ground cloves

1 tablespoon all purpose flour

1/2 cup heavy whipping cream

1/4 cup bourbon

STREUSEL TOPPING

3/4 cup all purpose flour

1/3 cup granulated sugar

1/3 cup firmly packed dark brown sugar

1/4 teaspoon ground cinnamon

1/2 teaspoon salt

1/2 cup (1 stick) chilled unsalted butter

Line a 10-inch tart pan with the tart dough. Preheat the oven to 350°F.

To make the filling: Spoon the pumpkin into a large bowl. Whisk in the eggs, one at a time, until thoroughly incorporated. Add both sugars, the salt, cinnamon, ginger, cloves, and flour; whisk vigorously about 30 seconds. Whisk in the cream and bourbon.

To make the topping: Combine the flour, both sugars, the cinnamon, and salt in the bowl of a food processor fitted with a metal blade. Cut the butter into small cubes and add to the flour mixture. Pulse 3 to 5 times, until the mixture is crumbly.

Pour the pumpkin mixture into the prepared tart crust. Spoon the streusel topping evenly over the pumpkin mixture. (Don't worry, it won't fall to the bottom of the tart.) Bake for 45 to 50 minutes, until the filling is set. Let the tart cool at least 1 hour before serving. Serve warm or at room temperature.

Tip: Don't overlook the simple efficiency of the wire whisk. You may dismiss it as hopelessly low-tech, but it's easy to use, is less complicated to set up and clean than an electric mixer, and takes up little storage space. I use whisks for everything from whipping together pie fillings to the Herculean job of mixing brownies. There's something magical about the physical labor of baking with simple, "uplugged" tools. It keeps you connected to what you're making and, at least in my case, keeps my arms toned. With a busy bakery and café to run, who has time to go to the gym?

Fredericksburg Peach Cream Cheese Tart

When the local peaches ripen in spring, I top this showstopping tart with peaches. When apples and pears reach their peak in the fall, I use them instead. The fabulously rich cream cheese filling never changes. And no matter what the season, my customers happily devour thick slices of it.

Although this tart has changed considerably over the years, the inspiration for it came from a recipe that originated with Karen Lerner, who hired me for my first professional baking job at A Fare Extraordinaire, almost fifteen years ago.

YIELD: 8 TO 10 SERVINGS

LEMON ZEST TART CRUST

- 2 cups all purpose flour
- 1/2 teaspoon salt
- 1/3 cup sugar
- 1 teaspoon lemon zest, preferably organic
- 2/3 cup (11 tablespoons) chilled unsalted butter
- 1 large egg, lightly beaten
- 1/4 cup chilled heavy whipping cream (more as needed)

CHEESE FILLING

- 8 ounces cream cheese, at room temperature
- 1/2 cup sugar
- 1/2 cup mascarpone cheese
- 1 tablespoon vanilla extract
- 2 large eggs
- 1/2 cup all purpose flour
- 1/4 teaspoon salt

FRUIT TOPPING

- 2 teaspoons ground cinnamon
- 1/2 cup sugar
- 5 to 6 large fresh peaches, pears, or apples

GLAZE

- 1/2 cup apricot jam
- 3 tablespoons brandy
- 3 tablespoons water

To MAKE THE TART CRUST: Using a mixer fitted with a paddle attachment, mix the flour, salt, sugar, and lemon zest in a large bowl on low speed about 30 seconds. Cut the chilled butter into 1/2-inch pieces. Add the butter to the flour mixture and combine on low speed about 1 to 1 1/2 minutes, until the mixture looks crumbly, with bits of dough the size of dried peas.

Whisk the egg with the cream and add to the flour mixture, mixing on low speed until the dough is just combined. Continue mixing for 10 seconds longer. If the dough is too dry to form a ball, add more cream, 1 tablespoon at a time. Gently mold the dough into a disk, wrap in plastic wrap, and refrigerate for at least 1 hour.

Roll the dough out to ⅛-inch thickness on a generously floured flat surface. Fold it over the rolling pin and gently transfer the dough to a 10-inch tart pan. Press it lightly into place.

Preheat the oven to 375°F.

To MAKE THE FILLING: Using a mixer fitted with a paddle attachment, beat the cream cheese and sugar in a large bowl on medium speed until fluffy. Add the mascarpone and vanilla and beat on medium speed until combined. Add the eggs and beat on medium-high for about 1 minute. Add the flour and salt; mix on low speed until combined. Spoon the cream cheese mixture into the unbaked tart crust.

To MAKE THE FRUIT TOPPING: In a medium bowl, stir the cinnamon and sugar together until combined. Peel and pit the peaches, or peel and core the apples or pears, and cut them in half. Score the outside of each half diagonally from top to bottom, starting at the top left corner and making 3 evenly spaced lines ending at the bottom right corner. (Score only 7 halves. The remaining fruit will be diced later.) Repeat with three scores, starting at the top right corner and extending to the bottom left. Coat the fruit in the cinnamon-sugar mixture. Arrange 6 halves around the outer edge of the pie. Place the seventh half in the center. Cut the remaining fruit in ½-inch dice and coat with the remaining cinnamon-sugar mixture. Spoon the diced fruit into the spaces between the fruit halves so that the cream cheese filling is completely covered.

Bake for 50 to 55 minutes.

To MAKE THE GLAZE: About 10 minutes before the tart is finished baking, stir the apricot jam, brandy, and water together in a small saucepan set over medium heat. Continue heating until the mixture thickens slightly, about 5 minutes. Cool for about 5 minutes.

Remove the tart from the oven and brush the glaze over the top. Let cool at least 1 hour before serving. When completely cool, this tart may be tightly covered and refrigerated for up to 2 days. Serve at room temperature.

Frangelico-Hazelnut Fruit Tart

This is a new take on an almond fruit tart we used to make at Anthony's in the 1990s, which I think was adapted from a recipe in Gourmet magazine. Topping this tart with a combination of pears and blueberries gives it a dramatic look that impresses even those who are blasé about dessert.

YIELD: 8 TO 10 SERVINGS

1 Lemon Zest Tart Crust (page 40)

HAZELNUT FILLING

1 cup hazelnuts

1½ cups (3 sticks) unsalted butter, at room temperature

¾ cup sugar

1 large egg

2 teaspoons vanilla extract

5 tablespoons Frangelico

6 tablespoons all purpose flour

¼ teaspoon salt

GLAZED FRUIT TOPPING

½ cup currant jelly

1 tablespoon Frangelico

1 cup fresh blueberries or frozen blueberries, defrosted and drained

2 to 3 ripe pears, peeled, cored, and sliced

Line a 10-inch tart pan with the tart dough.

To MAKE THE HAZELNUT FILLING: Preheat the oven to 350°F. Arrange the hazelnuts on a baking sheet in a single layer and toast them in the oven for 7 to 9 minutes, until golden brown and aromatic. Immediately gather the nuts in a kitchen towel and rub vigorously to remove the skins. Cool the nuts for 5 minutes, then coarsely grind in a food processor.

Using a mixer fitted with a paddle attachment, cream the butter and sugar in a large bowl on medium speed for 1 minute. Add the egg and beat on medium-high about 30 seconds. Add the hazelnuts, vanilla, Frangelico, flour, and salt; mix on low speed just until incorporated.

Spoon the batter into the unbaked crust. Bake about 40 minutes, until the top is brown and puffy. (The tart filling will deflate as the tart cools.) Cool the tart on a rack for 30 minutes.

To MAKE THE GLAZED TOPPING: Combine the currant jelly and Frangelico in a small saucepan set over low heat, stirring until the jelly melts. Use a pastry brush to coat the top of the tart evenly. If you are using defrosted and drained blueberries, arrange them in a single layer on paper towels to absorb the last bit of moisture.

Arrange 1 row of blueberries around the outer edge of the tart. Continue with 2 rows of pear slices set in a pinwheel formation, then pile the rest of the blueberries in the center of the tart. Use a pastry brush to coat the fruit evenly with the jelly glaze.

Refrigerate the tart at least 1 hour, or cover and store up to 2 days in the refrigerator. Serve cool or at room temperature.

Black-and-White Cranberry Tarts

This dessert has evolved from a white chocolate–raspberry tart in a standard butter and flour pie crust, a recipe of forgotten provenance, to a fresh cranberry tart in a chocolate cookie crust. (The raspberry tarts were a favorite of former Texas governor Mark White, who used to request them frequently.) The current version is a great holiday dessert with an unusual bonus: no baking necessary.

YIELD: 8 TARTS

CRUST

1 (16-ounce) package crème filled chocolate cookies (about 33 cookies)

1/2 cup (1 stick) unsalted butter, melted

WHITE CHOCOLATE-CRANBERRY FILLING

16 ounces white chocolate, chopped into small pieces

1 cup heavy whipping cream

1/4 cup (1/2 stick) unsalted butter

2 tablespoons light corn syrup

2 cups fresh cranberries

1/4 cup water

1/4 cup sugar

Mint leaves, for garnish (optional)

To MAKE THE CRUSTS: Process the cookies in a food processor fitted with a metal blade until ground to coarse crumbs. Pour in the melted butter and pulse until the butter is thoroughly combined. Press the mixture over the bottom of eight 4⅜-inch, 1-cup capacity disposable foil tartlet pans.

To MAKE THE FILLING: Put the chopped white chocolate in a large bowl. In a medium saucepan, heat the cream, butter, and corn syrup to the boiling point. Pour the hot cream mixture over the white chocolate and whisk until smooth. Combine the cranberries, water, and sugar in a medium saucepan and warm over low heat about 5 minutes. (Do not let the cranberries get hot enough to pop.) Drain the cranberries well, discarding the liquid. Fold the cranberries into the

(continued)

43

white chocolate mixture and pour evenly into the chocolate tart crusts. Refrigerate at least 2 hours or overnight. Garnish with mint leaves, and serve chilled. I love the dramatic look of a large individual tart, and so do my customers. Nevertheless, you may want to cut the tarts in half to double the servings.

Rather Sweet Variation

Finding fresh cranberries can be difficult in the spring and summer, but that shouldn't stop you from making this tart year-round. Substitute fresh, pitted cherries or raspberries and omit the water and sugar, as well as the step that calls for cooking the cranberries.

Tip: Not to name names, but historically the traditional chocolate crème cookie has been made with hydrogenated oils—a nutritional no-no, food experts say, that may be worse for our hearts than the fats in butter and cream. Why waste calories on man-made stuff that has no taste advantage and is probably worse for your health? Look for Newman's Own brand crème-filled chocolate cookies, with organic ingredients and no hydrogenated oils.

Buttermilk Pecan Pie

Brenda Greene Mitchell and I met when our children attended the same school. She is a for-mer owner of Wunsche Bros. Cafe in Spring, Texas, founded in 1902. According to the cafe's official website, "The Wunsche Brothers, railroad men themselves, built the Wunsche Bros. Hotel and Saloon to accommodate railroad employees overnight. In 1923, Houston and Great Northern (now called Missouri Pacific) moved the Spring railyard to Houston. By 1926 most of the town's wood buildings were salvaged for barn construction and firewood. The Wunsche Bros. Cafe and Saloon was the first two-story building erected in Spring and remains the old-est survivor of the past." The cafe is still open.

Adapted from the Wunsche Bros. Cafe Cookbook, *this is not your average pecan pie. The buttermilk gives the pie a lovely tang and mixes with the other ingredients to form a won-derful bumpy crust on top.*

YIELD: 8 SERVINGS

1 unbaked Basic Pie Crust (page 50)

1½ cups pecan halves

½ cup (1 stick) unsalted butter, at room temperature

1¼ cups granulated sugar

¼ cup firmly packed golden brown sugar

2 teaspoons vanilla extract

3 large eggs

3 tablespoons all purpose flour

½ teaspoon salt

1 cup buttermilk

Position an oven rack in the center of the oven and preheat to 350°F. Line a 9-inch deep-dish pie plate with the pie crust. Arrange the pecans on a baking sheet in a single layer and toast them for 7 to 9 min-utes, until golden brown and aromatic. Chop the pecans coarsely, leaving some in halves and others in quarters. Decrease the oven temperature to 300°F.

Using a mixer fitted with a paddle attach-ment, cream the butter with both sugars in a large bowl on medium-high speed until fluffy. Add the vanilla and then the eggs, one at a time, beating for 20 seconds on medium speed after each addition. Add the flour and salt and beat until incorporated, about 20 seconds. Add the buttermilk and beat for 20 seconds longer, until the batter is well mixed. Stir in the pecans. Pour the batter into the unbaked pie crust and bake for 1 hour and 20 minutes. As the pie cooks, a lovely golden crust will form on top. Cool the pie at least 30 minutes before serving.

Tip: The sugary crust that forms on the top of the pie can make it tricky to cut. Use a very sharp knife to cut through it, and don't worry if it crumbles. Cover and refrigerate the pie up to 3 days if you don't finish it the first time it's served.

Fourth of July Fried Pies

Fried pies have been a Southern tradition for years. I make them every Independence Day and stick little toothpick flags in them. I choose the fruit fillings specifically for their patriotic color scheme. Almost any fruit will do; let your imagination guide you. And see the variations (page 48) for making savory fried pies.

My friend David, who used to supply the coffee at my Austin bakery, told me that his great-aunt and her husband built a business on fried pies. In the early 1900s, they ran a barbecue place in a downtown Dallas penny arcade. A decision to offer dessert in the form of fried pies changed their business forever. Their fried pies became a runaway hit, selling for ten to fifteen cents apiece at the fantastic clip of four hundred a day. The demand was so great that they decided to chuck the barbecue business and concentrate on fried pies.

YIELD: 12 INDIVIDUAL PIES

BLUEBERRY, PEACH, AND CHERRY FILLINGS

- 1/2 pint fresh blueberries
- 1/4 cup blueberry preserves
- 2 white peaches, peeled and chopped into 1/2-inch dice
- 1/4 cup peach preserves
- 1 cup fresh cherries, pitted and chopped
- 1/4 cup cherry preserves

DOUGH

- 6 cups all purpose flour
- 4 teaspoons baking powder
- 1 tablepoon salt
- 1 cup (2 sticks) chilled unsalted butter
- 1 1/2 cups ice water

- Safflower oil, for deep-frying

GLAZE

- 1 cup powdered sugar
- 2 tablespoons milk
- 1/2 teaspoon vanilla extract

To make the fruit fillings: In 3 separate bowls, combine the blueberries with their matching preserves, the peaches with theirs, and the cherries with theirs.

To make the dough: Combine the flour, baking powder, and salt in a large bowl. Cut the butter into 1/2-inch cubes. Work the butter into the dry ingredients with a pastry cutter or your fingers until the mixture resembles cornmeal. Add the ice water and gently form the dough into a ball. Divide the dough into thirds (each ball should be about the size of an orange). Sprinkle a thin layer of flour on a pastry board or other flat, smooth surface. Roll out each portion of dough to 1/16-inch thickness, a little thicker than a tortilla. Cut out dough circles with a 5-inch-diameter cutter (the plastic top of a 1-quart yogurt container works well). Each ball of dough should make 4 rounds. Put 1 tablespoonful of 1 filling flavor in the center of each dough round. Fold the dough

(continued)

rounds in half; wet your fingers and press to seal the edges with water. Crimp the edges with the tines of a fork.

To fry the pies, pour about 3 inches of safflower oil into a deep-frying pan and set it over medium-high heat. The oil is hot enough when a scrap of dough dropped in the pan sizzles and bubbles. Fry the pies, a few at a time, until golden brown (they float, so this should take about 2 to 3 minutes per side). Drain the pies on paper towels.

To MAKE THE GLAZE: Whisk together the powdered sugar, milk, and vanilla extract. Using a pastry brush, glaze the warm pies. Serve immediately.

Rather Sweet Variations

For baked pies, if deep-frying seems daunting, preheat the oven to 375°F. Beat 1 egg with 2 tablespoons water. Brush the top of each pie with the egg wash. Bake them on a greased or parchment-lined baking sheet for about 12 minutes, until golden brown. Sprinkle with powdered sugar. These are best if served warm and best eaten on the same day they are made, but if necessary, the pies can be reheated at 325°F for 5 to 10 minutes.

Savory Fried Pies: Fill pies with sliced ham or turkey and cheese; sautéed spinach and crumbled feta cheese; scrambled eggs with bacon bits and shredded cheese; or goat cheese with sun-dried or roasted tomatoes. You can also make "pizza" fried pies with tomato sauce, pepperoni, and shredded mozzarella.

Tip: Cherry pitters can be found at any gourmet kitchen shop. They make the tedious work of pitting cherries go quickly and easily.

Aunt Mollie's Coconut Cream Pie

I adored my aunt Mollie (who, as my grandmother's sister, was really my great-aunt Mollie). My favorite cousin recently sent me several of her recipes, including her signature coconut cream pie. My cousin wrote, "Our mother, Mollie Wright Mitchell, was widowed when young—leaving her with four very young, hungry children to raise alone. She was a Practical Nurse and managed to work full-time six days a week at the local hospital, sometimes doing night private duty—and then feed, clothe, clean, and care for us four children. Because of her job, Mama never got to attend morning church services, but she made certain all four of her children were in Sunday school and church every week in nice clothes she had sewn for us, and then she would attend the evening service. She seldom got to attend funerals, but always sent her famous coconut cream pies."

I remember Aunt Mollie as just one of those special grandmas, big and round and always making baby dolls. She always had one for me, and it was always smiling. I have made a few changes to her cream pie, but whenever I bake it, I'm like one of those little baby dolls she used to make—always smiling.

YIELD: 8 SERVINGS

BASIC PIE CRUST

- 2 cups all purpose flour
- 1/2 teaspoon salt
- 2 tablespoons sugar
- 2/3 cup (11 tablespoons) chilled unsalted butter
- 4 to 5 tablespoons ice water

COCONUT CUSTARD FILLING

- 3 large egg yolks (reserve the egg whites for the meringue)
- 2 1/2 cups heavy whipping cream
- 1 1/2 cups sugar
- 3 heaping tablespoons all purpose flour
- 1 tablespoon unsalted butter
- 1 cup sweetened flaked coconut
- 1 tablespoon vanilla extract

MERINGUE TOPPING

- 3 large egg whites
- 1 cup sugar

To MAKE THE CRUST: Preheat the oven to 425°F. Using a mixer fitted with a paddle attachment, combine the flour, salt, and sugar on low speed about 30 seconds. Cut the chilled butter into 1/2-inch cubes. Add the butter to the flour mixture and combine on low speed about 1 to 1 1/2 minutes, until the mixture looks crumbly, with bits of dough the size of peas. Add 4 tablespoons ice water, 1 tablespoon at a time, mixing on low speed for 10 seconds after each addition. After the last addition, the dough should begin to clump together in a ball. If it doesn't, continue mixing about 10 seconds longer. If it still looks too dry, add an additional 1 tablespoon ice water. Gently mold the dough into a disk, wrap in plastic wrap, and refrigerate at least 1 hour.

Transfer the unwrapped dough to a lightly floured flat surface. Roll it into a $1/8$-inch-thick circle large enough to cover the bottom and sides of a 9-inch deep-dish pie plate. (To keep the dough from sticking, gently pick it up periodically as you roll it out and rotate it in place, adding more flour underneath if necessary.) Wrap the dough lightly over the rolling pin and set it in the ungreased pie plate. Press it into place and crimp the outside edges with your fingers or a fork. Use a fork to prick the bottom of the crust. Cover the bottom and sides of the crust with a sheet of parchment paper and fill the crust with pie weights or dried beans. (I use the cheapest red beans I can find.)

Bake the crust for 10 minutes. Remove the parchment and weights. If the crust is not golden brown, return it to the oven for 1 to 3 minutes. Cool on a rack until the filling is ready. Decrease oven temperature to 350°F.

To MAKE THE FILLING: Whisk together the egg yolks and cream in a medium bowl. Combine the sugar and flour in large saucepan. Pour the yolk-cream mixture into the saucepan, whisking over medium heat until smooth. Bring the mixture to a simmer, whisking constantly about 10 minutes, until it thickens. Stir in the butter, coconut, and vanilla. Remove from the heat.

To MAKE THE MERINGUE: Set a large, perfectly clean metal bowl over a pot of simmerimg water. Pour in the egg whites and sugar. (If there is trace of fat in the bowl, the eggs won't reach their proper volume.) Heat the egg white mixture while whisking constantly until the sugar melts and there are no visible grains in the meringue. Take a little meringue mixture and rub it between your fingers to make sure all sugar grains have melted. Remove the meringue from over the simmering water and whip it with a mixer fitted with a whisk attachment on low speed for 5 minutes; increase the speed to high and beat 5 minutes longer, until the meringue is stiff and shiny.

Pour the filling into the pie crust. Spoon the meringue over the pie, covering the filling completely and sealing the edges of the pie crust with the meringue. Dip the back of a spoon quickly into the meringue to make little spikes. Bake for 15 minutes, or until the meringue is golden brown.

Tip: This topping recipe makes just enough meringue to cover the top of the pie. If you wish to create high peaks for a more dramatic presentation, double the amounts of egg whites and sugar.

The pie-baking mother of a friend of mine had a wonderful idea to use up the inevitable pie dough scraps. She'd roll them out in $1/8$-inch-thick circles, cut them into strips, dust them generously with cinnamon sugar, and pop them in a 425°F oven about 10 minutes, until brown on the edges. They rarely lasted the day.

Chef Mark's
Southern Comfort Apple Pie

Mark Cox, the executive chef when I worked at Tony's in Houston, gave me this recipe. We made it frequently at the restaurant. I loved the way he approached baking and just about everything. We developed a lot of recipes together. I bounced a lot of ideas off him; he was great about brainstorming. He would give me books to read, and he helped me become a better pastry chef. He encouraged me to be creative, but would guide me as well. We worked hard, but we always had a lot of fun, too.

Mark was a great executive chef. He was humble—a real working chef, always in the kitchen. I think he's one of the most talented chefs I've worked with. He now has his own restaurant, top-rated Mark's American Cuisine, in Houston.

This pie is delicious served topped with cinnamon ice cream, whipped cream, or rum-spiked Caramel Sauce (page 97).

YIELD: 8 TO 10 SERVINGS

TOPPING

1/2 **cup pecans**

1/3 **cup granulated sugar**

3 **tablespoons firmly packed dark brown sugar**

1/2 **teaspoon ground cinnamon**

1/4 **teaspoon salt**

1/3 **cup all purpose flour**

1/3 **cup (5**1/3 **tablespoons) chilled unsalted butter**

1 **unbaked Basic Pie Crust (page 50)**

APPLE FILLING

5 **to 6 medium-size tart apples, such as Braeburn, Cortland, or Winesap**

1/2 **cup (1 stick) unsalted butter**

3 **tablespoons ground cinnamon**

1 **cup sugar**

3/4 **cup Southern Comfort liqueur**

1/2 **cup heavy whipping cream**

To MAKE THE TOPPING: Preheat the oven to 350°F. Arrange the pecans on a baking sheet in a single layer and toast them in the oven for 7 to 9 minutes, until golden brown and aromatic. Coarsely chop the nuts.

In a food processor fitted with a metal blade, process both sugars, the cinnamon, salt, and flour for about 1 minute. Cut the butter into small pieces and add to the sugar-flour mixture. Pulse about 10 to 15 times, until the mixture is crumbly. Stir in the pecans. Refrigerate the topping, covered, in a medium bowl until ready to use.

Line a 9-inch deep-dish pie plate with the pie dough. Press it into place and crimp the outside edges with your fingers or a fork.

(continued)

To MAKE THE FILLING: Increase the oven temperature to 375°F. Peel, core, and cut the apples into ¼-inch-thick slices. Melt the butter in a large skillet over medium-high heat. When the butter starts to foam, add the apples and sauté for 5 to 8 minutes. In a small bowl, stir together the cinnamon and sugar; sprinkle it on the apples and stir to combine. Simmer the apples over medium-low heat about 1 minute longer. Remove the apples from the skillet with a slotted spoon, leaving as much of the butter-sugar mixture in the skillet as possible. Transfer the apples to a baking sheet and arrange in a single layer. (If heaped in a pile, the hot apples will steam-cook and become soggy.)

Pour the Southern Comfort into the butter-sugar mixture in the skillet. Simmer the mixture over medium heat at least 5 minutes, until the alcohol burns off (carefully sniff the mixture at close range; if it burns the insides of your nostrils, the vapors are still burning off). Add the cream and continue cooking about 5 to 10 minutes, until the mixture is as thick as pourable caramel. Return the apples to the skillet.

Pour the apple filling into the unbaked pie crust and sprinkle the topping evenly over the apples. Bake for 50 to 60 minutes, until the filling is bubbling and the topping is brown. Serve the pie warm or at room temperature.

Silken Chocolate-Walnut Tart

6/3 = EMR
excellent!

This is like a flourless chocolate cake in tart form; the rich filling contrasts ultrasmooth chocolate with a layer of toasted nuts. Use the best chocolate you can afford and you will be rewarded with results that will leave your friends begging for the recipe. I like to use a mixture of semisweet and bittersweet, but almost any combination or a single type of chocolate will work well. (One exception: steer clear of using milk chocolate, which could make the filling too sweet.)

YIELD: 8 TO 10 SERVINGS

1 unbaked Lemon Zest Tart Crust, lemon zest omitted (page 40)

1½ cups coarsely chopped walnuts

¾ cup (1½ sticks) unsalted butter *½ 2*

14 ounces chopped chocolate, semisweet or bittersweet, or any combination

1½ cups sugar

3 large eggs

2 teaspoons vanilla extract

½ teaspoon salt

⅔ cup heavy whipping cream

2 tablespoons dark rum or whiskey (optional)

used Trestford

didn't do

Line a 10-inch tart pan with the tart dough. Press it into place and crimp the outside edges with your fingers or a fork.

Preheat the oven to 350°F. Place the walnuts on a baking sheet in a single layer and bake for 7 to 9 minutes, until golden brown and aromatic. Set aside to cool.

Put the butter and chocolate in a microwave-safe bowl and heat on medium-high for 1 minute. Remove from the microwave and stir. If the chocolate is not completely melted, keep heating for 30-second increments. Stir until blended. (Or combine the butter and chocolate in a metal bowl set over a saucepan filled with 3 inches of simmering water. Stir until melted and combined. Remove the pan from the simmering water.) Whisk the sugar into the butter-chocolate mixture. Add the eggs, one at a time, whisking until smooth after each addition. Whisk in the vanilla, salt, cream, and rum.

Spread the nuts in the bottom of the pie crust. Pour the chocolate mixture over the nuts without stirring. Bake for 50 minutes. The pie will seem undercooked and jiggly in the middle, but remove it from the oven anyway. The pie will set as it cools. Do not cut the pie until it has cooled at room temperature for at least 2 hours; or refrigerate it so it will set up more quickly.

Tip: Use a sharp, pointed knife to cut this pie, and make sure that it is fully cooled before slicing. Cut very thin slices, but never refuse requests for seconds.

Grasshopper Pie

I have Sakowitz Department Store to thank for my love of grasshopper pie. Every fall my mother and I would dress up and head to the style show at Sakowitz, one of Houston's grand old department stores, which, sadly, is no longer in business. We'd head straight to the Terrace Room to eat lunch and watch a parade of models sporting the latest fashions. I loved the fashions, but for me, the big thing at the Terrace Room was the grasshopper pie, served with a healthy ladleful of hot fudge sauce. Dee Winchester, a beautiful friend of my mother's, modeled for Sakowitz, and she'd always stop by to say hello, adding to the magic and glamour of the event. Many of my favorite foods are linked to childhood memories, and surely this is one of them. With this recipe, I've come as close as I can to re-creating that beloved childhood dessert.

Keep the pie frozen until you're ready to serve it. Cut it into thick wedges and smother it in hot fudge sauce.

YIELD: 8 SERVINGS

COOKIE CRUST

- 1 (16-ounce) package crème-filled chocolate cookies (about 33 cookies)
- 1/2 cup plus 2 tablespoons (1 1/4 sticks) unsalted butter, melted

FILLING

- 4 large egg yolks
- 1 large egg
- 1 envelope plain gelatin
- 2 tablespoons green crème de menthe
- 1/3 cup water
- 1 cup sugar
- 1/2 jar (about 3.5 ounces) marshmallow crème
- 1/4 teaspoon mint extract (optional)
- 2 cups chilled heavy whipping cream

Hot Fudge Sauce (page 196)

To MAKE THE CRUST: Process the cookies in a food processor fitted with a metal blade until ground to coarse crumbs. Pour in the melted butter and pulse until the butter is thoroughly combined. Press the mixture evenly over the bottom and up the sides of a 9-inch pie plate.

To MAKE THE FILLING: Using a mixer fitted with a paddle attachment, beat the yolks and the egg in a large bowl on high speed about 5 minutes, until thick. In a small bowl, combine the gelatin and crème de menthe; let soften for 5 minutes. In a medium saucepan, combine the water and sugar and simmer until the mixture reaches the soft-ball stage, registering between 234° and 240°F on a candy thermometer. In a slow, thin stream, add the sugar mixture to the egg mixture, mixing on low speed the entire time. Add the crème de menthe mixture and beat on medium-high speed about 5 minutes, until the mixture has thickened and cooled. Add the marsh-mallow crème and mint extract; continue beating on medium speed about 2 minutes. The mixture will be very gooey.

In another large bowl, whip the cream on high speed, using a mixer fitted with a whisk attachment, until stiff peaks form. Fold the whipped cream into the marsh-mallow mixture and pile it into the pre-pared crust. (There will be enough filling to mound it higher than the edges of the pie plate, which gives it a great look.) Cover the pie and freeze at least 6 hours or overnight. The pie will keep in the freezer, well wrapped, for 2 to 3 weeks. Serve it frozen. Slice it and cover the slices with warmed fudge sauce.

Rather Sweet Variation

To make grasshopper parfaits, layer stem-med glasses or sundae glasses with spoon-fuls of ground-up cookie crumbs (omit the melted butter), hot fudge sauce, and filling. Each parfait should have at least two layers of each component. Top the parfaits with 1 tablespoon cookie crumbs mixed with 1 tablespoon crushed peppermint candies. Freeze for at least 3 hours and serve frozen, accompanied by a pitcher of warmed fudge sauce to be drizzled over the top. Makes about 8 parfaits.

EVERYDAY
Desserts AND Candies

THIS CHAPTER CONTAINS some of my oldest, simplest-to-make standbys. The Mexican Chocolate Fudge–Pecan Cake got me through high school algebra. Today, if it's not among the desserts in my pastry case, I hear about it. Home cooks will appreciate this cake for its rich chocolate flavor and for its ease of preparation—just combine the ingredients in a single saucepan and stir. Oatmeal Crisps—buttery, brown sugar–sweetened bar cookies—come from the handwritten recipe book that I compiled during my high school years.

Totally Rummy Pound Cake was a favorite of my mother's, and Orange-Date Bundt Cake comes from my grandmother's extensive collection of recipes. Hill Country Peach Cobbler takes so little time to assemble that it may become one of your favorite weeknight desserts.

I've made Emergency Fruit Crostatas so often, I sometimes wonder if I could do them blindfolded. I've also thrown them together in three minutes on television. Made with a simple, sweet flour and butter dough, sprinkled with fruit and sugar, and baked, crostatas are easy enough for under-age cooks to tackle.

Years ago, I was hired to prepare dessert for a private art opening. I arrived mid-party loaded up with flour, sugar, berries, and butter. The hostess went wild. "You are going to make this in *my* kitchen? While my guests are here?"

I headed for the kitchen and whipped up the dessert while the guests ate dinner. The house filled with the fragrance of my creation. Before I knew it, several of the guests had followed the scent into the kitchen. They kept me company until I plucked the crostatas out of the oven.

Although that long-ago hostess didn't feel comfortable having me in her kitchen, my customers have no qualms about hanging around in mine. Some walk right in through the back door. Others wander in from the downstairs dining room. Maybe it's all the old-fashioned comfort food that makes them feel so at home.

Recently, we decided to close the restaurant for two weeks to take a long-needed vacation. Some of our regulars took it as an affront. They stared at us in disbelief. "Where will I eat?" asked ninety-four-year-old Uncle Albert plaintively.

The men's breakfast coffee club insisted they'd desert us for good if we didn't give them a key to the place while we were gone. They badgered us daily the week before we closed. "Do you have our key made yet? We'll just come in, make our coffee, have our talk time, and leave."

Others feel so connected that they help in unexpected and unbelievable ways. Early on, longtime customer Kim Robertson pitched in to wash dishes during one of our lunchtime rushes. When she was done, she noticed that our towels were in terrible shape. She headed out to Wal-Mart and bought us a new set. She returned with the new towels, bought a bunch of cookies and pastries from the front counter, and left. And she'd do it again today, except now we have linen service.

Emergency Fruit Crostatas

Perfect for dessert emergencies, crostatas can be made quickly and easily with pantry staples—butter, sugar, flour—and just about any fruit you have on hand. I've used apples, plums, pears, peaches, fresh figs, and berries (fresh or frozen). Don't forget to defrost and drain thoroughly all frozen fruits before placing them on the dough. A topping of whipped cream or ice cream would be a nice finishing touch.

YIELD: ABOUT 4 SERVINGS

1 cup sugar

2 cups all purpose flour

1/4 teaspoon salt

1 cup (2 sticks) chilled butter, cut into
      small pieces

4 tablespoons ice water

1 cup fruit

Preheat the oven to 450°F. Line a baking sheet with parchment paper or butter it generously. In a food processor fitted with a metal blade, pulse together 1/2 cup of the sugar with the flour and salt. Add the butter and pulse 3 to 5 times, until the mixture is crumbly. Pour the water through the feed tube, 1 tablespoon at a time, and pulse until the dough begins to hold together. Remove the dough, shape it into a ball, wrap it in plastic wrap, and refrigerate for 1 hour. (If you are in a huge hurry—which I often am—freeze the wrapped dough just long enough to prepare the fruit filling. It will be a little harder to work with, but it's an acceptable trade-off when time is short.)

Divide the dough into 4 equal pieces and roll each into a ball. Use your hands to press the dough into 1/4-inch-thick rounds on the prepared baking sheet. Each round should be about 6 inches in diameter. If you are using berries, leave the fruit whole. Larger fruits can be left unpeeled, but must be sliced so they can fit neatly in the center of the crostata. Spoon 1/4 cup of the fruit into the center of each round, leaving a 1 1/2-inch border all around the edge. (If using larger fruits, place 3 to 4 slices of fruit in the center of each crostata.). Sprinkle the remaining 1/2 cup sugar evenly over the fruit on each crostata. Fold the dough edges toward the center, making 3 separate flaps. With your thumb and forefinger, firmly pinch together the seams between the folds.

Bake the crostatas for 12 to 14 minutes, until brown around the edges. Cool the crostatas on the baking sheet for no more than 10 minutes or they will be difficult to remove whole. Serve warm or at room temperature.

(continued)

Rather Sweet Variation

If I have a little extra time, I make apple crostatas this way: Core and slice 2 medium apples. Put 3 tablespoons butter in a medium sauté pan. Add the apples and ¼ cup firmly packed brown sugar, and stir over medium heat until the apples have softened, about 3 minutes. Put one-quarter of the apple mixture on each of the dough rounds and proceed as directed above.

Tip: Strawberries and bananas are two common fruits that do not work in this recipe. Baking strawberries makes them watery; bananas become dried out.

Petite Pavlovas with Lemon Cream and Fresh Fruit

Here's another one of my emergency recipes: I prepare the components ahead and then throw them together at the last minute. These look impressive, and people will think you worked really hard to make them. (I'll never tell.) If you're truly pressed for time, buy a jar of ready-made lemon curd and fold it into the whipped cream.

This is a terrific light dessert for spring or summer. Although it isn't exactly low-fat, it feels like it, making it a perfect choice for the reluctant dessert eater who resists throwing caution to the wind.

YIELD: 4 SERVINGS

MERINGUE

4 large egg whites, 3 yolks (saved for the filling)

1/2 teaspoon cream of tartar

Pinch of salt

1 1/4 cups sugar

FILLING

3 large egg yolks

2 large eggs

1/3 cup granulated sugar

1/4 cup freshly squeezed lemon juice

1/4 cup champagne or brut sparkling wine

3 tablespoons chilled unsalted butter

1/2 cup chilled heavy whipping cream

2 tablespoons powdered sugar

1 cup fresh fruit, sliced and pitted, if necessary

To MAKE THE MERINGUE: Preheat the oven to 300°F. Line 2 baking sheets with parchment paper. Trace 4 evenly spaced 4-inch-diameter circles on each parchment sheet. Using a mixer fitted with a whisk attachment, beat the egg whites, cream of tartar, and salt on high speed about 2 minutes, until soft peaks form. Add the sugar, 2 tablespoons at a time, and continue beating on high speed until stiff peaks form.

Spoon the meringue onto the baking sheets using the traced circles as a guide. Use the back of a spoon to build up a 1-inch rim on each meringue round. Bake the meringues for 1 hour. Turn off the oven and leave them inside the closed oven for 1 hour longer, or overnight if that is more convenient. Well wrapped, the meringues will keep for 2 days at room temperature, or they can be frozen up to 3 weeks.

To MAKE THE FILLING: Whisk the egg yolks, eggs, granulated sugar, lemon juice, and champagne in a large bowl set over a saucepan filled with 2 inches of simmering water. Cook about 15 minutes, whisking occasionally, until the mixture thickens. Cut the butter into 4 pieces. Whisk the butter into the lemon mixture, one piece at a time. Cook about 10 minutes longer, whisking occasionally. The lemon filling will be thick and puddinglike. Cover the filling with plastic wrap, pressing the wrap into the surface of the curd, sealing it and leaving no air between the wrap and the filling. Refrigerate it for at least 1 hour, or for up to 3 days.

Using an electric mixer fitted with a whisk attachment, beat the cream in a large bowl on high speed until soft peaks form. Add the powdered sugar and beat until thoroughly combined. Fold the whipped cream into the cooled lemon filling. Spoon the lemon filling into the meringue shells and top with the fruit. Serve immediately.

Hill Country Peach Cobbler

Springtime is peach time in the Texas Hill Country, and peaches appear in every form imaginable—from crisps and cobblers to homemade jams and salsas. This cobbler is a Texas standard; a version of it appears in any number of local community or church cookbooks. I've been making this one for so long, I'm not sure where my tattered, peach-stained copy originated. But I am certain it is as easy to make as it is delicious.

YIELD: 6 TO 8 SERVINGS

½ cup (1 stick) unsalted butter

1 cup granulated sugar

1 cup all purpose flour

1 tablespoon baking powder

¾ cup milk (low-fat works)

3 cups sliced fresh peaches, peels left on

½ cup firmly packed golden brown sugar

Preheat the oven to 350°F. Melt the butter in a medium sauté pan set over medium-high heat until it bubbles and turns a nut-brown color. Watch the butter closely, as it can go from browned to burned in a few seconds. Pour the butter into an 8-inch-square baking dish. In a medium bowl, stir together the granulated sugar, flour, baking powder, and milk. Pour the milk mixture on top of the melted butter. *Do not stir.* Without mixing, arrange the peaches evenly on top of the batter. Evenly sprinkle the brown sugar over the cobbler.

Bake the cobbler for 40 to 45 minutes, until the top turns golden brown. Miraculously, the batter will migrate from the bottom of the pan to cover the peach slices partially. Serve warm or at room temperature.

♕ Tip: Fresh raspberries, blueberries, boysenberries, nectarines, and blackberries—either alone or in combination—are equally luscious in this recipe. Frozen fruit works fine as long as it is defrosted and drained before using.

Individual
Pear-Maple Cobblers

I have taught many a class at Austin's upscale Central Market grocery store. It has a wonderful, well-equipped instructional kitchen, and my classes there almost always sell out. I came up with this recipe for the chain's Foodie *newsletter, which is sent to customers all over Central Texas. The cobblers are best when topped off with a dollop of whipped cream, and you can add a drizzle of maple syrup too, if you like.*

YIELD: 6 SERVINGS

FILLING

3 pears, peeled, cored, and quartered

²/₃ cup pure maple syrup

2 tablespoons all purpose flour

¼ teaspoon salt

1 teaspoon vanilla extract

¼ teaspoon ground nutmeg

2 tablespoons chilled unsalted butter, sliced into 6 even pats

COBBLER TOPPING

1¹/₂ cups all purpose flour

2¹/₄ teaspoons baking powder

¹/₂ teaspoon ground nutmeg

¹/₂ cup (1 stick) chilled unsalted butter

9 tablespoons heavy whipping cream

9 tablespoons pure maple syrup

1 teaspoon vanilla extract

3 tablespoons sugar

To MAKE THE FILLING: Preheat the oven to 425°F. Combine the pears, maple syrup, flour, salt, vanilla, and nutmeg in a bowl and stir well. Divide the pear mixture evenly among six ³/₄-cup capacity custard cups or individual soufflé dishes. Top each dish with 1 pat of butter. Bake until heated through, about 18 to 20 minutes.

To MAKE THE TOPPING: In the bowl of a food processor fitted with a metal blade, combine the flour, baking powder, and ¼ teaspoon of the nutmeg. Melt 2 tablespoons of the butter and set aside for brushing the cobbler dough. Cut the remaining 6 tablespoons of butter into 6 pieces and add them to the flour mixture. Process the butter and flour mixture until fine crumbs form. Add the cream, maple syrup, and vanilla; process until just combined. Drop by spoonfuls onto the hot fruit filling. Brush the topping with the reserved melted butter. Combine the sugar and remaining ¼ teaspoon nutmeg in a small bowl. Sprinkle the sugar mixture evenly over the cobblers.

Bake for 14 minutes, or until golden brown and firm to the touch. Serve warm.

Mexican Chocolate Fudge-Pecan Cake

This cake saved me from failing algebra. I was struggling in class and, in desperation, I made the cake for my high school math teacher. Miraculously, I passed the course. Was it the cake? I'll never know. I do know that I've never met anyone who didn't fall for this cake.

This recipe works equally well whether it's baked in a Bundt or tube pan or in individual muffin cups. I highly recommend Baker's Joy spray, a mixture of flour and oil available in many grocery stores. This cake sticks to the pan more than most, and I have found that Baker's Joy ensures the most stick-free results, especially if you bake the cake in a Bundt pan.

YIELD: 12 SERVINGS FOR CAKE, 18 STANDARD CUPCAKES, 12 TEXAS-SIZE CUPCAKES

CAKE

- 1 cup (2 sticks) unsalted butter
- 1/2 cup unsweetened **Dutch-process** cocoa powder
- 3/4 cup water
- 2 cups sugar
- 2 large eggs
- 1 cup buttermilk
- 2 tablespoons vanilla extract
- 2 cups all purpose flour
- 1 teaspoon baking soda
- 1 1/2 teaspoons ground cinnamon
- 1/4 teaspoon salt

CHOCOLATE-PECAN GLAZE

- 1 cup pecans
- 1/2 cup (1 stick) unsalted butter
- 1/4 cup whole milk
- 1/2 cup high-quality dark cocoa powder, such as **Scharffen Berger**
- 2 cups sifted powdered sugar (sifted then measured)
- 1 tablespoon vanilla extract
- 1/4 teaspoon salt

Preheat the oven to 350°F. Grease a 9-inch tube pan or a 10- to 12-cup Bundt pan with butter, sprinkle lightly with flour and tap over the sink to remove any excess flour (or spray evenly with Baker's Joy spray). For cupcakes, line standard-size muffin pans with muffin wrappers or spray Texas-size (3 1/2 inches in diameter and 2 inches deep) muffin cups with Baker's Joy.

Melt the butter in a large saucepan over medium-low heat. Add the cocoa and whisk until smooth. Add the water and whisk until smooth. Be careful not to boil the mixture. Remove the saucepan from the heat. Add the sugar, eggs, buttermilk, and vanilla to the warm cocoa mixture all at once; whisk until smooth. Add the flour, baking soda, cinnamon, and salt all at once; whisk until the dry ingredients are completely incorporated. Don't worry if there are some small lumps. Pour the batter into the pan.

(continued)

If using muffin pans, fill each cup two-thirds full.

Bake for 40 to 45 minutes; the cake is done when it has pulled away slightly from the sides of the pan and feels firm to the touch. For cupcakes, check for doneness after about 20 minutes.

Let the cake cool in the pan about 20 minutes. Cupcakes need only a total of 10 minutes cooling time.

MEANWHILE, MAKE THE GLAZE: Arrange the pecans on a baking sheet in a single layer and toast them in the 350° oven for 7 to 9 minutes, until golden brown and aromatic. Chop the pecans.

Melt the butter over low heat in a medium saucepan. Add the milk, cocoa, and powdered sugar and whisk until glossy. Remove the saucepan from the heat and whisk in the vanilla, salt, and pecans.

Loosen the cake with a knife or spatula and overturn it onto a serving plate. Spoon the glaze over the cooled cake, covering it thoroughly. Don't worry if some of the glaze pools inside and around the cake. For cupcakes, remove them from the pan, and peel off the paper liners. Invert each cupcake onto a small serving plate—this way they look like tiny cakes—and cover with glaze.

This cake will keep up to 3 days, covered, at room temperature. Unglazed and well wrapped, it will keep frozen up to 3 weeks. When frozen, bring the cake to room temperature and glaze just before serving.

Rather Sweet Variation

For a simple summer dessert, I make cupcakes, invert them on individual serving plates, and serve them with sliced fresh strawberries and ice cream or lightly sweetened whipped cream.

Tip: Alkali has been added to Dutch-process cocoa powder to aid in neutralizing chocolate's natural acidity. This lends a richer, fuller chocolate flavor to baked goods. If you do not have Dutch-process cocoa on hand, add ½ teaspoon of baking soda along with the other dry ingredients, unless you are using an artisanal brand of cocoa. The highest-quality cocoas (such as Scharffen Berger) have been fermented and processed with such care that they are naturally balanced and have a mellow, rich flavor without the addition of baking soda.

I like to use the high-quality cocoa for both the cake and glaze if I have enough on hand; when I don't, I use the good stuff for the glaze and go with standard-issue cocoa for the cake.

Mahogany Cake

This is yet another of the recipes given to me by my grandmother. I have adapted it by adding an extra shot of coffee flavor. Where she used to add raisins, I substitute chopped coffee-flavored chocolate. As the cake bakes, the chocolate migrates to the bottom of the cake. When the cake is inverted for icing and serving, the melted chocolate bars form a beautiful, dark stripe of mocha nestled near the top edge. Both Scharffen Berger and Ghirardelli make coffee-flavored chocolate bars.

YIELD: 12 SERVINGS

CAKE

1 cup (2 sticks) unsalted butter, at room temperature

1½ cups sugar

3 large eggs

½ cup boiling water

1 rounded tablespoon instant espresso powder

½ cup unsweetened cocoa powder

1 cup sour cream

1 teaspoon vanilla extract

2 cups sifted cake flour (sifted then measured)

1 teaspoon baking powder

¼ teaspoon baking soda

¼ teaspoon salt

4 ounces dark chocolate flavored with coffee, coarsely chopped

MAHOGANY ICING

¼ cup boiling water

2 tablespoons instant espresso powder

2 tablespoons unsweetened cocoa powder

2 tablespoons unsalted butter, melted

1 tablespoon vanilla extract

¼ teaspoon salt

2 cups sifted powdered sugar (sifted then measured)

To MAKE THE CAKE: Preheat the oven to 350°F. Grease a 10- to 12-cup Bundt pan with butter or cooking spray, sprinkle lightly with all purpose flour, and tap over the sink to remove any excess flour (or spray evenly with Baker's Joy). Using a mixer fitted with a paddle attachment, cream the butter and sugar in a large bowl on medium speed about 2 minutes, until fluffy. Add the eggs, one at a time, beating on medium speed about 20 seconds after each addition.

Pour the boiling water into a medium bowl. Stir in the espresso powder and then the cocoa, stirring until smooth after each addition. Stir in the sour cream and vanilla. Place the sifted flour in another medium bowl; stir in the baking powder, baking soda, and salt. Add about one-third of the flour mixture to the butter-sugar mixture and beat on medium speed until just incorporated. Add half of the cocoa–sour cream mixture and beat until just incorporated. Continue adding the dry and wet ingredients alternately, ending with dry ingredients. Stir in the chopped chocolate.

Spoon the batter, which will be thick, into the prepared pan. Bake for 40 to 45 minutes,

until a toothpick inserted into the center comes out clean. (After about 40 minutes, the cake may crack slightly around the middle, and the crack may look slightly wet. Test with a toothpick anyway; the cake may be done.) If overbaked the cake will dry out. Cool for 5 minutes in the pan, invert onto a rack, and cool for 20 minutes before icing.

To MAKE THE ICING: Pour the boiling water into a medium bowl. Stir in the espresso powder and then the cocoa, stirring until smooth after each addition. Stir in the butter and vanilla and add the salt and powdered sugar. Stir until smooth.

Set the cooled cake on a large serving plate and spoon the icing over it, covering it completely. The icing will pool in the hole in the middle of the cake as well as on the outside edges of the cake plate. (Resist the urge to dip your finger in for a taste unless you are confident you can hide the evidence of icing tampering.) The icing will cool within 30 minutes, making it possible to cover the cake with plastic wrap without smearing it.

The covered glazed cake will keep at least 2 days at room temperature. It can be frozen up to 3 weeks.

Orange-Date Bundt Cake

I recently stumbled across a tattered spiral notebook from my high school years. Stocked with my hand-copied renditions of family recipes, it included this long-forgotten cake. Later, I found the yellowed original copy in my grandmother's handwriting. I made it on the spot and remembered why she adored it. It's an old-fashioned comfort cake, and I love it, too. I did change one thing: Grandma used Crisco but I use butter.

YIELD: 12 SERVINGS

CAKE

- ½ cup (1 stick) unsalted butter, at room temperature
- 1 cup sugar
- 2 large eggs
- Grated zest of 1 medium orange, preferably organic
- 1 teaspoon vanilla extract
- 2 cups all purpose flour
- ½ teaspoon baking soda
- ½ teaspoon salt
- ⅔ cup buttermilk
- 1 cup chopped dates
- ½ cup coarsely chopped pecans

GLAZE

- 1 cup sugar
- ½ cup freshly squeezed orange juice
- 1 tablespoon grated orange zest, preferably organic

To MAKE THE CAKE: Preheat the oven to 350°F. Grease a 10- to 12-cup Bundt pan, sprinkle lightly with all purpose flour, and tap over the sink to remove any excess flour (or spray evenly with Baker's Joy). Using a mixer fitted with a paddle attachment, cream the butter in a large bowl on medium-high speed about 1 minute, until fluffy. Add the sugar and cream on medium-high speed about 30 seconds. Add the eggs all at once and continue creaming for 1 minute. Add the orange zest and vanilla; beat until combined. Add about half the flour, the baking soda, and the salt; mix on medium-low speed until just combined. Add the buttermilk and mix on medium-low speed until just combined. Add the rest of the flour and mix until just combined. Gently stir in the dates and pecans.

Spoon the batter evenly into the pan (it will be too thick to pour). Bake for 40 to 45 minutes, until the cake is brown around the edges and a toothpick inserted into the center comes out clean. Let the cake cool in the pan about 10 minutes. Invert it onto a rack and cool at least 20 minutes before glazing. Transfer the cake to a serving plate and gently pierce the cake many times with a toothpick; or, if you want the glaze to penetrate more deeply, use a wooden skewer.

To MAKE THE GLAZE: Combine the sugar and orange juice in a small saucepan and bring to a boil over medium heat. Stir until the sugar melts. Remove from the heat and stir in the zest. Pour the glaze carefully over the cooled cake.

Serve immediately or at room temperature. The glazed cake will keep for 2 to 3 days at room temperature, well wrapped. It can also be frozen up to 3 weeks.

Tip: It's easiest to buy prepackaged, chopped dates, but if you have only whole dates on hand, pit them and put them in a food processor fitted with a metal blade. Add 1 tablespoon sugar and pulse until the dates are coarsely chopped. The sugar will keep them from sticking together in a lump.

A HOUSE IS BEAUTIFUL NOT BECAUSE OF ITS WALLS, BUT BECAUSE OF IT'S CAKES.

— OLD RUSSIAN PROVERB

Totally Rummy Pound Cake

How much rum can a cake take without getting sloppy or downright nasty? It may seem like there's a lot in this recipe, but this is one cake that can hold its liquor. The unmistakable rum flavor melds with the buttery cake to make a very grown-up dessert.

YIELD: 12 SERVINGS

CAKE

1 1/4 cups pecans

1 cup (2 sticks) unsalted butter, at room temperature

2 1/2 cups sugar

5 large eggs

3 cups all purpose flour

1 teaspoon baking powder

1/2 teaspoon salt

2/3 cup sour cream

1 tablespoon vanilla extract

1/2 cup dark rum, such as Myers's

GLAZE

1/4 cup (1/2 stick) unsalted butter

1/4 cup water

1/2 cup sugar

1 tablespoon freshly squeezed lemon juice

1/4 cup dark rum, such as Myers's

To MAKE THE CAKE: Preheat the oven to 350°F. Grease a 10-inch tube pan or 10- to 12-cup Bundt pan with butter or cooking spray.

Arrange the pecans on a baking sheet in a single layer and toast them in the oven for 7 to 9 minutes, until golden brown and aromatic. Cool the nuts for 5 minutes. Coarsely grind ¼ cup of the pecans in a food processor fitted with a metal blade. Coarsely chop the remaining 1 cup of pecans.

Sprinkle the greased pan with the ground pecans and shake it until the pan is lightly coated with nuts. Hold the pan upside down over the sink and tap it lightly to discard any excess nuts. Using a mixer fitted with a paddle attachment, beat the butter in a large bowl on medium-high speed about 1 minute, until fluffy. With a rubber spatula, scrape down any butter clinging to the sides and bottom of the mixing bowl. Add the sugar and beat on medium-high speed about 2 minutes, until incorporated.

Scrape down the bowl with the spatula. Add the eggs, one at a time, and continue to beat on medium-high speed 1 to 2 minutes, until the mixture is fluffy and light yellow in color. In a medium bowl combine the flour, baking powder, and salt. Add one-third of the flour mixture to the batter and mix on low speed until the flour is no longer visible. Add half of the sour cream and mix on low speed until it is combined. Continue to add the flour and sour cream alternately, ending with the last third of the flour. Stir in the vanilla, rum, and the 1 cup coarsely chopped pecans.

Spoon the batter evenly into the pan and bake about 1 hour and 20 minutes, until it springs back when touched lightly (if the top starts to brown too quickly, cover it loosely with a sheet of aluminum foil). Let the cake cool at least 15 minutes before removing it from the pan. Invert it onto a cooling rack, and then invert it again back into the pan and then from the pan onto a cake plate when cool.

To MAKE THE GLAZE: Stir the butter, water, sugar, lemon juice, and rum in a small saucepan over medium heat until melted and combined. Boil the mixture about 1 minute.

Transfer the cake to a serving plate and gently pierce the cake many times with a toothpick; or, if you want the glaze to penetrate more deeply, use a wooden skewer. Pour the glaze over the cake. Let the cake cool at least 1 hour before serving. The glazed cake can be frozen up to 3 weeks if well wrapped in a layer of plastic wrap and a layer of foil.

Tip: Dense pound cakes mellow if given time to rest after baking. If you have time, make the cake the day before serving, let it cool completely, and wrap it securely with plastic wrap. It will taste great at room temperature for at least 2 days.

Glazed Lemon-Cranberry Loaf Cake

When Karen Lerner—co-owner of Houston catering powerhouse A Fare Extraordinaire—gave me my first professional cooking job, she was just starting out herself. I worked with three other women in a bitty kitchen. I did desserts and pastries and everything else, including washing dishes, scrubbing floors, serving, and delivering. I learned a ton from working with her. She was very specific about the way she wanted things to look, and they always looked beautiful. She was incredibly hardworking then, and I'm sure that hasn't changed. Her business certainly has—she routinely plans grand events and caters for the city's top hosts and hostesses.

I still use this loaf cake recipe of Karen's for catering jobs of my own. I freeze the loaves, cut them into thin slices, and arrange them neatly on a platter.

For a more caramel-like flavor, substitute dark brown sugar for the granulated sugar in both the loaf cake and the glaze recipes.

YIELD: 1 LOAF

LOAF CAKE

- **1 cup fresh cranberries**
- **1²/₃ cups all purpose flour, plus 1 tablespoon for dredging cranberries**
- **½ cup (1 stick) unsalted butter, at room temperature**
- **1 cup sugar**
- **2 large eggs**
- **1½ teaspoons baking powder**
- **¼ teaspoon salt**
- **½ cup milk**
- **1 tablespoon grated lemon zest, preferably organic**

LEMON GLAZE

- **¼ cup sugar**
- **¼ cup freshly squeezed lemon juice**

To MAKE THE CAKE: Preheat the oven to 350°F. Grease a 9 by 5-inch loaf pan with butter, sprinkle lightly with flour, and tap over the sink to remove any excess flour (or spray evenly with Baker's Joy spray).

Toss the cranberries with the 1 tablespoon flour in a small bowl. Using a mixer fitted with a paddle attachment, cream the butter and sugar in a large bowl on medium-high speed about 1 minute, until fluffy. Add the eggs and beat on medium-high speed for 1 minute. Add half of the remaining flour, the baking powder, and the salt; mix on low speed just until combined. Add half of the milk and mix on low speed just until combined. Add the remaining flour, mix just until combined, and then mix in the remainder of the milk. Fold in the lemon zest and the cranberries.

Pour the batter into the pan and bake about 1 hour, until a toothpick stuck into the middle of the loaf comes out clean. Cool the loaf for about 15 minutes, then remove it from the pan.

To MAKE THE LEMON GLAZE: Combine the sugar and lemon juice in a small saucepan set over medium-high heat; bring the mixture to a boil and cook about 30 seconds. Remove the pan from the heat.

Gently pierce the top of the loaf cake many times with a toothpick. Use a pastry brush to apply the warm glaze evenly over the top of the loaf.

Oatmeal Crisps

"These are crunchy and wonderful for tea parties." That's what I wrote in my high school recipe notebook, and it is still true these many years later. (Does anyone have tea parties anymore?) It takes a little more than half an hour to whip these together, including baking time. Well wrapped, they'll keep for 1 week at room temperature and a month in the freezer.

YIELD: 24 BARS

- 1/2 cup (1 stick) unsalted butter
- 1/2 cup firmly packed dark brown sugar
- 1 tablespoon light corn syrup
- 2 cups old-fashioned rolled oats
- 1 teaspoon baking powder
- 1/4 teaspoon salt
- 1/3 cup sweetened shredded coconut
- 1/2 cup bittersweet chocolate chips (optional)

Preheat the oven to 350°F. Grease a 9 by 13-inch pan with butter or cooking spray. Melt the butter, brown sugar, and corn syrup in a saucepan set over medium heat. Stir 1 to 2 minutes, until the brown sugar is no longer grainy. Remove the pan from the heat. In a medium bowl, stir together the oats, baking powder, salt, and coconut. Add the butter mixture and stir to combine.

Spoon the dough into the pan. Lightly coat your fingers with cooking spray or butter and press the mixture evenly into the pan.

Bake for 20 to 25 minutes. Cool for 20 minutes and cut into narrow fingers. In a small, heavy saucepan, melt the chocolate chips over low heat, stirring constantly. Drizzle over the bars.

Tip: I prefer the heartier bite of old-fashioned rolled oats for cooking and baking, but you should have no problem substituting quick-cooking rolled oats in this recipe if that's all you have on hand. Do not use instant oatmeal, which has been precooked and then dried, leaving it with little character or texture.

Cappuccino Cheesecakes

These individual cheesecakes are among our biggest sellers at the bakery. I tried rotating them off the schedule to make room for something new, but a persistent, vocal group of regulars finally cured me for good. Now I make sure we have a batch on hand daily. You may wish to cut these generously sized cheesecakes in half to double the servings.

YIELD: 8 INDIVIDUAL CHEESECAKES

CRUST

1 (16-ounce) package crème-filled
    chocolate cookies (about 33 cookies)

1/2 cup (1 stick) unsalted butter, melted

FILLING

2 teaspoons instant espresso powder

1 tablespoon boiling water

2 (8-ounce) packages cream cheese,
    at room temperature

1 cup sugar

1/4 teaspoon salt

3 large eggs

1 cup semisweet chocolate chips

GANACHE

4 ounces high-quality bittersweet
    chocolate

1/2 cup heavy whipping cream

2 tablespoons light corn syrup

1 teaspoon vanilla extract

To MAKE THE CRUSTS: Preheat the oven to 350°F. Process the cookies in a food processor fitted with a metal blade until ground to coarse crumbs. Pour in the melted butter and pulse until the butter is thoroughly combined. Press the mixture over the bottom of eight 4³/₈-inch, 1-cup capacity disposable foil tartlet pans.

To MAKE THE FILLING: Combine the espresso powder with the boiling water in a small bowl. Using a mixer fitted with a paddle attachment, combine the cream cheese, sugar, salt, and coffee mixture in a large bowl on medium-high speed. Add the eggs all at once and beat on medium-high about 1 minute. Stir in the chocolate chips. Pour the cream cheese mixture over the chocolate crusts, leaving about 1/4 inch at the top for the chocolate ganache.

Bake the cakes for 35 to 40 minutes, until the filling is set. Cool for 20 minutes before topping with the ganache.

To MAKE THE GANACHE: Chop the chocolate into small pieces and place in a medium bowl. Heat the cream in a small saucepan until it is very hot and just beginning to steam. Pour the hot cream over the chocolate and stir until it is completely melted. Stir in the corn syrup and vanilla. Pour the glaze into a medium pitcher or measuring cup and let it cool for 10 minutes.

Pour an even layer of ganache atop the cheesecakes, being sure to cover the cream cheese filling. Refrigerate for at least 4 hours or up to 3 days. Press up on the bottom of the tart pans to release the tarts. Serve chilled.

Mrs. Chisholm's Divinity

Mrs. Chisholm lived next door to my grandmother. Whenever we visited, she would arrive at the door with her divinity. We were considered "company," and Mrs. Chisholm believed that company deserved divinity. We never argued.

Mrs. Chisholm wouldn't have added chocolate nibs—the bean-like morsels from cacao pods that are fermented, roasted, then ground into chocolate—but I like their nutlike crunch, richness, and earthy chocolate hit in my divinity.

YIELD: 20 TWO-INCH PIECES

½ cup nuts, such as almonds, pecans, or walnuts

3 cups sugar

½ cup light corn syrup or Lyle's Golden Syrup (see tip on page 17)

½ cup water

3 large egg whites

½ cup dried fruit (such as dried cranberries or cherries or chopped dried apricots)

½ cup chocolate nibs (optional)

Preheat the oven to 350°F. Arrange the nuts on a baking sheet in a single layer and toast them for 7 to 9 minutes, until golden brown and aromatic. Chop the nuts. Line a large baking sheet with parchment paper.

Boil the sugar, corn syrup, and water without stirring in a large heavy-bottomed saucepan until it registers 223° to 234°F on a candy thermometer, or it forms a thin thread when dropped into a small glass filled with cold water. While the syrup is cooking, use a mixer fitted with a whisk attachment to beat the egg whites on high speed until stiff peaks form. Pour the heated syrup into a 4-cup glass measuring cup. Slowly pour half the syrup into the egg whites, mixing constantly on medium-low speed. Return the remaining syrup to the saucepan and boil over medium-high heat until it reaches the hard crack stage, 300° to 310°F, or turns into hard, brittle threads when dropped into a small glass filled with cold water. Slowly pour the syrup into the egg white mixture, mixing constantly on medium-low speed. Add the fruit, nuts, and chocolate; combine on low speed until a small portion of the mixture drops slowly and easily from a spoon. Drop tablespoon-fuls onto the prepared baking sheet.

The divinity will cool quickly and should be stored in an airtight container with waxed paper between the layers. It should be eaten within 2 days.

Tip: For candy-making novices, a candy thermometer takes the guesswork out of determining the proper temperature for cooking the syrup.

Coconut Cream Flan

This recipe is a takeoff on one given to me by my second mother in life, Peggy Wood. She and my father married about the time I went to college. I remained close to my family and visited often. Peggy loves to cook and has even more cookbooks than I do. She cooked for all of us, and she has always tried to make it special.

My dad didn't cook much, but when he became sick, all he did was watch the Food Network. He'd call and tell me about it. Soon he began sending away for things. Once he sent all kinds of obscure flours to me. Peggy finally had to confiscate his credit card.

YIELD: 8 SERVINGS

1 cup sugar

6 large eggs

1 (14-ounce) can sweetened condensed milk

1 (15-ounce) can cream of coconut, such as Coco Lopez

1 cup half-and-half

1 teaspoon vanilla extract

1/4 cup dark rum, such as Myers's

Preheat the oven to 325°F.

Place the sugar in a small, uncoated skillet. Heat the sugar over medium-high heat until melted and golden brown. Pour it into a 1-quart baking dish or distribute it evenly among eight 1-cup capacity ramekins (about 2 tablespoons per ramekin). Tip and turn the dish or ramekins to coat the bottom(s) and sides with the melted sugar.

Whisk the eggs in a large bowl until foamy. Stir in the condensed milk, cream of coconut, half-and-half, vanilla, and rum. Pour the mixture into the baking dish. Put the baking dish in a larger baking pan and set it in the oven. Pour enough boiling water into the larger pan to reach halfway up the sides of the baking dish or ramekins.

Bake 1 hour for the 1-quart or 45 minutes for the ramekins, until the center is almost set. Remove the flan(s) from the pan of water and cool on a rack. Invert onto a serving plate; cover and refrigerate at least 1 hour before serving. The flan(s) will keep for 3 days in the refrigerator.

Texas Pralines

My mother loved parties, and she loved pralines. Whenever she threw a party, she stirred up a batch of pralines, which meant that we had a steady supply of this Southern delicacy. Who knows where my mother got this recipe. I found it on a scrap of paper with her makeup list scrawled on the back: Maybelline Hi-Fi Eyeliner, Scandia Be Natural Wild something-or-other, and medium-brown eyebrow pencil.

2¹/₂ cups whole pecans

1 cup buttermilk

1 teaspoon baking soda

3 cups sugar

2 tablespoons light corn syrup

¹/₄ cup (¹/₂ stick) unsalted butter

2 tablespoons vanilla extract

Preheat the oven to 350°F. Arrange the pecans on a baking sheet in a single layer and toast them for 7 to 9 minutes, until golden brown and aromatic.

Combine the buttermilk, baking soda, sugar, corn syrup, and butter in a heavy-bottomed 4-quart pot; cook slowly over medium heat, stirring occasionally, until it reaches the soft-ball stage, registering between 234° and 240°F on a candy thermometer, about 30 minutes. Remove the pot from the heat. Add the vanilla and pecans and beat the candy with a wooden spoon until it starts to lose its shine, becomes more opaque, and starts getting creamy, about 10 minutes. The candy should be thick enough to drop by tablespoonfuls onto waxed paper. Cool the candies thoroughly, then wrap them individually in plastic wrap. They will keep at room temperature for about 5 days.

DESSERTS FOR
Special Occasions AND Holidays

AT LEAST TWICE A WEEK, Mary and her husband, Bill, a retired engineer, make the forty-minute drive to Rather Sweet from Blanco. Mary takes my cakes and cookies to friends and neighbors. She gave her dentist a piece of my Larger-Than-Life Praline Cheesecake and told me that getting an appointment suddenly became easier.

I served Bananas Foster Shortcakes for our New Year's Eve dinner this year. They were so popular, I think they may have kicked off a new Rather Sweet tradition. My version starts with a sugar scone base that's topped with ice cream, sliced bananas, and a brown sugar sauce spiked with rum and liqueur.

Our old-fashioned layer cakes take top honors as the bakery's best sellers. We sell them by the piece, and we sell them whole. We sell them to desperate spouses who've forgotten their partner's birthday or anniversary. Last spring, a friend begged for a Strawberry Ricotta Cake at the last minute. I didn't have time to make it, and it took almost a year for him to forgive me.

I've noticed that many people are intimidated by the thought of making cakes from scratch. They don't attempt it, even though it is not as daunting, or as tedious, as it may seem. I rarely sift flour, I don't always take time to measure ingredients perfectly, and my cakes still turn out fine. They don't look like the overly styled cakes in wedding magazines. That's not what matters to me; I care about flavor. If the cake leans a bit, don't obsess about it. Early on in my career, I suffered from cake lean. If it happens to you, just cut the cake in the kitchen and serve it. No one will know the difference.

Try the White-on-White Buttermilk Cake with Jack Daniel's Buttercream, a foolproof cake that I've been making since I started baking for a living. It always comes out in three flat layers, making it possible for an amateur to frost with ease.

My Tuxedo Cake—a moist chocolate cake frosted with whipped cream and partially coated with melted chocolate—outsells all others. One customer convinced me to send one all the way to her home in Southern California. It was a lot easier to make it than it was to freeze, wrap, and package it for shipping. But I'd be happy to do it for her, or any of my customers, again.

American Beauty Cake

I made this cake for Texas Monthly *magazine when they asked me to come up with a flour-less chocolate cake for Valentine's Day. I wanted to do something romantic, with contrasting flavors and more than one texture. I started with a dense flourless cake and lightened it by topping it with an airy milk chocolate mousse. The cake gets its shiny, finished look from its bittersweet chocolate glaze. It looks lovely garnished with rose petals.*

This is an excellent make-ahead cake. The cake and mousse combination must be frozen for at least six hours before glazing, and if wrapped tightly, it will keep in the freezer for three weeks. Once the ingredients are assembled, the glaze can be made in less than five minutes. Just pour it over the cake and freeze until ready to serve. For a simpler dessert, skip the mousse and glaze the cake alone. It is wickedly rich, so start with small servings.

You can make this cake in any shape you like. I've used four-inch heart molds (you'll need four for this recipe), tart pans, ramekins, or a single nine-inch cake pan.

YIELD: 14 TO 16 SERVINGS

CAKE

- 1 cup (2 sticks) unsalted butter
- 12 ounces premium-quality bittersweet chocolate, chopped into small pieces
- 6 large eggs
- 1 cup sugar
- 1 tablespoon vanilla extract
- 2 tablespoons dark rum, such as Myers's or the liqueur of your choice, such as Kahlúa or Grand Marnier (optional)

MILK CHOCOLATE MOUSSE

- 1/4 cup unsalted butter
- 10 ounces premium-quality milk chocolate
- 3 large eggs, separated
- 3 tablespoons sugar
- 1 tablespoon vanilla extract
- 1 cup chilled heavy whipping cream

DARK CHOCOLATE GLAZE

- 4 ounces premium-quality bittersweet chocolate, chopped into small pieces
- 1/4 cup light corn syrup
- 1/2 cup heavy whipping cream
- 1 1/2 teaspoons vanilla extract

To MAKE THE CAKE: Preheat the oven to 350°F. Line the bottom of a 9-inch cake pan with a parchment paper round and coat evenly with cooking spray. Melt the butter and chocolate in a metal bowl set over a medium saucepan with 2 inches of simmering water. Stir until smooth. Remove the bowl from over the saucepan. Whisk the eggs and sugar in a large bowl. Whisk the chocolate mixture into the egg mixture until well combined. Stir in the vanilla and rum.

Pour the mixture into the prepared pan and place it in a larger roasting or baking pan. Fill the larger pan with enough hot water to come about two-thirds of the way up the sides of the cake pan. Bake for 35 to 40 minutes. The cake is done when it is firm to the touch. It will rise while baking and settle down to its original size when removed from the oven. Cool the cake completely in the pan on a rack.

To MAKE THE MOUSSE: Melt the butter and milk chocolate in a metal bowl set over a saucepan of simmering water. Set the chocolate mixture aside to cool. Using a mixer or whisk, beat the egg yolks and sugar until smooth. Stir in the vanilla. Combine the egg yolk mixture with the chocolate mixture. In a clean bowl, beat the egg whites on high speed using a mixer fitted with a whisk attachment until shiny, stiff peaks form. Fold the egg whites into the chocolate mixture, one-third at a time, using a large rubber spatula. Using a mixer fitted with a whisk attachment, whip the cream on high speed just until soft peaks start to form. If you beat the cream more, the mousse will get lumpy. Gently fold the whipped cream into the chocolate mixture.

Spread the mousse over the cooled cake, filling the pan to the top. Wrap with plastic wrap or aluminum foil and freeze at least 6 hours and preferably overnight.

At this point the cake can be kept in the freezer for up to 3 weeks.

To MAKE THE GLAZE: Place the chocolate in a medium mixing bowl. Combine the corn syrup, cream, and vanilla in a saucepan; bring to a boil. Immediately pour the cream mixture over the chopped chocolate and whisk until smooth. Keep the glaze at room temperature to ensure that it will pour. If the glaze is too thick, add more cream.

To assemble the dessert, remove the cake from the freezer. Dip the bottom of the pan in hot water to loosen, then invert it onto a plate. Invert the cake again onto a serving plate, so that the mousse is on top. Pour the glaze over the mousse, making sure it covers the sides. Let the glaze set at least 1 hour. Cover with plastic wrap and freeze until ready to serve. The dessert is best when removed from the freezer just a few minutes before cutting. If left at room temperature, it will begin to melt.

Tip: It is easiest to separate eggs when they are cold, but egg whites whip up best when beaten at room temperature. Separate the eggs as soon as they come out of the refrigerator, then let the whites sit on the counter until they reach room temperature, about 10 to 15 minutes. Note: the very young, the elderly, and anyone immunocompromised should avoid eating raw eggs.

Tuxedo Cake

This is the birthday cake of choice for many of my customers and the best-selling cake in the bakery. I made it for the daughter of Hollywood actress Madeleine Stowe, who owns a ranch near Fredericksburg. She loved it so much she wanted one for her own birthday. One small detail: she was celebrating in California. I froze the cake solid, wrapped it in multiple layers of plastic wrap and foil, packed it in dry ice, sent it via overnight mail, and held my breath. I heard she was happy with it.

YIELD: 12 TO 14 SERVINGS

CAKE

1 cup (2 sticks) unsalted butter

2 cups water

1 cup canola oil

4 cups sugar

1 cup high-quality unsweetened cocoa powder

4 cups all purpose flour

4 large eggs

1 cup buttermilk

1 tablespoon baking soda

1/2 teaspoon salt

1 tablespoon vanilla extract

WHIPPED CREAM FROSTING

4 cups chilled heavy whipping cream

1¼ cups powdered sugar

CHOCOLATE GLAZE

4 ounces high-quality bittersweet chocolate, chopped into small pieces

1/2 cup heavy whipping cream

1/4 cup Lyle's Golden Syrup (see Tip on page 17)

2 teaspoons vanilla

To MAKE THE CAKE: For a 3-layer cake, place one baking rack one-third from the bottom of the oven and the second two-thirds from the bottom. Preheat the oven to 350°F. Line the bottom of three 9-inch or two 10-inch cake pans with parchment paper rounds, grease with butter, and dust with flour (or spray with Baker's Joy).

Combine the butter, water, and canola oil in a medium saucepan set over medium heat. In a large bowl, stir together the sugar, cocoa, and flour. Pour the butter mixture into the sugar mixture and whisk until smooth. Whisk in the eggs, one at a time, then whisk in the buttermilk. Whisk in the baking soda, salt, and vanilla all at once. Transfer the batter to the prepared pans. For a 3-layer cake, stagger the cake layers on the oven racks so that no layer is directly over another. Set two layers on one rack and the third on the other. For a 2-layer cake, stagger the layers on the middle rack with one placed more toward the front of the oven and one toward the back. Bake for

(continued)

35 to 40 minutes, or until a toothpick inserted in the middle of each layer comes out clean. Monitor the layers carefully for doneness; each one may be done at a different time.

Remove the cakes from the oven and cool on racks for about 15 minutes before inverting onto baking racks. Cool the cakes completely, at least 2 hours, before frosting.

To MAKE THE FROSTING: Using a mixer fitted with a whisk attachment, whip the cream in a large bowl on high speed until soft peaks form. Add the powdered sugar and whip until thoroughly combined.

Place 1 cake layer on a platter and spread some of the frosting over the top. Top with the remaining layer or layers, thickly coating the top and sides of each with frosting.

Refrigerate the cake until the whipped cream frosting has stabilized, at least 1 hour.

To MAKE THE GLAZE: Place the chocolate in a medium bowl. Heat the cream in a small saucepan over medium heat until it is very hot and just beginning to steam. Pour the hot cream over the chocolate and stir until it has melted completely. Stir in the syrup and vanilla. Pour the glaze into a medium pitcher or measuring cup and let cool for 10 minutes. Do not let the glaze sit longer because it will stiffen and become difficult to pour over the cake. Slowly pour the glaze over the cake, ensuring that it covers the top and drizzles down the sides. Cover the top of the cake entirely, but make sure some of the cream frosting shows through the drizzles on the sides. (If the glaze doesn't flow easily over the edge of the cake don't be afraid to add an extra tablespoon or two of Lyle's Golden Syrup.)

Refrigerate the cake until the glaze is set and the whipped cream frosting is firm, at least 1 hour. Slice the cake with a long serrated knife, dipping it in a tall glass of hot water between each slice. The refrigerated cake will keep for about 2 days.

Tip: Whipped cream usually begins to separate shortly after it has been beaten. The secret to this frosting—and its stability—is the powdered sugar. Powdered sugar has added cornstarch, which stabilizes the cream. This cake sat on my counter on a warm spring night for more than 30 minutes and still looked as good as it had just after icing.

Larger-than-Life Praline Cheesecake

This is a big, gorgeous cheesecake perfect for the most glamorous holiday feast. The spiced pumpkin–cream cheese filling is topped with a deep brown blanket of praline sauce, and underneath lies a buttery gingersnap crust.

Remember to make this dessert in advance. It needs to chill in the refrigerator for several hours before serving.

YIELD: 14 TO 16 SERVINGS

GINGER CRUST

- 2 cups crushed gingersnap cookies (about 40 cookies)
- 1/2 cup (1 stick) unsalted butter, melted
- 1/4 cup sugar
- 1 tablespoon ground cinnamon

PUMPKIN FILLING

- 3 (8-ounce) packages cream cheese, at room temperature
- 1 1/3 cups sugar
- 3 large eggs
- 1 teaspoon vanilla extract
- 1 (15-ounce) can pure pumpkin
- 1/2 teaspoon ground cinnamon
- 1/2 teaspoon ground nutmeg
- 1/2 teaspoon ground ginger

PRALINE TOPPING

- 1 cup pecans
- 1/2 cup firmly packed golden brown sugar
- 3/4 cup heavy whipping cream
- 1 tablespoon unsalted butter
- 1 tablespoon vanilla extract
- 1/4 teaspoon salt

To MAKE THE CRUST: Line the bottom of a 9- or 10-inch springform pan with parchment paper and coat with cooking spray or Baker's Joy. In a large bowl, stir together the crushed gingersnaps with the melted butter, sugar, and cinnamon. Press into the bottom of the prepared pan.

Preheat the oven to 350°F.

To MAKE THE FILLING: Using a mixer fitted with a paddle attachment, beat the cream cheese in a large bowl on medium-high speed about 1 minute, until fluffy. Add the sugar and beat until smooth, about 1 minute. Add the eggs, one at a time, beating on medium-high for 20 seconds after each addition. Add the vanilla, pumpkin, cinnamon, nutmeg, and ginger; beat on medium speed about 1 minute, until incorporated.

Pour the filling over the crust. Put the springform pan into a larger baking pan and set it on the center rack of the oven. Pour enough boiling water into the larger pan to reach halfway up the sides of the

(continued)

springform pan. Bake about 1 hour, until the filling is set and golden brown on top. Cool the cheesecake on a rack about 30 minutes, then chill for several hours or overnight. Remove the cheesecake from the springform pan and set it on a serving plate.

To MAKE THE PRALINE TOPPING: Preheat the oven to 350°F. Arrange the pecans on a baking sheet in a single layer and toast them for 7 to 9 minutes, until golden brown and aromatic. Coarsely chop the nuts.

Stir together the brown sugar, cream, and butter in a saucepan set over medium heat. Boil the mixture for about 1½ minutes, adjusting the heat to make sure it does not boil over. Do not stir. Remove the pan from the heat and stir in the vanilla, salt, and pecans. Cool the topping at least 15 minutes before pouring over the top of the chilled cheesecake. Serve immediately, or cover and chill until ready to serve. The cheesecake will keep, well wrapped, in the refrigerator for 3 to 4 days.

Bananas Foster Shortcakes

I first encountered Bananas Foster Shortcakes at the famous New Orleans restaurant Commander's Palace. I loved the idea, and when I got home, I developed my own version.

Ideally, the shortcakes should be served warm, with the biscuits straight out of the oven— but this is often impossible, especially when entertaining. Instead, make the biscuits in the morning, cool completely, and cover with plastic wrap. When ready to serve, heat the biscuits in a 325°F oven for five minutes, assemble the shortcakes, and serve.

YIELD: 8 SERVINGS

BISCUITS

- 1/2 cup pecans (optional)
- 2 cups all purpose flour
- 2 teaspoons baking powder
- 1/2 teaspoon salt
- 1/3 cup granulated sugar
- 1/2 cup (1 stick) chilled unsalted butter
- 1 teaspoon vanilla extract
- 3/4 cup heavy whipping cream
- Coarse sugar, such as decorating sugar or raw sugar, for coating

BANANA SYRUP

- 1 cup (2 sticks) unsalted butter
- 1½ cups firmly packed golden brown sugar
- 1/2 teaspoon ground cinnamon
- 1/4 cup banana liqueur, such as crème de banane
- 1/4 cup dark rum, such as Myers's
- 8 barely ripe bananas, sliced into 1/4-inch rounds

- 8 scoops vanilla ice cream

Preheat the oven to 350°F. Arrange the pecans on a baking sheet in a single layer and toast them for 7 to 9 minutes, until golden brown and aromatic. Cool the nuts completely.

To MAKE THE BISCUITS: Increase the oven temperature to 425°F. Combine the flour, baking powder, salt, and granulated sugar in a food processor fitted with a metal blade. Process about 30 seconds. Cut the butter into 16 pieces and add to the flour mixture. Pulse about 15 times, until the mixture is crumbly. Add the pecans, turn on the processor, and pour in the cream through the feed tube in a thin, steady stream. Stop the machine. Pulse until the mixture begins to form a ball.

Remove the dough and place on a flat surface that has been sprinkled with flour. Gently form the dough into a ½-inch-thick disk. (It may be slightly crumbly. Push it gently together, handling it as lightly and as little as possible.) Use a 4-inch biscuit cutter, a round cookie cutter, or a glass to cut the dough into rounds. Roll the biscuits in the coarse sugar and set on an ungreased baking sheet. (Eight biscuits should fit on a standard-size sheet. They will rise a little, but won't spread much.)

Bake for 10 to 12 minutes, until the short-cakes begin to turn golden brown, especially around the edges. Cool for 5 minutes on the baking sheet, then use a spatula to transfer the biscuits to individual serving plates. If you do not plan to serve them immediately, cool on racks.

To MAKE THE BANANA SYRUP: Melt the butter, brown sugar, and cinnamon in a large sauté pan set over medium-high heat, about 3 minutes. The mixture should not be heated beyond a simmer; if it begins to boil over, decrease the heat. The syrup may be made ahead up to this point. Store it in a clean glass jar in the refrigerator up to 1 week. Before serving, reheat the syrup; add the banana liqueur, rum, and sliced bananas.

If the biscuits were made ahead, preheat the oven to 325°F and reheat for 5 to 7 minutes. Split the biscuits in half with a fork and set them on individual plates. Place a scoop of ice cream on the bottom halves; spoon over some banana syrup. Set the top halves of the biscuits atop the ice cream and spoon more banana syrup on top. Serve the shortcakes immediately.

Strawberry Ricotta Cake

When I worked at Tony's in Houston, a freelance baker used to sell us a similar cake. I always liked it, but never got the recipe. After opening Rather Sweet, I came up with a version of my own.

The angel food cake recipe comes from my friend Jonnie Stansbury and, like everything she makes, it is first-rate. Superfine sugar is available in most grocery stores, but you can make you own by whirling regular sugar in a food processor fitted with a metal blade. If you are desperate for time, you can buy a ten-inch store-bought angel food cake instead.

YIELD: 10 TO 12 SERVINGS

ANGEL FOOD CAKE

- 1⅓ cups sifted cake flour (sifted then measured)
- ¼ teaspoon salt
- 1¾ cups superfine sugar
- 2 tablespoons freshly squeezed lemon juice
- Zest of 2 oranges, preferably organic
- Zest of 2 lemons, preferably organic
- 14 large egg whites (1¾ cups), at room temperature
- 1 teaspoon cream of tartar

FILLING

- 4 cups whole or part-skim ricotta cheese
- 2 tablespoons heavy whipping cream
- 1 teaspoon vanilla extract
- 1 cup powdered sugar
- ⅛ teaspoon salt

WHIPPED CREAM FROSTING

- 2½ cups chilled heavy whipping cream
- ½ cup powdered sugar
- ½ teaspoon vanilla extract

- 25 medium-size fresh strawberries
- Powdered sugar, for garnish

To MAKE THE ANGEL FOOD CAKE: Set the oven rack on the lowest level and preheat the oven to 350°F. Combine the flour, salt, and ¼ cup of the sugar into a medium bowl. Combine the lemon juice and zests in a small bowl.

Using a mixer fitted with a whisk attachment, mix the egg whites and cream of tartar in a large bowl on low speed until frothy. Add the remaining 1½ cups sugar, 1 tablespoon at a time, beating on high speed until all of the sugar is added and the egg whites are stiff and shiny. Overbeating will create a tough crumb and a dry cake. Use a large rubber spatula to gently but thoroughly fold in the flour mixture and the lemon juice and zest. Spoon the batter into an ungreased 10-inch tube pan. (The cake will not rise properly unless the pan is grease free.)

Bake the cake for about 45 minutes, until it is golden brown and a wooden skewer inserted in the center comes out clean. Invert the cake pan and place the neck of a large soda bottle through the pan's center hole to hang the cake upside down. (The idea is to keep the cake from touching any surface as it cools.) Cool completely, 1 to 2 hours.

To MAKE THE FILLING: Line a 2-quart bowl with plastic wrap. (Don't obsess about the bowl's size; I use a slightly larger 72-ounce plastic bowl with fine results.) Combine the ricotta, cream, vanilla, powdered sugar, and salt in a medium bowl. Stir vigorously until well mixed. Using a serrated knife, cut the angel food cake horizontally into 3 layers. Press the bottom layer lightly into the bottom of the prepared bowl. Spoon half of the ricotta mixture, about 1½ cups, evenly over the cake layer. Top with the middle layer of cake and use the remaining ricotta mixture to cover it. Lightly press the last layer of cake on top.

At this point you may cover and refrigerate the cake up to 1 day. When ready to assemble, flip the cake over onto a serving plate (remove any plastic wrap that has stuck to the top). You'll have a perfect little domed cake.

To MAKE THE FROSTING: Using a mixer fitted with a whisk attachment, whip the cream in a medium bowl on high speed until thick, with medium-soft peaks forming when you lift the mixer out of the bowl (this takes about 1½ to 2 minutes with a handheld mixer, and even less time with a stand mixer). Be careful not to overwhip the cream, or it will separate. Stir in the powdered sugar and vanilla extract.

Use a spatula to cover the cake with the whipped cream frosting, mounding a little extra on the top to accentuate the dome shape. Wash the strawberries and dry them thoroughly with paper towels. Cut off the green stems, set each strawberry stem end down, and cut each into as many thin, vertical slices as possible. Starting at the top of the dome, push the strawberry slices gently into the whipped cream frosting in vertical lines. The tops and bottoms of the slices should overlap as you decorate the cake with strawberries. (Visualize the way roof shingles are laid.) Using this method, cover the entire cake with the sliced strawberries. Sprinkle the cake lightly with powdered sugar. This cake is best served immediately. It will keep for several hours in the refrigerator, but it should be eaten the day you make it.

Rather Sweet Variation

For a Valentine's Day treat, make the cake in a heart mold (with at least a 2-quart capacity). Line it with plastic wrap and follow the recipe.

For an almond-flavored version, substitute equal amounts of pure almond extract—never imitation almond flavoring—for the vanilla extract in both the filling and frosting recipes, and omit all of the citrus ingredients from the cake recipe.

Peach Queen Cake with Dulce de Leche Buttercream Frosting

I love a challenge. When my friend, Pat Sharpe, a senior editor at Texas Monthly *requested an original recipe using peaches, I agreed. Forget the usual cobbler, crisp, or pie, I thought. I soon learned I had very little time to submit the recipe. I gulped hard and spent the next two days locked in my kitchen developing this dramatic triple-layer cake. Don't be daunted by the recipe's length or seeming complexity. Take one step at a time, and you'll find it's simple enough for a novice baker.*

YIELD: 12 TO 14 SERVINGS

DULCE DE LECHE

1 (14-ounce) can sweetened condensed milk

CAKE

2 cups coarsely chopped pecans

1 cup pecan halves

1½ cups (3 sticks) unsalted butter, at room temperature

3 cups sugar

6 large eggs

1 cup sour cream

2 teaspoons vanilla extract

3 cups cake flour

1¼ teaspoons baking soda

¼ teaspoon salt

1 cup peeled, chopped peaches, fresh or frozen

PEACH FILLING

10-ounces jar high-quality peach preserves

1¾ cups peeled, chopped peaches, fresh or frozen, defrosted and drained if frozen

DULCE DE LECHE BUTTERCREAM

1½ cups (3 sticks) unsalted butter, at room temperature

3 tablespoons heavy whipping cream

1 teaspoon vanilla extract

4 cups powdered sugar

Dulce de leche (above)

To make the dulce de leche: Remove the paper wrapper from the can of sweetened condensed milk. Use a can opener to make two small punctures on opposite sides of the top of the can. Set the can of milk in a medium saucepan, puncture side up. Fill the saucepan with water to reach two-thirds of the way up the sides of the can. Cover the saucepan and bring the water to a boil over high heat. Lower the heat until the water simmers. Simmer the milk about 1 hour. Check the saucepan periodically, adding water to ensure that the water level does not drop below halfway. A bit of milk may seep out of the small holes in the can. Cook until the milk pooled on top of the can has turned a deep golden brown. (You may have heard that boiling the can of sweetened condensed milk unopened is a shortcut. *Do not attempt this.* The milk expands when heated and may erupt with explosive results.)

Remove the can from the simmering water using a pot holder or tongs (it will be very hot). Open the can carefully and use a rubber spatula to spoon the cooked milk into a small bowl. It should have a puddinglike consistency. Set aside until completely cooled. Reserve the dulce de leche for the frosting.

To MAKE THE CAKE: Place one baking rack one-third from the bottom of the oven and the second two-thirds from the bottom. Preheat the oven to 350°F. Line the bottoms of three 9-inch cake pans with parchment paper rounds and grease with butter or cooking spray. Arrange the chopped pecans on a baking sheet in a single layer, and arrange the pecan halves on another baking sheet. Toast them in the oven for 7 to 9 minutes, until golden brown and aromatic. Cool the pecans for at least 10 minutes. Set the toasted pecan halves aside for decorating the cake. Leave the oven at 350°F.

Using a mixer fitted with a whisk attachment, cream the butter and sugar in a 6-quart bowl on medium-high speed about 2 minutes, until fluffy. Use a rubber spatula to scrape the mixture from the sides into the middle of the bowl. Add the eggs, 1 at a time, beating on medium-high speed between each addition. Add the sour cream and vanilla; beat until incorporated. In a medium mixing bowl, stir together the flour, baking soda, and salt. Add the flour mixture to the batter and beat on low speed

just until incorporated. Fold in the peaches and 1 cup of the chopped pecans (reserve the remaining chopped pecans for the filling). Pour or spoon the batter evenly into the prepared pans. Stagger the cake layers on the oven racks so that no layer is directly over another. Set two layers on one rack and the third on the other. Bake for 35 to 40 minutes, or until the cakes are light brown on top and firm to the touch. Cool for 10 minutes in the pans. Run a knife round the edges of the pans and invert the cakes onto a rack to cool completely, about 15 to 30 minutes.

The cake layers can be kept frozen, tightly wrapped in plastic wrap, up to 3 weeks.

To MAKE THE PEACH FILLING: Stir together the preserves, peaches, and reserved 1 cup pecans.

To MAKE THE BUTTERCREAM: Using a mixer fitted with a whisk attachment, beat the butter in a large bowl on medium-high speed about 2 minutes, until fluffy. Add the cream, vanilla, and powdered sugar and beat until incorporated. Add the cooled dulce de leche and beat until fluffy, about 2 minutes longer.

To assemble the cake, place 1 cake layer on a serving plate. Top with half of the peach filling. Add the second layer; top with the remaining peach filling. Add the third layer. Frost the top and sides of the cake with the buttercream. Press the toasted pecan halves in an even circle around the outer edge of the cake's top.

The frosted cake will keep for 2 days at room temperature, or 1 week in the refrigerator. Bring the cake to room temperature before serving.

Cream-Filled Pumpkin Roll

A welcome surprise to add to your Thanksgiving Day dessert repertoire, this airy, butterless cake is flavored with pumpkin and rolled up with a creamy, cinnamon-spiced filling. Serve it with homemade caramel sauce and a spoonful of whipped cream and it could become a festive Turkey Day tradition. Easy to transport and easy to make in advance, it is a great dessert to bring when it's someone else's turn to host the Thanksgiving feast.

YIELD: 10 TO 12 SERVINGS

CAKE

- 4 large eggs, separated
- 1/4 cup firmly packed light brown sugar
- 1/2 cup all purpose flour
- 1 teaspoon baking powder
- 1 teaspoon baking soda
- 1/2 teaspoon salt
- 1/2 teaspoon ground cinnamon
- 1/2 teaspoon ground allspice
- 1/2 cup canned pure pumpkin
- 1/4 cup granulated sugar

FILLING

- 2 (3.5-ounce) packages cream cheese, at room temperature
- 1 cup mascarpone cheese
- 1 cup powdered sugar
- 1 generous teaspoon vanilla extract
- 1/4 teaspoon ground allspice
- 1/2 teaspoon ground cinnamon
- 1/4 teaspoon ground nutmeg
- 1/8 teaspoon salt
- 1/2 cup toasted pecans or walnuts, coarsely chopped
- 1/2 cup heavy whipping cream

CARAMEL SAUCE

- 1 cup sugar
- 1/4 cup (1/2 stick) unsalted butter
- 3/4 cup chilled heavy whipping cream
- Pinch of salt
- 2 tablespoons dark rum, such as Myers's (optional)

GARNISH

- 1 cup chilled heavy whipping cream
- 1/4 cup powdered sugar
- 1/2 cup toasted pecan or walnut halves
- 2 ounces dark chocolate, for garnish
- 2 ounces white chocolate, for garnish

To MAKE THE CAKE: Preheat the oven to 350°F. Cover the bottom of a 12 by 17-inch rimmed baking pan with parchment paper and coat lightly with cooking spray. Using a mixer fitted with a whisk attachment, beat the egg yolks in a large bowl on medium-high speed about 2 minutes, until thick and frothy. Add the brown sugar and mix on medium speed for 1 minute longer. In a separate bowl, stir together the flour, baking powder, baking soda, salt, and spices. Add the dry ingredients to the egg yolk mixture one-third at a time, beating on medium speed between each addition until incorporated. Add the pumpkin and mix on low speed until combined.

(continued)

Pour the egg whites into a clean, large bowl. Using a mixer fitted with a whisk attachment, whip them on high speed about 1 to 2 minutes, until soft peaks form. Add the granulated sugar, 1 tablespoon at a time, beating on high speed after each addition until incorporated. Fold the egg whites gently into the batter. Spoon the batter evenly into the pan and smooth carefully; it will not even out as the cake bakes. Bake for 15 to 20 minutes, until the cake is golden brown and springs back when touched lightly. Let the cake cool for 15 minutes.

To MAKE THE FILLING: Using a mixer fitted with a paddle attachment, beat the cream cheese on medium speed until creamy. Add the mascarpone and beat until incorporated. Add the powdered sugar, vanilla, allspice, cinnamon, nutmeg, and salt; beat on medium-high speed about 1 minute, until combined. Stir in the nuts. In a separate large bowl, whip the cream using a mixer fitted with a whisk attachment on high speed about 1 to 2 minutes, until soft peaks form. Fold the whipped cream gently into the cream cheese-pecan mixture.

Remove the cake from the pan without peeling off the parchment paper. Top the cake with the filling. Begin peeling the cake away from the parchment paper as you roll it up, starting at the short end closest to you. When the cake is completely rolled up, set it on a rectangular serving plate or wrap it well and refrigerate it for up to 2 days.

To MAKE THE CARAMEL SAUCE: Heat the sugar over medium heat in a heavy-duty saucepan or iron skillet until it is completely melted and turns amber in color, about 5 minutes. Decrease the heat to low, add the butter all at once, and stir to combine. (It will bubble up.) Add the cream, a couple of tablespoons at a time, stirring to combine between each addition. Adding the cream slowly keeps the caramel from clumping. Continue stirring until the caramel sauce is melted and smooth. Remove from the heat and stir in the rum. You'll have about 1½ cups of caramel sauce. Caramel can be stored in a covered glass container in the refrigerator for up to 3 weeks. Reheat it in the microwave.

To MAKE THE TOPPING: Using a mixer fitted with a whisk attachment, beat the cream on medium-high speed until it is thick with medium-soft peaks forming. Beat in the powdered sugar. For a fancy flair, partially fill a pastry bag fitted with a star tip with the whipped cream and pipe a fat line down the middle of the roll. Arrange the nuts in a line on top of the piped whipped cream.

Place the dark and white chocolate in separate bowls and melt in the microwave on medium-high power, about 45 seconds. Stir and return to the microwave for 15 seconds more if not fully melted. Using a spoon for each, drizzle the melted dark and white chocolate over the top of cake in a zigzag pattern.

To serve, cut the roll with a serrated knife. Pass a pitcher of warm caramel sauce and a bowl of the remaining whipped cream and let guests serve themselves.

Tip: Caramel sauce can be a challenge. The trick is caramelizing the sugar without burning it. You need to watch constantly as the sugar heats. Once the sugar melts things happen very fast. I've burned mine plenty of times. If the kids are screaming, or the phone is ringing, reschedule your caramel sauce making. There are two cardinal rules for making caramel: Don't get the hot stuff on yourself—it will leave a nasty burn—and don't take it too far. You've gone too far if the sugar starts smoking, a sure sign that it has started to burn. (Toss it out. Believe me, it will not taste good.) The key is to melt the sugar until it turns medium amber in color, then reduce the heat and immediately add the butter and cream.

Make sure you use a heavy-duty saucepan without nonstick coating when making caramel. (Nonstick coating may disintegrate at the high heat needed to melt sugar.) Also, make sure the saucepan or skillet is completely dry before adding sugar. If not, the water in the pan could cause the sugar to crystallize, resulting in grainy caramel sauce. This recipe doubles, easily.

Mini Apple-Cinnamon Loaves with Calvados Glaze

During the holiday season, we wrap these luscious little quick breads in cellophane, tie them up with shimmering red bows, and sell them for holiday gift-giving. If you don't own mini loaf pans, buy disposable foil pans, available in most supermarkets around the holidays. Dimensions vary, but aim for pans that are about 6 by 4 by 2 inches.

Calvados is French apple brandy, but you can substitute any kind of apple brandy— known as applejack in the United States.

YIELD: 5 SMALL LOAVES

BREAD

- 1 cup pecans
- 1¼ cups light vegetable oil, such as canola or safflower
- 2 cups sugar
- 2 large eggs
- 1 teaspoon vanilla extract
- 3 cups all purpose flour
- ½ teaspoon ground cinnamon
- ½ teaspoon ground nutmeg
- ½ teaspoon baking soda
- 1 teaspoon salt
- 3 cups peeled, cored, diced apples (about 3 large apples)

GLAZE

- ¼ cup (½ stick) unsalted butter
- ⅓ cup firmly packed golden brown sugar
- 1 tablespoon light corn syrup or Lyle's Golden Syrup (see tip on page 17)
- 1 tablespoon Calvados

To MAKE THE BREAD: Preheat the oven to 350°F. Arrange the nuts on a baking sheet in a single layer and toast them for 7 to 9 minutes, until golden brown and aromatic. Cool the nuts and then coarsely chop.

(continued)

Grease five 6 by 4 by 2-inch mini loaf pans with butter or Baker's Joy. Whisk together the oil, sugar, eggs, and vanilla in a large bowl. In a separate bowl, combine the flour, cinnamon, nutmeg, baking soda, and salt. Stir the flour mixture into the oil mixture until incorporated. Stir in the apples and pecans. (The batter will be very stiff and difficult to stir.) Spoon the batter into the loaf pans, filling each about three-quarters of the way to the top. Bake for 50 minutes to 1 hour, or until a toothpick inserted into the middle of the bread comes out clean. Cool the loaves in their pans for 10 minutes, then turn them out onto baking racks for glazing.

To MAKE THE GLAZE: Melt the butter, brown sugar, syrup, and Calvados in a saucepan set over medium-high heat. Simmer the mixture over medium-low heat about 2 minutes, until it thickens slightly. Spoon the warm glaze over each loaf. Do not wrap the loaves until they are thoroughly cooled and the glaze has set, about 1 hour. Wrapped bread will keep up to 4 days at room temperature, or 1 month frozen.

Rather Sweet Variation

The batter can be cooked in a 9-inch Bundt pan. Bake at 350°F for 1 hour, or until a toothpick inserted into the middle comes out clean.

Espresso Crème Brûlée

One of my mottos as a pastry chef is, you're only as good as your last crème brûlée. I make this recipe weekly, and it always works without a hitch.

The custard can be made one to three days ahead and refrigerated. The topping should be caramelized just before serving.

YIELD: 6 SERVINGS

1/4 cup whole milk

2 3/4 cups heavy whipping cream

1 tablespoon espresso powder

1 vanilla bean

7 large egg yolks

2/3 cup plus 1/2 cup sugar

Preheat the oven to 300°F. Lightly coat six 6-ounce ramekins with cooking spray. To make the custard, pour the milk, cream, and espresso powder into a 1 1/2-quart, nonreactive, heavy-bottomed saucepan and warm over medium-high heat. While the cream mixture is heating, use a sharp paring knife to slice the vanilla bean pod in half lengthwise. Separate the beans from

(continued)

the pod by scraping the inside of the pod with the edge of the knife. Add the beans and pod to the heating cream mixture. Bring to a boil and immediately remove the saucepan from the heat. In a large mixing bowl, whisk the egg yolks and the ⅔ cup sugar until well combined. Continue to whisk while slowly pouring the hot cream into the egg mixture. Blend thoroughly. Pour the custard through a fine-mesh sieve to remove the vanilla bean pod and any bits of overcooked egg.

Place the prepared ramekins in a baking pan with sides that are at least 2 inches high. Pour the custard into the ramekins, filling each halfway. Transfer the baking pan carefully to the oven and fill the ramekins as close to the top as possible without spilling. Fill a measuring cup with hot water from the tap. Add enough hot water to the baking pan to reach three-quarters of the way up the sides of the ramekins. Bake the custards about 1 hour. Check periodically to make sure the custards are not browning or bubbling. If they are, decrease the oven temperature to 250°F. The custards are done when just set (they should tremble slightly when shaken). If they still look liquidy, return to the oven for 5 minutes longer, or until set. Remove the ramekins from the baking pan and cool for 30 to 40 minutes. Cover tightly and refrigerate at least 3 to 4 hours. (They can be prepared up to 3 days ahead.) The custards will fully firm up in the refrigerator.

Just before serving, use the ½ cup sugar to top each custard with a thin layer of sugar. It is important to spread the sugar evenly and to make sure the sugar layer is thick enough so that the custard does not show through. If you have a kitchen torch, use it to caramelize the sugar. If not, preheat the broiler. Place the ramekins 4 inches from the flame and broil, watching carefully, until the sugar is caramelized and lightly browned. Serve immediately.

Rather Sweet Variations

Crème brûlée purists—I know who you are—will want to omit the coffee flavoring and enjoy this dessert in its classic form. In another variation, I thinly slice a banana and arrange a single layer atop the crème brûlée, then add the sugar and caramelize it.

Tip: I swear by the tradition of using vanilla beans for crème brûlée, but if you're caught short or don't want to mess with slicing the bean pods in half and scraping them out, I recommend keeping a bottle of pure vanilla bean paste, made by Nielsen-Massey Vanillas, based in Waukegan, Illinois. Made with sugar, water, vanilla extract, and the tiny vanilla seeds, it is thick but still pourable. According to the instructions on the bottle, 1 tablespoon of paste is equivalent to 1 vanilla pod or 1 tablespoon of vanilla extract. Vanilla bean paste is very expensive, so I don't substitute it blindly, but I find it creates a slightly more robust vanilla flavor than standard extract and has the added advantage of flecking my finished goods with those appealing vanilla beans.

Toffee Bar Brownie Torte

This is one of my absolute richest desserts: three layers of deep chocolate brownie covered in a coffee-scented whipped cream and mascarpone cheese frosting and finished off with a thin layer of crushed toffee. I use whatever nut- or chocolate-covered toffee candy I happen to have around, from Heath bars to Almond Roca. They can be smashed with a rolling pin between two sheets of waxed paper, or pulsed in a food processor or blender.

YIELD: 12 TO 14 SERVINGS

BROWNIES

- 2 cups (4 sticks) unsalted butter
- 16 ounces bittersweet chocolate, chopped into small pieces
- 3 cups sugar
- 8 large eggs
- 2$\frac{1}{2}$ cups all purpose flour
- $\frac{1}{2}$ teaspoon salt
- 2 tablespoons vanilla extract

FROSTING

- 3 cups chilled heavy whipping cream
- $\frac{1}{3}$ cup powdered sugar
- 1 teaspoon vanilla extract
- 2 tablespoons instant espresso powder dissolved in 2 teaspoons boiling water, chilled

FILLING

- 2 (8-ounce) tubs mascarpone cheese
- 2 tablespoons instant espresso powder dissolved in 2 teaspoons boiling water
- $\frac{1}{2}$ cup powdered sugar
- 2 teaspoons vanilla extract
- $\frac{1}{8}$ teaspoon salt
- 1 cup frosting (above)

- 2 cups chopped toffee bars

To make the brownies: Preheat the oven to 350°F. Grease three 9-inch cake pans with butter and dust lightly with flour (or spray with Baker's Joy). Melt the butter and chocolate in a medium metal bowl set over a saucepan filled with 2 inches of simmering water. Stir until the chocolate has melted. Remove the bowl from over the saucepan. (Or melt the butter and chocolate in a medium microwave-safe bowl in the microwave for 1 minute on medium-high. Stir until the chocolate has melted completely. If the chocolate does not melt fully, microwave for an additional 30 seconds. Continue microwaving for 30-second intervals, stirring between each heating, until the mixture is smooth.) Add the sugar and eggs to the chocolate; whisk about 1 minute, until the mixture is glossy and smooth (you may use a hand mixer set on medium-high speed for this). Stir in the flour, salt, and vanilla. Do not overmix the batter.

Pour one-third of the batter into each pan and bake for 20 to 25 minutes, until the brownies are just firm to the touch. Cool the brownies in their pans for 30 minutes, then invert them onto racks to cool completely, about 30 minutes longer.

To MAKE THE FROSTING: Using a mixer fitted with a whisk attachment, whip the cream on high speed until medium-soft peaks form. Whip in the sugar, vanilla, and espresso, whipping until combined. Cover and refrigerate 1 cup of the frosting to use in the filling. Set aside the rest of the frosting.

To MAKE THE FILLING: Using a mixer fitted with a paddle attachment, beat the mascarpone, espresso liquid, sugar, vanilla, and salt on medium speed just until combined. Using a large spatula, fold in the 1 cup of reserved frosting.

To assemble the torte, transfer 1 brownie layer to a round, flat serving plate and spread half of the filling evenly over the top. Add the second layer and spread the remaining filling evenly over the top. Add the third layer and cover the top and sides with frosting. Press the toffee pieces into the frosting to thinly cover the sides of the torte and to create an even band of toffee around the edge of the top of the torte. Refrigerate until ready to serve. Cut the torte in thin slices—it is very rich—with a long serrated knife, dipping it in a tall glass of hot water between each cut. The cake is best served the day it is made, but leftovers will keep, covered, in the refrigerator for 2 days.

Tiramisù with Homemade Ladyfingers

The darling of the 1980s upscale restaurant scene, tiramisù seemed to pop up on just about every menu. Soon it inevitably suffered from overexposure. Nonetheless, my love has remained true. One of my favorite desserts, I adore making it almost as much as eating it.

Making your own ladyfingers may seem daunting, but I figure if you're going to all the trouble of making this dessert, you might as well go all the way. That said, store-bought ladyfingers do save time, and I guarantee the dessert will still be a stunner. I have given a range for the quantity of rum used in this recipe. Some people love a pronounced rum flavor, others just a hint. It's up to you.

This dessert must be made in advance. The flavors mellow and mingle as it cures in the refrigerator. It will keep covered for at least 2 weeks, but I'd be surprised if it lasted that long.

YIELD: 16 TO 20 SERVINGS

LADYFINGERS

½ cup powdered sugar for dusting the ladyfingers, plus extra for dusting the baking sheets

7 large eggs, separated

¾ cup plus 4 tablespoons granulated sugar

2 teaspoons vanilla extract

1 cup all purpose flour

SOAKING SYRUP

½ cup water

1½ cups sugar

2 teaspoons instant espresso powder

¼ cup coffee liqueur, such as **Kahlúa**

⅛ to ¼ cup dark rum, such as **Myers's**

1 tablespoon vanilla extract

FILLING

3 (8-ounce) packages cream cheese, at room temperature

2 cups sugar

1 (16-ounce) tub mascarpone cheese, at room temperature

1 tablespoon boiling water

2 tablespoons instant espresso powder

Dark cocoa powder or grated bittersweet chocolate, for dusting

To make the ladyfingers: Preheat the oven to 375°F. Line two 12 by 17-inch baking sheets with parchment paper. Use a fine-mesh sieve to dust the paper with a light coating of powdered sugar. Using a mixer fitted with a paddle attachment, beat the egg yolks, the ¾ cup granulated sugar, and the vanilla in a large bowl on high speed about 5 minutes, until the yolks become thick and pale yellow. In a separate clean, large bowl, use a mixer fitted with a whisk attachment to beat the egg whites on high speed until stiff peaks form. Add the 4 tablespoons granulated sugar, 1 tablespoon at a time, beating after each addition. Fold the egg white mixture gently into the egg yolk mixture. Use a sieve to sift the flour over the batter. Gently fold in the flour just until incorporated.

Spoon the batter into a pastry bag fitted with a large round tip. Pipe the batter onto the prepared baking sheets, making each ladyfinger about 4 inches long and 2 inches wide. (This takes a little practice. Don't worry if your first attempts are a little wobbly.) You'll be able to fit about 5 ladyfingers across and 4 down on each sheet. Bake about 10 minutes, until lightly browned. Sift the ½ cup powdered sugar over the ladyfingers just as they come out of oven. Cool for 5 minutes and use a spatula to transfer them from the baking sheet to cooling racks.

To MAKE THE SOAKING SYRUP: Simmer the water and sugar in a heavy saucepan set over medium heat about 10 minutes, until slightly thickened. Remove the mixture from the heat and stir in the espresso powder, liqueur, rum, and vanilla. Set aside to cool.

To MAKE THE FILLING: Using a mixer fitted with a paddle attachment, combine the cream cheese and sugar in a large bowl on high speed. Add the mascarpone and beat on medium speed just until incorporated. Combine the boiling water and espresso powder in a small bowl. Stir ¼ cup of the cooled soaking syrup and 1 tablespoon of the espresso liquid into the filling. Spoon half of the cream cheese mixture into a medium bowl. Stir the remaining 1 table-spoon of espresso liquid into the second bowl of cream cheese mixture. You will have 1 bowl of light brown cream cheese filling and 1 bowl of dark brown cream cheese filling.

Coat a 9 by 13-inch baking pan with cooking spray. Dip both sides of 1 ladyfinger in the cooled soaking syrup and place in the bottom of the pan. Repeat with more ladyfingers and syrup to line the whole pan. Spoon the light-colored cream cheese mixture evenly over the ladyfingers and smooth gently with a spatula. Cover with a second layer of dipped ladyfingers. Spoon on the dark-colored cream cheese mixture and smooth the top as before. (Leftover ladyfingers can be wrapped and frozen up to 1 month.) Use a fine-mesh sieve to dust the top with a light coating of dark cocoa, or sprinkle grated bittersweet chocolate evenly on top.

Cover the tiramisù and refrigerate for at least 2 hours or overnight. Serve cold from the refrigerator. Cut in squares and serve with a spatula.

Tip: The Microplane grater is the perfect tool for creating an even dusting of bittersweet chocolate over the tiramisù. Move the tool slowly over the dessert while you grate.

Dulce de Leche-Arborio Rice Pudding

A new twist on an old-fashioned favorite, my version of rice pudding is flavored with dulce de leche, *amaretto liqueur, and almonds. Dulce de leche has become such a popular ingredient that you can buy it ready-made in specialty foods stores. Naturally, it's cheaper to make it yourself out of a can of sweetened condensed milk. I make several cans at once, transfer the contents into glass jars, and keep them in the refrigerator until needed. It makes a delicious topping for ice cream, and I've given decorated jars of it to friends for the holidays.*

YIELD: 4 TO 6 SERVINGS

RICE PUDDING

- 1 (14-ounce) can sweetened condensed milk
- 1/2 cup **Arborio rice**
- 2 cups water
- 1 1/2 cups milk (low-fat will work)
- 4 large egg yolks
- 1/4 cup firmly packed golden brown sugar
- 1 1/2 cups heavy whipping cream
- 2 vanilla beans, split in half, seeds scraped out and reserved
- 3 tablespoons amaretto liqueur

GARNISH

- 1 cup slivered almonds
- 1 cup chilled heavy whipping cream
- 1/3 cup dulce de leche (above)

To make the pudding: Coat a 5- to 6-cup ovenproof casserole or soufflé dish with cooking spray.

Remove the paper wrapper from the can of sweetened condensed milk. Use a can opener to make two small punctures on opposite sides of the top of the can. Set the can of milk in a medium saucepan, puncture side up. Fill the medium saucepan with water to reach two-thirds of the way up the sides of the can. Cover the saucepan and bring the water to a boil over high heat. Lower the heat until the water simmers. Simmer the milk about 1 hour. Check the saucepan periodically, adding water to ensure that the water level does not drop below halfway. A bit of milk may seep out of the small holes in the can. Cook until the milk pooled on top of the can has turned a deep golden brown. (You may have heard that boiling the can of sweetened condensed milk unopened is a shortcut. *Do not attempt this.* The milk expands when heated and may erupt with explosive results.)

Remove the can from the simmering water using a pot holder or tongs (it will be very hot). Open the can carefully and use a rubber spatula to spoon 1 cup of the cooked milk into a measuring cup (save the rest to use in the whipped cream topping). It should have a puddinglike consistency.

Bring the rice and water to a boil in a medium saucepan and simmer for 5 minutes. Drain the rice in a colander, pour back into the saucepan, and add the milk. Cover and simmer the rice 20 to 25 minutes, until the milk is absorbed. Transfer the rice to a bowl.

Preheat the oven to 325°F. In a separate bowl, whisk together the egg yolks and brown sugar until smooth. In a medium saucepan set over medium heat, bring the cream, 1 cup dulce de leche, and vanilla bean pods and their beans to a boil. Remove the vanilla bean pods.

Whisk 2 tablespoons of the hot cream mixture into the egg yolk mixture (introduce the hot mixture slowly, or the yolks may begin to curdle). Pour the rest of the cream mixture in a slow, steady stream into the egg yolk mixture, whisking constantly. Stir in the amaretto. Add the cooked rice and mix to combine.

Pour the mixture into the prepared casserole dish. Bake for 45 to 50 minutes, until the top is browned and a toothpick stuck into the middle comes out almost clean. (The pudding may look a little wet on top.)

To MAKE THE GARNISH: Arrange the almond slivers on a baking sheet in a single layer and toast them in the oven for 7 to 9 minutes, until golden brown and aromatic.

Using a mixer fitted with a whisk attachment, beat the cream in a large bowl on high speed until soft peaks begin to form. Add 1/3 cup of the remaining dulce de leche, if desired, and beat until incorporated.

Serve the pudding warm or at room temperature with a dollop of dulce de leche whipped cream and a generous sprinkling of toasted almonds.

Muchas Leches Cake with Sugared Almonds

This is a loosely adapted version of a fabulous cake conceived by Jill Reedy, former pastry chef at Dallas's Star Canyon restaurant. (Aficionados of Latin American food will recognize it as a creative takeoff on pastel tres leches, *a popular cake in Nicaragua and Mexico that is soaked in three kinds of milk.) The first time I tried Jill's version, covered with a showstopping sugared almond garnish, I fell in love with it and asked for the recipe. It is one of my favorite special-occasion cakes, and I make it often for birthdays, anniversaries, and important dinners.*

The dramatic look and great taste of this flourless cake add up to very high "wow" rating— exactly what I'm looking for in a celebration cake. A few years ago, I served it at a dinner for a freelance writer who was visiting from New York to research a story that included my bakery. Shortly thereafter she moved to Texas and we became great friends. Was it the cake? Of course not. But it didn't hurt.

I like the look of a rectangular cake, so I use a 12 by 17-inch baking pan to bake mine (then I cut it in quarters to make four cake layers). Two 10-inch cake pans or three 9-inch pans will work as well.

One last word about this very unusual cake: It contains very little flour and no butter or oil. Finely ground blanched almonds fill in for the flour, and egg yolks provide the most concentrated source of fat. The result is a light, airy cake unlike any you've baked before. Once it is saturated with the cream-laden soaking liquid, it takes on an almost puddinglike consistency that I find irresistible.

YIELD: ABOUT 16 SERVINGS

(continued)

CAKE

4 cups (16 ounces) blanched almonds

1¼ cups plus ½ cup sugar

½ teaspoon ground cinnamon

14 large eggs, separated

¼ cup all purpose flour

½ teaspoon baking powder

SOAKING LIQUID

½ cup heavy whipping cream

¼ cup cajeta (caramelized goat's milk) or Dulce de Leche (page 94)

½ cup sweetened cream of coconut, such as Coco López

½ cup sweetened condensed milk

½ cup evaporated milk

1 tablespoon vanilla extract

SUGARED ALMONDS

4 large egg whites

4 cups sliced almonds

1 cup sugar

FROSTING

4 cups chilled heavy whipping cream

1½ cups powdered sugar, plus additional for dusting

Seasonal berries (optional)

To MAKE THE CAKE: Preheat the oven to 350°F. Line a 12 by 17-inch baking pan with parchment paper and coat it with butter or cooking spray. Finely grind the almonds with the ½ cup sugar and the cinnamon in a food processor fitted with a metal blade. Using a mixer fitted with a paddle attachment, beat the egg yolks and the 1¼ cups sugar in a large bowl on mdeium-high speed about 3 to 4 minutes, until the mixture lightens in color and becomes fluffy. Fold in the flour and baking powder. Fold in the ground almond mix-

ture. In a separate clean, large bowl, use a mixer fitted with a whisk attachment to beat the egg whites on high speed 1 to 2 minutes, until stiff peaks form. Gradually fold the beaten egg whites into the batter.

Spoon the batter into the prepared baking pan. Use a spatula to distribute the batter smoothly and evenly (this is an important step, because the batter will not even out in the pan as it bakes). Bake for 35 to 40 minutes, until the top is golden brown and the cake is firm to the touch. Cool for 5 minutes, then invert onto a rack that has been greased with a light coating of cooking spray. Decrease the oven temperature to 325°F.

To MAKE THE SOAKING LIQUID: Whisk together the cream, cajeta or dulce de leche, cream of coconut, milk, evaporated milk and vanilla in a medium bowl.

To MAKE THE SUGARED ALMONDS: Using a mixer fitted with a whisk attachment, beat the egg whites on high speed until foamy. Stir in the almonds and sugar, making sure the nuts are evenly coated. Spread the almonds evenly in a baking pan and bake until golden brown, 8 to 10 minutes. Stir the almonds to break them up and set aside to cool.

To MAKE THE FROSTING: Using a mixer fitted with a whisk attachment, whip the cream in a large bowl on high speed until soft peaks form. Add the powdered sugar and whip until incorporated and the frosting is thick enough to spread easily.

Cut the cooled cake carefully in half lengthwise and then cut each half in half widthwise, using a serrated knife. You'll have 4 rectangles (the assembled cake will be about 8 inches long and 5 inches tall). Place

1 cake quarter on a large serving plate. Brush it liberally with one-quarter of the soaking liquid. Frost the top with the whipped cream frosting. Set the second cake layer directly on top of the first. Brush with a quarter of the soaking liquid. Repeat with the remaining two quarters. Frost the sides of the cake with the remaining frosting. Press the cooled almonds gently into the frosting on the sides and top of the cake, covering it completely. Refrigerate the cake until ready to serve. Dust with a light coating of powdered sugar. Covered in plastic wrap, the cake will keep will keep in the refrigerator about 2 days. Garnish the cake with berries, slice, and serve.

Tip: Chilled heavy cream whips up more easily and, once whipped, holds its shape better. When whipping cream, do not remove the cream from the refrigerator until the last minute. If you are really serious about your whipped cream, refrigerate the mixing bowl and whip attachment about 5 minutes before use.

Almond Bliss German Chocolate Cake

My grandmother's German chocolate cake recipe differs little from the standard version found in many cookbooks. I've made a few small changes, including substituting bittersweet chocolate for German chocolate, but it got me wondering: what exactly is German chocolate? It's not a type of chocolate, but a brand name belonging to Baker's chocolate. Apparently Sam German, who worked for Baker's, developed this sweet baking chocolate in the mid-nineteenth century. The company called it German's Sweet chocolate.

I soon discovered that this rich, three-layer cake has a lot more to do with Texas than with Germany, to which it has no connection. (By most accounts, it turns out, German was an Englishman.) In the 1950s, a Dallas newspaper published a chocolate cake recipe using German's chocolate. The cake caused an immediate sensation. Soon it appeared in newspapers all over the country under the name German's Chocolate Cake. Who knows when the apostrophe disappeared and the cake showed up in cookbooks as that perennial American favorite, German chocolate cake.

Traditionally, the cake is frosted with a coconut-pecan frosting made with sweetened condensed milk or evaporated milk. The version we serve at the bakery is covered with a blanket of almond-flecked icing made with regular milk and sweetened cream of coconut.

YIELD: 12 TO 14 SERVINGS

CAKE

8 ounces bittersweet chocolate, chopped into small pieces

1/2 cup boiling water

1 cup (2 sticks) unsalted butter, at room temperature

2 cups sugar

4 large eggs, separated

1 teaspoon baking soda

1 cup buttermilk

2 1/2 cups all purpose flour

1/2 teaspoon salt

1 tablespoon vanilla extract

1 3/4 cups semisweet chocolate chips

CUSTARD ICING

1 1/2 cups sliced almonds

1 cup milk

1 1/2 cups sweetened cream of coconut, such as Coco López

1/2 cup (1 stick) unsalted butter

5 large egg yolks

3/4 cup sugar

3 tablespoons cornstarch

1 1/2 cups sweetened shredded coconut

1 cup sliced fresh strawberries (optional)

To MAKE THE CAKE: Place one baking rack one-third from the bottom of the oven and the second two-thirds from the bottom. Preheat the oven to 350°F. Line the bottom of three 9-inch cake pans with parchment paper rounds, grease with butter, and dust with flour (or spray the paper with the Baker's Joy).

Place the chocolate in a small saucepan, pour the boiling water over, and stir until the chocolate has dissolved completely. (If it doesn't completely dissolve, put the pan on the stovetop over low heat and stir until it does. Do not leave it unattended; chocolate burns easily.) Remove from the heat to cool.

Using a mixer fitted with a paddle attachment, beat the butter and sugar in a large bowl on medium-high speed about 2 minutes. Add the egg yolks and beat on medium-high for 1 minute. Stir the baking soda in the buttermilk until it dissolves. Add half of the buttermilk mixture alternately with the half of the flour, mixing on low speed after each addition. Repeat with the remaining buttermilk mixture and flour. Stir in the salt, chocolate mixture, and vanilla. Stir in the chocolate chips.

In a clean medium bowl, beat the egg whites on high speed, using a mixer fitted with a whisk attachment, until soft peaks form. Gently fold the egg whites into the chocolate batter using a large rubber spatula, which makes for lighter and easier folding.

Spoon the batter evenly into the prepared cake pans. Stagger the cake layers on the oven racks so that no layer is directly over another. Set two layers on one rack and the third on the other. Bake for 30 to 35 minutes, or until a toothpick inserted into the middle of the cakes comes out clean. Monitor the layers carefully for doneness; each one may be done at a different time. Cool the cakes in the pans for 5 minutes, then turn them out onto racks and cool completely.

To MAKE THE ICING: Arrange the almond slices on a baking sheet in a single layer and toast them for 5 to 7 minutes, until golden brown and aromatic. Cool the nuts completely.

Heat the milk, cream of coconut, and butter in a saucepan over medium heat until the butter has completely melted. In a medium bowl, whisk the egg yolks, sugar, and cornstarch until smooth. Slowly pour 3 tablespoons of the hot milk mixture, 1 tablespoon at a time, into the yolk mixture, whisking briskly until the yolks have absorbed the hot liquid. (Pouring in a little of the hot liquid helps to temper the eggs, which keeps them from curdling.) Slowly pour the tempered yolk mixture into the hot milk mixture still set over medium heat, whisking constantly. Continue whisking about 7 to 10 minutes, until the mixture thickens, takes on the consistency of custard, and seems thick enough to spread. Stir in the coconut and almonds. Let the icing cool at least 15 minutes.

Place 1 cake layer on a serving platter and cover the top generously with frosting. Add the second and third layers, frosting the top of each. Do not frost the sides of the cake, but it's okay if some of the icing oozes out.

(continued)

Decorate the top of the cake with sliced fresh strawberries.

To serve, cut the cake with a serrated knife, dipping it into a tall glass of hot water between each cut. Wrap the cake well if you do not plan to serve it within a few hours. It can be refrigerated up to 3 days.

Tip: Don't forget that leftover egg whites can be refrigerated at least two days. Use them to make meringues (see the Petite Pavlovas with Lemon Cream and Fresh Fruits, page 64), or if you're feeling guilty about last night's second helping of German chocolate cake, whip up an angelic egg white omelet for breakfast.

Seventh Heaven Chocolate Truffle Cake

The bakery version of this cake sports seven layers, but for home cooks it is simpler to cut it into six. I guarantee that six layers of this rich truffle-filled cake will be plenty to transport you to seventh heaven.

Planning is essential here, because once the cake is layered with truffle filling it must be refrigerated for at least two hours. And don't forget to make the ganache frosting early. It must sit at room temperature for at least two hours to reach the proper consistency for frosting the cake. If you're truly organized, make the whole thing in advance and refrigerate the well-wrapped cake up to three days, or freeze it up to three weeks.

YIELD: 10 TO 12 SERVINGS

CAKE

- 2¹/₃ cups cake flour
- 1¹/₂ teaspoons baking soda
- 1 teaspoon salt
- 1 ounce unsweetened chocolate
- ¹/₂ cup (1 stick) unsalted butter, at room temperature
- 2¹/₃ cups firmly packed golden brown sugar
- 3 large eggs
- 2 teaspoons vanilla extract
- 1 cup sour cream
- 1 cup boiling water

GANACHE FROSTING

- 24 ounces bittersweet chocolate (70 percent cacao), finely chopped
- ¹/₂ cup (1 stick) unsalted butter, at room temperature
- 2¹/₂ cups heavy whipping cream
- 2 teaspoons vanilla extract
- ¹/₄ cup light corn syrup

TRUFFLE FILLING

- 8 ounces semisweet chocolate, chopped into small pieces
- 3 ounces unsweetened chocolate, chopped into small pieces
- 1½ cups (3 sticks) unsalted butter
- ½ cup heavy whipping cream
- 6 large egg yolks
- ⅔ cup powdered sugar
- 1 tablespoon vanilla extract
- 2 tablespoons Grand Marnier (optional)

To MAKE THE CAKE: Preheat the oven to 350°F. Line two 12 by 17-inch rimmed baking pans with silicone mats or parchment paper and coat with nonstick cooking spray. Make sure the parchment paper is wrinkle-free or the cakes will be uneven when baked. Place one baking rack one-third from the bottom of the oven and the second two-thirds from the bottom. (If you only have one baking pan, you can bake the cakes separately on the middle rack of the oven, washing the pan after baking the first cake and preparing it as you did the first time.)

Sift together the flour, baking soda, and salt in a medium bowl. Coarsely chop the chocolate and melt it in a small metal bowl set over a saucepan with 2 inches of simmering water, or in the microwave. Stir the melted chocolate until smooth and remove it from the heat.

Using an electric mixer fitted with a paddle attachment, beat the butter and sugar in a large bowl on medium-high speed about 2 minutes, until light and creamy. Add the eggs, one at a time, beating on medium speed for 30 seconds after each addition. Add the melted chocolate and vanilla to the batter and beat until incorporated. Add

one-third of the flour mixture and beat on medium speed for 20 seconds. Add ½ cup of the sour cream and beat for another 20 seconds. Continue alternating additions until all of the dry ingredients and sour cream have been added. Add the boiling water and mix thoroughly on medium speed for 30 seconds.

Pour the batter into a large measuring cup. Pour half of the batter into each of the prepared pans. Bake for 7 to 12 minutes, until the cake springs back when touched lightly or a toothpick inserted into the center comes out clean. Monitor the layers carefully for doneness; they may be done at different times. Remove the cake from the oven and cool at least 30 minutes.

To MAKE THE GANACHE: Place the chocolate and butter in a medium bowl. Heat the cream in a small saucepan over medium heat until it is very hot and just begins to steam. Pour the hot cream over the chocolate and butter and stir until the mixture is smooth. Add the vanilla and corn syrup; stir until the ganache is smooth and glossy. The ganache will be too soft to frost the cake immediately; it must sit at room temperature about 2 hours to firm up. The ganache can be made the night before the cake is assembled and left, covered, at room temperature. (Do not refrigerate it, or it will become too hard to handle.)

To MAKE THE TRUFFLE FILLING: Melt both chocolates, the butter, and the cream in a large bowl set over a saucepan with 2 inches of simmering water. Remove from the heat to cool. Using a mixer fitted with a whisk attachment, whip the egg yolks in another

(continued)

large bowl on high speed about 5 minutes, until thick and light in color. Add the melted chocolate mixture and beat on medium-high speed for 1 minute. Add the powdered sugar, vanilla, and Grand Marnier and mix on medium speed until incorporated.

To ASSEMBLE THE CAKE: Invert the cooled cake onto a flat surface lined with waxed paper. Cut each cake into 3 equal rectangles (see Tip). You will have 6 rectangles of cake total. Put 1 cake layer on a cake plate, spread the top with a thick layer of truffle filling (about one-fifth of the filling), and cover the filling with another layer of cake. Continue with a layer of filling and a layer of cake until all of the cake layers are used, but do not spread filling over the top layer. Cover the cake with plastic wrap and refrigerate about 2 to 3 hours, until firm.

Remove the cake from the refrigerator and frost it with the cooled ganache. Cut the cake with a long serrated knife, dipping it in a tall glass of hot water between each slice. Well wrapped, the cake will keep in the refrigerator for up to 1 week or in the freezer for up to 3 weeks.

Tip: A ruler and dental floss can ease the job of cutting this cake into equal parts before frosting. Use the ruler to measure out three equal portions of each cake, measuring from one side of the cake's short end to the other. Stretch unflavored floss from one end of the cake to the other and push down lightly to mark a straight line. Follow the line with your knife to cut the cake into squares.

White Chocolate–Snickers Mousse

I developed this recipe when I worked for Tony Vallone, owner of several upscale Houston restaurants. Tony's executive chef, Mark Cox, used to tell us, "Utilization is the key to success." He wouldn't let a carrot peel go into the garbage. I had some white chocolate I needed to use up and a bag of Snickers. With Mark's words reverberating in my head, I came up with this dessert.

The recipe involves several steps, but it can be made up to two weeks in advance. Don't leave it until the last minute: it must freeze at least six to eight hours before serving. Make a splash at your next dinner party by serving the mousse just as we did in Houston—in an edible almond tuile cup.

YIELD: 6 TO 8 SERVINGS

ALMOND TUILES

- 1/4 cup (1/2 stick) unsalted butter
- 1 cup sliced almonds
- 1/2 cup sugar
- 5 tablespoons white corn syrup or Lyle's Golden Syrup (see Tip on page 17)
- 1/4 teaspoon salt
- 1/4 cup flour

MOUSSE

- 9 ounces high-quality white chocolate, chopped into small pieces
- 2 cups chilled heavy whipping cream
- 2 tablespoons crème de cacao (optional)
- 1/2 cup sugar
- 1/4 cup water
- 4 large egg whites, at room temperature
- 2 large Snickers bars or 8 Fun Snack–size Snickers, chopped into 1/2-inch pieces

To MAKE THE TUILES: Preheat the oven to 350°F. Line 2 baking sheets with parchment paper or silicone mats. Stir the butter, almonds, sugar, and syrup in a medium saucepan set over low heat. Once the butter has melted completely remove the pan from the heat and stir in the salt and flour.

Drop the dough, 2 tablespoons at a time, on parepared baking sheets, spacing each cookie at least 4 inches apart. (They will flatten and spread as they bake.) Only 2 cookies will fit on a 12 by 17-inch baking sheet. Bake for 10 to 14 minutes, until the cookies are flat and golden brown.

Let the tuiles cool on the baking sheets for 3 to 5 minutes. The trick is to remove them with a spatula while they are still warm and pliable. Immediately center each cookie over the base of an inverted drinking glass or jar that is about 2 inches in diameter and at least 3½ inches tall, letting the sides of the cookie drape around the glass or jar.

Gently press the edges of the cookie to hug the sides of the glass or jar. If the tuiles are too hot when you do this, they will fall apart when you try to remove them from the baking sheet. If they are too cool, they'll crack when you try to drape them. If the tuiles become too hard to drape, put them back on the baking sheets and return them to the oven for 30 to 60 seconds until they are pliable.

Cool the tuiles on the inverted glasses until they are hard enough to hold their shape, about 5 minutes. Store in an airtight container for up to 3 days.

To MAKE THE MOUSSE: Place the white chocolate in a large bowl. Pour ½ cup of the cream in a medium saucepan and bring it just to boiling over medium heat. (Keep the remaining 1½ cups cream in the refrigerator until ready to use.) Pour the hot cream over the chopped chocolate. Whisk until smooth. Let the chocolate mixture sit until cooled. Stir in the crème de cacao.

Heat the sugar and water in a saucepan over medium-high heat and boil for 3 to 5 minutes, until the syrup reaches the soft ball stage (registering between 234° and 240°F on a candy thermometer, or forms a soft-ball when a little bit is dribbled into a glass of cold water). Remove the saucepan from the heat.

Using a mixer fitted with a whisk attachment, beat the egg whites in a medium bowl on high speed until soft peaks form. Continue beating on high speed while pouring the hot sugar syrup into the egg whites in a slow, steady stream. Beat the mixture on medium speed about 2 minutes, until it is thick, shiny, and slightly cooler. Using a large rubber spatula, fold a dollop of egg white mixture into the white chocolate mixture, then gently fold in the rest of the egg whites. Using a mixer fitted with a whisk attachment, whip the remaining 1½ cups chilled cream in a large bowl on high speed just until soft peaks begin to form. Do not overbeat, or the mousse will be lumpy. Fold the whipped cream gently into the white chocolate mixture using a large rubber spatula. Stir the chopped Snickers gently into the mousse.

Spoon the mousse into a container with a cover; cover and freeze at least 6 hours and up to 2 weeks. Scoop the frozen mousse into the tuile cups, stemmed glasses, or sundae glasses and serve.

Tip: It is important to use high-quality white chocolate in this recipe, such as Lindt Swiss White Tablette Blanche or Bernard Callebaut's White Chocolate Drops, which have the added advantage of not needing much chopping. These white chocolates employ cocoa butter as their source of fat, not the hydrogenated oils used in cheaper versions. Check the ingredients on the label.

For a refreshing summer dessert, tuiles can be also filled with chopped fresh fruit, sorbet, or ice cream.

White-on-White Buttermilk Cake with Jack Daniel's Buttercream

One of the finest pastry chefs at Houston's renowned Café Annie, Jeannie Hemwattakit was running the pastry department at an upscale supermarket when we met. We both were single mothers—our babies were born in the same year—and we connected immediately. I ran a wedding cake business from my home. She took me under her wing, and gave me this recipe. I have been making it ever since for birthday parties, weddings, and other special events.

Jeannie is one of the most generous chefs I've ever met. She is always quick to share her recipes and her knowledge. Now, it's my turn—until now, I have refused repeated requests for this recipe. I love this cake because it is a moist, snow-white cake and the layers always come out flat on top, making it a dream to frost. Decorated with edible flowers, such as pansies or nasturtiums, this cake looks as fabulous as it tastes.

YIELD: 12 TO 14 SERVINGS

CAKE

- 1¹/₂ cups (3 sticks) unsalted butter, at room temperature
- 2¹/₃ cups sugar
- 3 large egg whites
- 2 teaspoons vanilla extract
- 3 cups cake flour
- ³/₄ teaspoon baking soda
- ³/₄ teaspoon salt
- 1¹/₂ teaspoons baking powder
- 1¹/₂ cups buttermilk

BUTTERCREAM

- 3 large eggs
- 4 large egg yolks
- ¹/₂ cup water
- 2 cups sugar
- 3 cups (6 sticks) unsalted butter, at room temperature
- ¹/₂ teaspoon salt
- 3 tablespoons Jack Daniel's whiskey

To MAKE THE CAKE: Place one baking rack one-third from the bottom of the oven and the second two-thirds from the bottom. Preheat the oven to 350°F. Line three 9-inch cake pans with parchment paper rounds, grease with butter, and dust with flour (or spray with Baker's Joy).

Using a mixer fitted with a paddle attachment, beat the butter and sugar in a large bowl on medium speed about 2 minutes, until light and fluffy. Scrape down the sides of the bowl. Add the egg whites and vanilla and beat on medium speed for about 1 minute. Combine the flour, baking soda, salt, and baking powder in a medium bowl. Add about one-third of the flour mixture to the batter and beat on medium speed until incorporated. Add about half of the buttermilk and beat on medium speed until incorporated. Continue adding dry and wet ingredients alternately, scraping the bowl down and beating until incorporated after each addition. End with the dry ingredients. The batter will be thick and glossy.

Spoon the batter evenly into the prepared cake pans. Stagger the cake layers on the oven racks so that no layer is directly over another. Set two layers on one rack and the third on the other. Bake for 25 to 35 minutes, until a toothpick inserted into the middle of the cakes comes out clean and the tops are flat and browned. Monitor the layers carefully for doneness; each one may be done at a different time.

Set the cake pans on racks to cool for 10 minutes. Invert the cakes onto the racks and cool completely before frosting. At this point the cakes can be tightly wrapped in a layer of plastic wrap and a layer of aluminum foil and frozen up to 3 weeks.

To MAKE THE BUTTERCREAM: Using a mixer fitted with a whisk attachment, whip the eggs and yolks in a large bowl on high speed about 5 minutes. In a medium saucepan, combine the water and sugar; simmer until it reaches the soft-ball stage, registering between 234° and 240°F on a candy thermometer. Immediately transfer the syrup to a large heatproof liquid measuring cup. In a slow, thin stream, add the sugar mixture to the egg mixture, mixing on low speed the entire time. Increase the speed to medium and beat about 7 minutes, until the syrup has cooled (the bowl should be barely warm to the touch). Add the butter, half a stick at a time, beating on medium speed about 20 seconds after each addition. Once all of the butter has been added, beat on medium speed until the frosting thickens

slightly, about 3 minutes. Stir in the salt and whiskey.

Place 1 cake layer on a serving plate and spread a thick blanket of frosting on top. Add the second layer and spread thickly with frosting. Add the third layer and cover the top and sides of the cake with an even layer of frosting. Covered, the cake will keep for 2 days at room temperature.

Rather Sweet Variation

Any flavored liqueur can be substituted for the Jack Daniel's in the frosting. Some of my favorites include Grand Marnier and amaretto. For chocolate-flavored buttercream, substitute 8 ounces of melted bittersweet chocolate for the Jack Daniel's. Make sure to cool the melted chocolate for at least 15 minutes before adding it to the buttercream.

When you want to celebrate without quite as much drama (or work), there's a two-layer version of this cake. Simply substitute the reduced amounts that follow and pour the batter into two 9-inch cake pans: Bake both pans on the middle rack in the oven, staggering them so that one is toward the front of the oven and the other toward the back. The pans should not be touching. For the batter, use 1¼ cups unsalted butter, 1¾ cups sugar, 2 large egg whites, 1 teaspoon vanilla extract, 2⅓ cups cake flour, ¼ teaspoon baking soda, ½ teaspoon salt, ½ teaspoon baking powder, and 1 cup plus 3 tablespoons buttermilk. For the buttercream, use 2 large eggs, 2 large egg yolks, ¼ cup water, 1 cup sugar, 1½ cups butter, ¼ teaspoon salt and 1 tablespoon whiskey.

Tropical Carrot Cake with Coconut-Cream Cheese Frosting

I love a moist carrot cake with lots of cream cheese frosting that's not too sweet. Apparently so do my customers. The addition of toasted macadamia nuts, crushed pineapple, and cream of coconut gives this cake a different twist. A great cake to make for a large crowd, this rich, triple-layer confection guarantees there will be plenty for all.

YIELD: 12 TO 14 SERVINGS

CARROT CAKE

- 1 cup macadamia nuts
- 3 cups all purpose flour
- 3 cups sugar
- 1 tablespoon baking soda
- 1 teaspoon salt
- 1 tablespoon ground cinnamon
- 1/2 teaspoon ground nutmeg
- 1 1/2 cups sweetened flaked coconut
- 4 large eggs
- 2 tablespoons vanilla
- 1 1/2 cups vegetable oil, such as canola or safflower
- 1 1/2 cups shredded peeled carrots
- 1 1/2 cups diced fresh pineapple or drained crushed canned pineapple
- 1/2 cup sweetened cream of coconut, such as Coco López

COCONUT-CREAM CHEESE FROSTING

- 3 (8-ounce) packages cream cheese, at room temperature
- 1 1/2 cups powdered sugar
- 1/4 cup heavy whipping cream
- 1/4 cup sweetened cream of coconut, such as Coco López
- 1/2 teaspoon salt

To make the cake: Preheat the oven to 350°F. Arrange the nuts on a baking sheet in a single layer and toast them for 7 to 9 minutes, until golden and aromatic. Set aside to cool.

Place one oven rack one-third from the bottom of the oven and the second two-thirds from the bottom. Preheat the oven to 350°F. Line three 9-inch cake pans with parchment paper rounds, grease with butter, and dust with flour (or spray with Baker's Joy).

Stir together the flour, sugar, baking soda, salt, cinnamon, nutmeg, coconut, and nuts in a large bowl. In another large bowl, whisk together the eggs, vanilla, oil, carrots, pineapple, and cream of coconut. Pour the egg mixture into the flour mixture and stir until combined.

Pour the batter into the prepared cake pans. Stagger the cake layers on the oven racks so that no layer is directly over another. Set 2 layers on one rack and the third on the other. Bake for 30 to 35 minutes. The cakes are done when they are golden brown on top and a toothpick inserted into the center comes out clean. Cool the cakes in their pans on racks for 5 minutes, then invert them onto the racks and cool completely, about 15 to 20 minutes.

To MAKE THE FROSTING: Using a mixer fitted with a paddle attachment, beat the cream cheese and powdered sugar in a large bowl on medium-high speed about 1 minute. Add the whipping cream, cream of coconut, and salt; beat until combined.

Place 1 cake layer on a serving plate and spread a thick blanket of frosting on top. Add the second layer, spread thickly with frosting, and top with the third layer. Cover the top and sides of the cake with an even layer of frosting. If you're feeling energetic and there is frosting left over, use a pastry bag fitted with a decorative tip to pipe a decoration around the top rim of the cake.

The cake can be covered with plastic wrap and refrigerated up to 4 days. Let it cool in the refrigerator about 1 hour before covering, to ensure the frosting has hardened and will not stick to the plastic wrap.

COOKIES, Brownies, AND Bars

COOKIES AND BARS are my downfall. I cannot keep away from them—especially brownies and chocolate chip cookies. More frequently than I'd like to admit, I steal over to the baking rack near the commercial oven to nab a broken cookie or a brownie remnant. (I've trained the staff to cut away the brownies' corners and edges before slicing them into the huge squares that will be stacked like giant chocolate dominoes in the bakery's front pastry case. As a result, there is an unending supply of irresistible brownie morsels.)

The other night, I asked one of my customers to name his favorite cookie. "I kinda liked Cookie Simpson from high school," he said, straightfaced. Then he added, "Your chocolate chip cookies are hard to beat."

I've been making cookies and bars for so long, I can't remember when I didn't. I started baking for all of my friends when we were in high school. They consistently asked for brownies and oatmeal cookies. Now my best sellers include Triple-Threat Chocolate Chip Cookies—made with three kinds of chocolate—bittersweet, semisweet, and unsweetened—and Blackberry Pie Bars, a fruit pie taste-alike without the bother of rolling out a crust.

We are known for our Texas-size cookies—they're about the size of CDs—and customers razz us about it all the time. "Where are the *big* cookies?" they ask with faux innocence. Everyone knows things are bigger in Texas, but mostly our customers like getting the most for their money.

People love our cookies. They pick up dozens of them for parties. Nurses from the local hospital call ahead for them.

I'm such a cookie nut that I've even started baking cookies for the horses at Lane's barn (where I'm known as the horse-cookie lady). My horse cookies are made from carrots, sweet grains, barley, oats, and honey. Now, whenever the horses see me coming, they start whinnying, confirming what I've known for a long time—cookies make you popular in every circle.

Many home cooks use two teaspoons for spooning cookie dough onto baking sheets: one to scoop the dough up, the other to push it onto the baking sheet. This is a tedious and inexact process. There is a better way. Use metal ice cream scoops to ensure that cookies come out in uniform sizes and shapes. Scoops come in many sizes, allowing you to make cookies as large or small as your fancy dictates. The scoops have a small lever attached to the base, which activates a metal ring that pushes out the dough quickly and easily.

Silicone baking mats are another time-saving must-have. You'll never have to grease another baking sheet, and they can be used again and again. Simply buy one that covers your whole baking sheet, scoop cookies onto it, and once they are baked they'll slide off with little effort. Wash the mats with soapy water, dry them thoroughly, and put them in a drawer until you're ready to use them again. Cookie-size ice cream scoops and silicone baking mats are available at most kitchen stores.

My Favorite
Chocolate Chip Cookies

I love these cookies. They are not too chewy and not too crunchy—they are just right. I've taken to giving a free chocolate chip cookie to the girls from Fredericksburg High who drive here for lunch. (The school is about one mile away.) It's great to see them come in with their blue jeans and backpacks. They call ahead to order—mostly half sandwiches with soup or salad—so they can make it back to school on time. The food is on the table by the time they arrive.

YIELD: ABOUT 5 DOZEN

1½ cups walnuts

1½ cups pecans

1 cup (2 sticks) unsalted butter, at room temperature

1 cup firmly packed dark brown sugar

1 cup granulated sugar

2 large eggs

1 tablespoon vanilla extract

2⅓ cups all purpose flour

1¼ teaspoons baking soda

1 scant teaspoon salt

3 cups chocolate chips

Preheat the oven to 350°F. Arrange the nuts on a baking sheet in a single layer and toast them for 7 to 9 minutes, until golden brown and aromatic. Cool the nuts and then coarsely chop.

Line baking sheets with parchment paper or silicone mats, or grease generously with butter or cooking spray. Using a mixer fitted with a paddle attachment, cream the butter and both sugars in a large bowl on medium speed about 1 minute, until fluffy. Add the eggs and vanilla and beat on medium speed for 1 minute. Add the flour, baking soda, and salt. Mix on medium-low speed until incorporated. Stir in the walnuts, pecans, and chocolate chips. The dough is relatively stiff, so don't be surprised if this takes some muscle (your triceps will thank you later).

Drop the dough onto the prepared baking sheets using a 1¾-inch-diameter ice cream scoop (this will make mounds of dough about the size of a golf ball). Space the cookies about 1½ inches apart as they will spread. Bake for 10 to 12 minutes, until the cookies are medium brown around the edges. (As long as the edges are brown, don't worry about a little bit of raw-looking dough in the middle. It will disappear as the cookies cool.) The cookies will spread to about 3½ inches in diameter.

Tip: Here's a time-saving trick for those with a heavy-duty electric mixer equipped with at least a 525-watt motor. Add the flour, baking soda, salt, walnuts, pecans, and chocolate chips all at once. Use a paddle attachment and turn the mixer on and off every 5 seconds or so, until all of the ingredients are thoroughly incorporated. (Your triceps will thank you now.)

Triple-Threat
Chocolate Chip Cookies

Crisp on the outside and chewy on the inside, these cookies include three kinds of chocolate. This recipe makes a lot of cookies, but if well wrapped in a layer of plastic wrap and a layer of foil, they'll keep for about three weeks in the freezer. Otherwise, they're at their chocolaty, chewy best when eaten within three days. Regular customer Don Parrish says you have to eat these in the morning or you won't sleep at night. He's not the only one who loves them. Kids, especially teens, go wild over them.

YIELD: ABOUT 4 DOZEN

1 cup chopped pecans

1 cup chopped walnuts

6 tablespoons unsalted butter

8 ounces bittersweet chocolate, coarsely chopped

3 ounces unsweetened chocolate, coarsely chopped

3 large eggs

1 cup sugar

1 tablespoon vanilla extract

1/3 cup all purpose flour

1/4 teaspoon baking powder

1/4 teaspoon salt

1 1/2 cups semisweet or milk chocolate chips

Preheat the oven to 350°F. Arrange the pecans and walnuts on a baking sheet in a single layer and toast for 7 to 9 minutes, until golden brown and aromatic. Cool the nuts completely.

Line baking sheets with parchment paper or silicone mats, or grease generously with butter or cooking spray.

Melt the butter, bittersweet chocolate, and unsweetened chocolate in a small saucepan set over low heat. Stir occasionally, watching carefully to make sure the chocolate does not burn. Remove the pan from the heat to cool.

Using a mixer fitted with a paddle attachment, beat the eggs and sugar in a large bowl on medium speed about 3 minutes, until fluffy. Add the vanilla and melted chocolate. Beat on medium speed about 2 minutes, until the dough is thick and glossy. Add the flour, baking powder, and salt to the chocolate mixture, stirring just until incorporated. Stir in the nuts and chocolate chips. Let the dough rest for 20 minutes, which makes it easier to scoop.

Use a 1 3/4-inch-diameter scoop to drop spoonfuls of dough on the prepared baking sheets, spacing them at least 1 1/2 inches apart. Wet your fingertips lightly with water and gently flatten the cookie dough (no

(continued)

Triple
Chocolate
Cookies
$2.5

need to press hard; just press out the hump). Bake for 10 to 12 minutes, until the tops begin to crack and look glossy. Cool the cookies for 10 minutes before removing them from the baking sheets.

(pictured on previous page)

Rather Sweet Variation

For Triple-Threat Rocky Road Cookies, a favorite with elementary school kids, add 1 cup quartered mini marshmallows to the dough along with the nuts and chocolate chips. Bake as directed.

Sugar Saucers

At Rather Sweet, we bake these cookies big—you've got it, as big as saucers. A variation on the traditional sugar cookie, these are crisp on the outside but real softies on the inside. You decide how big you want them: two-inch dainties, perfect for a ladies' lunch, or saucer-size monsters for the bottomless-pit stomachs of teens who might be hanging around. Just remember, the bigger they are, the longer they bake.

Virginia Wood, food editor and columnist for the Austin Chronicle, *gave me this recipe. It has become a Rather Sweet Bakery standard.*

YIELD: 1 DOZEN 4-INCH COOKIES OR 2 DOZEN 2-INCH COOKIES

- ¹/₂ cup (1 stick) unsalted butter, at room temperature
- ¹/₂ cup vegetable oil, such as canola or sunflower
- ¹/₂ cup granulated sugar, plus additional for sugaring tops
- ¹/₂ cup powdered sugar
- 1 large egg
- 2 teaspoons vanilla extract
- 2 cups all purpose flour
- ¹/₂ teaspoon baking soda
- ¹/₄ teaspoon salt

Preheat the oven to 350°F. Line baking sheets with parchment paper, or silicone mats, or grease generously with butter or cooking spray. Using a mixer fitted with a paddle attachment, beat the butter in a large bowl on medium speed about 1 minute. One ingredient at a time, add the vegetable oil, granulated sugar, powdered sugar, egg, and vanilla, beating on medium speed after each addition until completely incorporated. Stir in the flour, baking soda, and salt all at once, using a wooden spoon or the mixer set on low. (The dough will be soft.) Refrigerate the dough about 1 hour or freeze for 15 minutes to make it easier to handle.

Using a standard-size ice cream scoop for giant cookies or a tablespoon-size scoop for 2-inchers, drop the dough onto the prepared baking sheets. The cookies should be spaced about 2 inches apart. Press the dough evenly with your fingers or palm to flatten the cookies to ¼-inch thickness. Sprinkle sugar over the tops of the cookies. Bake for 8 to 10 minutes for small cookies or 12 to 14 minutes for large ones, until the edges turn golden. If you like your cookies on the crisp side, bake them 1 or 2 minutes longer. Let the cookies cool on the baking sheets at least 10 minutes before transferring to racks to cool completely. The cookies will keep for up to 3 days if stored in an airtight container, or they can be frozen for up to 1 month.

Rather Sweet Variation

To make lemon saucers, add a little class to this simple cookie by adding the juice and grated zest of 1 lemon to the dough in place of the vanilla. Then ice with lemon icing: Combine 1 cup powdered sugar with the juice and grated zest of 1 lemon. Stir until smooth and spread over the cooled cookies. Or dip the baked, cooled cookies into melted bittersweet chocolate, covering half the cookie in chocolate. Place the cookies on waxed paper in a single layer and let sit until the chocolate sets, about 30 minutes.

Chock-Full-of-Nuts Cookies

A small percentage of people do not like the taste of almond extract. If someone in your family has such an aversion, skip it and double the quantity of vanilla. Feel free to adjust the proportion of nut types according to your taste, too, but be sure to keep the total amount consistent—these cookies are meant to be nutty.

YIELD: 6 1/2 DOZEN

3 cups pecan pieces

1¹/₂ cups chopped macadamia nuts

1¹/₂ cups chopped walnuts

1¹/₂ cups slivered blanched almonds

1¹/₂ cups (3 sticks) butter, at room temperature

1¹/₂ cups granulated sugar

1¹/₂ cups firmly packed golden brown sugar

3 large eggs

1 tablespoon vanilla extract

1 tablespoon almond extract

3¹/₂ cups all purpose flour

1¹/₂ teaspoons baking soda

1 teaspoon salt

Preheat the oven to 350°F. Arrange the nuts on baking sheets in a single layer and toast them for 7 to 9 minutes, until golden brown and aromatic. Cool the nuts for 5 minutes. Chop the macadamia nuts, walnuts, and almonds.

Line baking sheets with parchment paper or silicone mats, or grease generously with butter or cooking spray.

Using a mixer fitted with a paddle attachment, cream the butter and both sugars in a large bowl on medium-high speed about 1 minute, until light and fluffy. Add the eggs, vanilla extract, and almond extract; beat on medium speed for 1 minute. Add the flour, baking soda, and salt. Beat for 30 seconds, just until the ingredients are thoroughly mixed. Stir in the nuts until combined.

Using a 1³/₄-inch scoop or forming the dough into rounds about the size of a golf ball, set the cookies about 2 inches apart on baking sheets. (I fit 3 cookies across and 4 cookies down for a total of 12 cookies on a 12 by 17-inch baking sheet.) Bake for 10 to 12 minutes, until the cookies are wrinkly and golden brown around the edges, with no raw-looking dough in the middle. They will have spread to about 3 inches in diameter. Cool for 10 minutes on the baking sheets before transferring to a rack. The cookies will keep for 3 to 4 days in an airtight container and can be frozen, well wrapped, for up to 1 month.

Tip: Cooks in a rush may be tempted to skip the step of oven-toasting nuts when using them in baked goods. You have my permission to do so. But once you taste how a little toasting time brings out their flavor and aroma, you may decide the extra work is worth it. Organized types may even decide to toast big batches of nuts, cool them, and freeze them in airtight containers until needed.

Café Chocolate-Cherry Bites

With their strong coffee flavor, these always seemed to me distinctly adult cookies, but a friend of mine's preteen daughter changed my mind by repeatedly requesting "the cherry cookies." It turns out that lots of other kids like them too.

1 cup pecans

1 cup (2 sticks) unsalted butter, at room temperature

1¼ cups firmly packed golden brown sugar

2 large eggs

1 tablespoon instant espresso powder

1 tablespoon boiling water

1 tablespoon vanilla extract

1¼ cups all purpose flour

¼ cup unsweetened cocoa powder

1 teaspoon baking powder

¼ teaspoon salt

1 cup bittersweet or semisweet chocolate chips

1½ cups dried cherries, halved or quartered

Preheat the oven to 350°F. Arrange the pecans on a baking sheet in a single layer and toast for 7 to 9 minutes, until golden brown and aromatic. Cool the nuts for 5 minutes, then coarsely chop.

Line baking sheets with parchment paper or silicone mats, or grease generously with butter or cooking spray. Using a mixer fitted with a paddle attachment, beat the butter and sugar in a large bowl on medium speed about 1 minute, until fluffy. Add the eggs and beat on medium speed about 30 seconds. In a small bowl, stir the espresso powder into the boiling water until dissolved. Add the espresso liquid and the vanilla to the cookie batter and beat for 30 seconds. Add the flour, cocoa, baking soda, and salt all at once, mixing on low speed just until incorporated. Stir in the pecans, chocolate chips, and cherries. (The dough will be softer and wetter than the average cookie dough.)

Using a 1¾-inch-diameter scoop, drop the cookie dough on the prepared baking sheets, spacing 1¾ inches apart. Bake for 8 to 10 minutes, until the cookies have spread and have no lighter-colored, raw-looking dough in the middle. Cool the cookies on the baking sheets about 10 minutes, until they are no longer too soft to remove. Transfer the cookies to racks and cool completely before serving. The cookies will keep for 2 to 3 days in an airtight container and can be frozen, well wrapped, for up to 1 month.

Tip: Heed the one-minute rule: It can take as little as sixty seconds for cookies to turn from underdone to overbaked. To ensure the best results, start checking cookies about a minute before the end of the specified cooking time, and check every minute from then on.

Caramel-Filled Brownies

Incredibly rich and absolutely irresistible, these brownies leave chocolate lovers begging for more. I made them once for a large fund-raiser in Austin and served them with vanilla bean ice cream topped with whiskey-spiked chocolate sauce. Hundreds of my brownie sundaes disappeared in just three hours. I've also served them drizzled with rum-spiked Caramel Sauce (page 97), as pictured. Equally fabulous plain, they can be kept individually wrapped in the freezer for middle-of-the-night chocolate cravings.

The base for this brownie has been adapted from one I made when I worked for Doreen and Richard Kaplan at Acute Events & Catering. My daughter, Frances, spent three years in a playpen under the pastry table at their place. Our little girls were the same age. (Now they're thinking about college.) Richard was the first in a long line of wonderful mentors who have guided me throughout my career. To this day, he claims he taught me everything I know.

YIELD: 2 DOZEN

1½ cups pecans

1 cup (2 sticks) unsalted butter

12 ounces bittersweet chocolate, coarsely chopped

1½ cups sugar

4 large eggs

1 tablespoon vanilla extract

1¼ cups all purpose flour

½ teaspoon salt

14 ounces caramel candies, unwrapped

⅓ cup heavy whipping cream

1 cup semisweet chocolate chips

Preheat the oven to 350°F. Arrange the pecans on a baking sheet in a single layer and toast for 7 to 9 minutes, until golden brown and aromatic. Coarsely chop the nuts.

Line a 9 by 13-inch baking pan with aluminum foil, leaving several inches hanging over the short ends of the pan. Grease the foil with butter or cooking spray. Be sure to grease the sides of the foil-covered pan thoroughly, or the caramel layer in the middle of the brownies will stick. Combine the butter and chocolate in a heavy-bottomed medium saucepan set over low heat, stirring occasionally until melted and smooth. (Do not leave the chocolate mixture unattended for long or it may burn, and you'll have to throw it out and start over.) Transfer the chocolate mixture to a large bowl. Add the sugar, eggs, and vanilla mixing until thick and glossy. This will take 1 to 2 minutes of vigorous mixing with a wire whisk (my implement of choice) or about 1 minute using a mixer fitted with a paddle attachment set on medium-high speed. Whisk or stir in the flour and salt. Transfer half the batter (about 2½ cups) to the baking pan and spread evenly. Bake for 20 minutes. Let the brownies cool about 20 minutes.

Stir the caramels and cream in a heavy medium saucepan over low heat until melted and smooth. Remove from the heat

(continued)

and stir in half the pecans. Immediately spread the caramel mixture over the brownies (if you let it sit, it will get hard and difficult to spread). Pour the remaining brownie batter evenly over the caramel mixture and spread gently to cover (do not pour it in a clump, or it will be difficult to spread over the hot caramel without mixing up the layers). Sprinkle the chocolate chips and remaining pecans on top of the brownie layer. Bake for 20 minutes. Cool the brownies completely in the pan (for quicker cooling, set the pan in the freezer for 30 minutes).

Grab the foil edges and lift the brownies out of the pan. Cut them into squares. If individually wrapped in plastic wrap, the brownies will keep for 1 week at room temperature or for 1 month in the freezer. (Hint: They are great straight from the freezer on a hot summer day.)

Rather Sweet Variation

To make plain, old-fashioned brownies, follow the directions as above but omit the caramel filling, and stir all of the chocolate chips and pecans into the batter. Pour the batter into the baking pan (the same pan works for both recipes) and bake for 25 minutes at 350°F. Cool the brownies before cutting into squares.

Tip: Looks can be deceptive, especially when you're attempting to divide batter evenly and accurately. If you have trouble eyeballing the called-for amount, invest in a large glass measuring cup (at least 8 cups). Those made for pancake batter are ideal. Coat the measuring cup with cooking spray and pour in all the batter. Pour out however much you need. The cooking spray will ensure that the batter doesn't cling to the sides when you pour it into the pan. This technique also works wonderfully for dividing cake batter to fill multiple pans.

Turbo-Charged Brownies with Praline Topping

You may not get a caffeine buzz from these espresso-laced brownies, but adding coffee does provide an extra jolt of flavor, and a sugary layer of praline lends them their Texas twang. Slimmer than average, they're just one more reason to believe in that old saying: you can never be too rich or too thin. These qualify on both counts.

YIELD: ABOUT 2 DOZEN

BROWNIES

3/4 cup (1 1/2 sticks) unsalted butter

3 ounces unsweetened chocolate

1 cup granulated sugar

3/4 cup firmly packed dark brown sugar

3 large eggs

1 tablespoon vanilla extract

1 tablespoon instant espresso powder

1 tablespoon boiling water

1 cup all purpose flour

1/4 teaspoon salt

PRALINE TOPPING

1 cup pecans

1/2 cup heavy whipping cream

1 cup firmly packed golden brown sugar

2 tablespoons unsalted butter

1 tablespoon light corn syrup

1 tablespoon vanilla extract

To MAKE THE BROWNIES: Preheat the oven to 350°F. Line a 9 by 13-inch baking pan with aluminum foil, leaving several inches hanging over the short ends of the pan. Grease the foil with butter or cooking spray.

In a large metal bowl set over a pan filled with 2 inches of simmering water, melt the butter and chocolate (or melt the butter and chocolate in the microwave on medium-high about 1 minute, or longer if necessary). Stir until the chocolate has completely melted. Stir in both sugars. Add the eggs and vanilla all at once and stir until the batter is smooth and shiny. In a small bowl, combine the espresso powder and the boiling water; stir into the brownie mixture. Stir in the flour and salt.

Pour the batter into the prepared pan, smoothing it evenly. Bake about 30 minutes, or until the brownies have just begun to shrink slightly away from the sides of the pan. Do not overbake; the brownies should be slightly wet inside. Cool completely while making the praline topping, about 1 hour at room temperature or 15 minutes in the freezer. Leave the oven at 350°F.

To MAKE THE TOPPING: Arrange the pecans on a baking sheet in a single layer and toast for 7 to 9 minutes, until golden brown and aromatic. Break the nuts into large pieces.

Combine the cream, brown sugar, butter, and corn syrup in a 2 1/2-quart saucepan and

(continued)

stir over medium-low heat until the mixture is smooth and the butter has melted. Bring to a slow boil; boil without stirring about 6 minutes. (If the mixture starts to boil over, you've set the heat too high. Turn the burner down a notch.) Remove the mixture from the heat and let cool about 5 minutes. Stir in the vanilla and pecans.

Pour the topping over the cooled brownies, spreading it with a knife or spatula to cover evenly.

Let the topping cool at least 15 minutes at room temperature. Lift the brownies, still in the foil, out of the pan. Cut them into small, 2-inch squares—these babies are rich.

Double-Ginger Chews

Crystallized ginger, available in the spice section of most grocery stores, adds a touch of class to these rich and chewy little two-inch cookies. If you're feeling flush, spring for the plump, moist Australian crystallized ginger available from Williams-Sonoma.

These cookies become unmanageably floppy if made too large. Use only about a tablespoon of dough for each cookie. This recipe doubles easily.

YIELD: 4 DOZEN

3/4 cup (1 1/2 sticks) unsalted butter

1/2 cup firmly packed dark brown sugar

1/2 cup granulated sugar

1/4 cup molasses

1 large egg

1 1/2 cups all purpose flour

1 teaspoon ground ginger

1 teaspoon ground cinnamon

1/2 teaspoon baking soda

1/4 teaspoon salt

1/2 cup chopped crystallized ginger

Preheat the oven to 350°F. Line baking sheets with parchment paper or silicone mats, or grease generously with butter or cooking spray. Melt the butter in a small saucepan. Pour the butter into a medium bowl and add both sugars and the molasses. Beat the mixture to combine, using a wire whisk or a handheld electric mixer on medium speed. Add the egg and whisk or beat vigorously. Add the flour, ground ginger, cinnamon, baking soda, and salt, stirring until combined. Stir in the crystallized ginger.

Use a 1 1/4-inch-diameter scoop to drop generous tablespoonfuls of dough onto the baking sheets, spacing them at least 1 inch apart. (The cookies will spread.) Bake for 7 to 9 minutes. The cookies will puff up in the oven and flatten when cooled. Remove them from the oven when the edges are just a little more browned than the middles.

Store the cookies in an airtight container at room temperature up to 1 week. They'll keep for 1 month in the freezer if tightly wrapped in foil or plastic wrap.

Rather Sweet Variation

For a special treat, use the ginger chews to make pint-size ice cream sandwiches. Spoon slightly softened green tea or vanilla bean ice cream onto the bottom of a cookie and cover with a second cookie, top side up. Press slightly so the ice cream is evenly distributed without protruding from the edges of the cookies. Wrap each sandwich tightly in plastic wrap. Freeze for up to 1 month.

Ruby-Flecked Florentines

These lacy cookies studded with red and gold dried fruit are naturals for Christmastime serving and giving. They are easy to make and keep well in an airtight container for several days. Do not leave them out in humid weather or they'll lose their distinctive crisp snap. The white chocolate decorations make them particularly festive, but the cookies taste great without them. English-made Lyle's Golden Syrup, available at upscale grocery stores and specialty shops, is worth seeking out for this recipe. It adds a distinctive caramel flavor to the cookies.

YIELD: ABOUT 45

2 cups sliced blanched almonds

¹/₂ cup (1 stick) unsalted butter

1 cup sugar

¹/₂ cup dried cranberries

¹/₂ cup golden raisins

Zest of ¹/₂ orange, preferably organic

¹/₂ cup Lyle's Golden Syrup (see Tip page 17) or light corn syrup

³/₄ cup all purpose flour

¹/₂ cup white chocolate chips, for decorating (optional)

Preheat the oven to 350°F. Line baking sheets with parchment paper or silicone mats, or grease generously with butter or cooking spray.

Process ¹/₂ cup of the almonds in a blender or food processor fitted with a metal blade until they are finely ground. Melt the butter over low heat in a medium saucepan. Remove the saucepan from the heat and add, one at a time, the sugar, cranberries, raisins, zest, syrup, and flour, stirring after each addition. Stir in the ground and the sliced almonds.

Using about 1 tablespoonful of dough per cookie, roll the mixture into balls. The dough will be sticky. The cookies will spread, so space them at least 3 inches apart on the prepared baking sheets. Bake the cookies for 12 to 15 minutes, until golden brown. Cool the cookies on the baking sheets for 10 minutes before gently transfering them to wire racks to cool 10 minutes longer. Let them cool thoroughly on racks before stacking them on serving plates or decorating them with white chocolate.

To decorate the cookies, melt the white chocolate chips in a metal bowl set over a saucepan with 2 inches of simmering water. Stir frequently until the chocolate has melted completely. Dip a dinner fork into the warm chocolate and hold it about 1 to 2 inches above each cookie. Move the fork around, letting the white chocolate dribble and drip onto the cookie. No need to be precise here, any pattern looks great (think Jackson Pollock). Let the chocolate harden for 30 minutes to 1 hour before stacking the cookies on a plate. They will keep in an airtight container up to 4 days or frozen, well wrapped, for 1 month.

Dulce de Leche Macaroons

Dulce de leche, a popular South American dessert, means "sweet milk" and is made by gently heating milk and sugar until thickened and caramelized. It comes in many guises, including cajeta, *a Mexican variation often made with goat's milk. Here I've given all-American coconut macaroons a sumptuous Latin accent by simmering sweetened condensed milk until it takes on a deep caramel tan.*

YIELD: ABOUT 1 1/2 DOZEN

1 (14-ounce) can sweetened condensed milk

3 cups lightly packed sweetened flaked coconut

1 teaspoon vanilla extract

1 cup semisweet or bittersweet chocolate chips or 1 cup toasted slivered almonds

Line baking sheets with parchment paper or silicone mats, or grease generously with butter or cooking spray.

Remove the paper wrapper from the can of sweetened condensed milk. Use a can opener to make two small punctures in the top of the can on opposite sides. Set the can of milk in a medium saucepan, puncture side up. Fill the saucepan with water to reach two-thirds of the way up the sides of the can. Cover the saucepan and bring the water to a boil over high heat. Decrease the heat until the water simmers and simmer about 1 hour. Check the sauce-pan periodically, adding water to ensure that the level does not drop below halfway. A bit of milk may seep out of the small holes in the can. Cook until the milk pooled on top of the can has turned a deep golden brown. (You may have heard that boiling the can of sweetened condensed milk unopened is a shortcut. *Do not attempt this.* The milk expands when heated and may erupt with explosive results.)

Preheat the oven to 350°F. Remove the can from the simmering water using a pot holder or tongs (it will be very hot). Carefully open the can and use a rubber spatula to spoon the cooked milk into a medium bowl. Let it cool at least 10 minutes. Add the coconut, vanilla, and chocolate chips, stirring until combined.

Use a firmly packed 1¾-inch-diameter scoop to drop the spoonfuls of dough on the prepared baking sheets, spacing them 1½ inches apart. Wet your fingertips lightly with water and gently flatten the cookie dough (no need to press hard; just press out the hump). Bake for 12 to 14 minutes, until the edges are dark brown and crisp. Let the cookies cool for 10 to 15 minutes. Store the cookies for about 1 week in an airtight tin, or freeze for 1 month. Separate the layers of cookies with waxed paper or they will stick together.

Rather Sweet Variation

To make chocolate-dipped macaroons, melt 4 ounces chopped bittersweet chocolate in a small bowl in a microwave on medium high. Check every 30 seconds to ensure the chocolate does not burn. Stir until smooth. Dip each cookie into the warm chocolate, covering half the macaroon. (The bottom side of the cookie will be covered in chocolate, too.) Set the cookies on waxed paper until the chocolate hardens, at least 30 minutes.

Snow-Tipped Sand Tarts

I created these for a Food & Wine *article about Christmas cookies. Dipping them in white chocolate and rolling them in chopped pistachios keeps them in line with the holiday color scheme. This makes a large batch, but there's no need to bake them all at once. Well wrapped, the dough will keep in the refrigerator at least one week and in the freezer at least one month.*

YIELD: 4 DOZEN

2 cups (4 sticks) unsalted butter, at room temperature

1¹/₃ cups powdered sugar, plus extra for dusting (optional)

2 tablespoons almond extract

4 cups all purpose flour

3 cups shelled, coarsely chopped pistachio nuts

8 ounces white chocolate

Preheat the oven to 325°F. Line baking sheets with parchment paper or silicone mats, or grease generously with butter or cooking spray. Using a mixer fitted with a paddle attachment, cream the butter and the 1⅓ cups powdered sugar in a large bowl on medium speed until light and fluffy. Add the almond extract and beat until combined. Stir in the flour until combined. Stir in 2 cups of the pistachios.

Roll the dough into 2-inch-long, ½-inch logs and shape each log into a crescent. Arrange the crescents on the prepared baking sheets about 1 inch apart. (They spread minimally.) Bake for 20 minutes, just until light golden brown. Cool the cookies for 15 to 20 minutes before removing from the baking sheet. Transfer to racks to cool completely.

Chop the white chocolate coarsely and place it in a medium bowl set over a saucepan with 2 inches of simmering water. Stir until the chocolate has melted. Dip the end of each cooled cookie in the melted white chocolate and immediately roll the chocolate-covered part in the remaining 1 cup pistachios. Place the dipped cookies on waxed paper. Use a small fine-mesh sieve to sprinkle powdered sugar over the portion of the cookies that have not been dipped in chocolate.

The chocolate will harden in about 45 minutes at room temperature or 10 minutes in the refrigerator. The cookies will keep in an airtight container about 4 days.

Texas Pecan Pie Bars

I don't know what it is about these bars that makes them so addictive; they never fail to disappear quickly. This recipe makes a lot of bars, but they're so popular and versatile, I think it's worth the trouble to make a large batch. I make them for school functions, parties, teacher gifts, and catering jobs. They are easy to make and cut and people just flip over them. If you can't use all of them immediately, wrap them up and stow them in the freezer for up to three weeks.

YIELD: ABOUT 2 1/2 DOZEN

CRUST

- 1½ cups (3 sticks) unsalted butter, at room temperature
- 1 cup firmly packed golden brown sugar
- 4 cups all purpose flour
- 1 teaspoon salt

FILLING

- 8 large eggs
- 6 cups firmly packed golden brown sugar
- ¼ cup bourbon (optional)
- 6 tablespoons unsalted butter, melted
- 2 tablespoons vanilla extract
- 1 cup all purpose flour
- 1 teaspoon salt
- 2 cups sweetened flaked coconut
- 2 cups pecan halves

To MAKE THE CRUST: Preheat the oven to 350°F. Grease a 12 by 17-inch baking pan with butter or cooking spray. Using a mixer fitted with a paddle attachment, beat the butter in a large bowl on medium speed about 1 minute. Add the sugar and beat about 1 minute, until fluffy. Add the flour and salt; mix on low speed until evenly incorporated but still crumbly. Press the mixture evenly over the bottom of the prepared pan. Bake the crust for 15 to 20 minutes, until it has darkened to a deep golden brown. Leave the oven at 350°F.

To MAKE THE FILLING: Whisk the eggs and sugar in a large bowl until blended. Stir in the bourbon, butter, vanilla, flour, and salt, then the coconut and pecans. Pour the filling over the crust, spreading evenly. Bake until set, 25 to 30 minutes. Cool thoroughly, at least 30 minutes, before cutting into 3-inch squares or diamonds.

Rather Sweet Variations

To make Chocolate–Pecan Pie Bars, melt 2 tablespoons unsalted butter with 4 ounces bittersweet chocolate in a small saucepan over low heat. Add the cooled chocolate-butter mixture to the filling's egg and brown sugar mixture and follow the recipe as directed.

Tip: It isn't always hip to be square. For a change, cut bars into a diamonds. Cut diagonally, going from the southeast corner to the northwest corner. Continue making parallel cuts about 1½ inches apart. Repeat, cutting in strips going from southwest to northeast.

Blackberry Pie Bars

Fear of making pie crust is a common affliction, but almost everyone loves pie. What's a phobic pie baker to do? Here's a solution for those who live in terror that their homemade pie crust will not pass muster with Grandma, Uncle Joe, or the neighborhood domestic goddess. No need to roll out pastry, no worries about sodden crust. Just press the dough into the bottom of a pan, pour on the fruit filling, sprinkle with topping, and bake. Yum! Whoever said pie isn't for breakfast?

This versatile dessert can also be spooned out of the pan warm and served cobbler style, with a scoop of ice cream on top.

YIELD: 2 DOZEN

CRUST AND TOPPING

3 cups all purpose flour

1¹⁄₂ cups sugar

¹⁄₄ teaspoon salt

1¹⁄₂ cups (3 sticks) chilled unsalted butter

FRUIT FILLING

4 large eggs

2 cups sugar

1 cup sour cream

³⁄₄ cup all purpose flour

Pinch of salt

2 (16-ounce) packages frozen blackberries, defrosted and drained

To MAKE THE CRUST AND TOPPING: Preheat the oven to 350°F. Grease a 9 by 13-inch baking pan with butter or cooking spray. Combine the flour, sugar, and salt in the bowl of a food processor fitted with a metal blade; process until combined, about 45 seconds. Cut the butter into ¹⁄₂-inch cubes. Process the butter with the flour mixture for 30 to 60 seconds, until the butter is evenly distributed but the mixture is still crumbly. (If you do not have a food processor, you can use an electric mixer fitted with a paddle attachment. Combine the ingredients on medium speed until the mixture looks dry and crumbly.) Reserve 1¹⁄₂ cups of the crust mixture to use as the topping. Press the remaining mixture into the bottom of the pan. Bake the crust for 12 to 15 minutes until it is golden brown. Cool for at least 10 minutes.

To MAKE THE FILLING: Whisk the eggs in a large bowl, then add the sugar, sour cream, flour, and salt. Gently fold in the blackberries. Spoon the mixture evenly over the crust. Sprinkle the reserved crust mixture evenly over the filling. Bake for 45 to 55 minutes, until the top is lightly browned. Cool at least 1 hour before cutting into bars.

Tip: Defrosting berries may take longer than you think. These bars come together in a hurry unless you need to wait a few hours for the berries to thaw and drain. Put the bags of berries into a plastic grocery bag so the thawed juice does not get all over the place and leave them in the refrigerator overnight. They'll be thawed and ready to drain the next day.

Lemon-Champagne Bars with Strawberry Brûlée Topping

yuck!
5/08

The idea for these unusual bars grew out of a lemon-champagne tart I made when I was a pastry chef in Houston. I noticed then that champagne took the edge off the flavor of lemon, bringing out its softer side. It works that magic on these lemon bars, giving them a luscious flavor that sets them apart from other lemon squares.

The strawberries are a salute to my mother, whose favorite party drink was a glass of champagne garnished at the last minute with a fresh strawberry. She served this lively libation at almost every party she hosted, and to this day, any mention of champagne reminds me of strawberries—especially the one lodged in the bottom of my mother's glass as she raised it to toast her guests.

YIELD: ABOUT 2 DOZEN

CRUST

- 1 cup (2 sticks) unsalted butter, at room temperature
- 1 cup sugar
- 2 cups all purpose flour
- 1/4 teaspoon salt
- Zest of 2 lemons, preferably organic
- 1/2 cup raspberry or strawberry jam (optional)

LEMON FILLING

- 6 large egg yolks
- 6 large eggs
- 1 3/4 cups sugar
- 1 cup freshly squeezed lemon juice
- 1/2 cup champagne or brut sparkling wine
- 3/4 cup (1 1/2 sticks) chilled unsalted butter

STRAWBERRY BRÛLÉE TOPPING

- 1 pint fresh strawberries, hulled
- 1/2 cup sugar

To MAKE THE CRUST: Preheat the oven to 375°F. Coat a 9 by 13-inch baking pan with cooking spray. Using a mixer fitted with a paddle attachment, beat the butter and sugar in a large bowl on medium speed about 3 minutes, until creamy. Add the flour, salt, and zest. Beat on medium-low speed just until incorporated. Press the dough evenly into the bottom of the prepared pan. Bake for 12 to 15 minutes, until the crust is golden brown. Let cool about 10 minutes. Spread the jam evenly over the cooled crust. Turn the oven down to 350°F.

To MAKE THE LEMON FILLING: Whisk the egg yolks, eggs, sugar, lemon juice, and champagne in a large bowl set over a saucepan with 2 inches of simmering water. Cook about 15 minutes, whisking occasionally,

(continued)

until the mixture thickens. Cut the cold butter into tablespoon-size pieces. Whisk the butter, one piece at a time, into the lemon mixture. Cook about 10 minutes longer, whisking occasionally. The mixture will be thick and puddinglike.

Pour the filling over the crust and bake for 10 to 12 minutes. Cool the bars, then refrigerate at least 2 hours or overnight. (If you are in a hurry, they'll get sufficiently cold after 1 hour in the freezer.)

To MAKE THE TOPPING: Slice the strawberries thinly and arrange them in a single layer on top of the lemon filling. Sprinkle the sugar evenly over the strawberries. Use a kitchen torch to melt the sugar until it is brown and crackly; or put the bars under a hot broiler for about 1 minute, until the sugar melts and browns.

Tip: I've always believed in using the best, the freshest, the highest-quality ingredients in my cooking. In this case, however, feel free to save the Veuve Clicquot for New Year's. Use an inexpensive champagne or brut sparkling wine, such as a Cava from Spain. Since the recipe calls for only half a cup, look for sparkling wine splits, which often go on sale during the holiday season.

Bunches of Biscotti

These are inspired by the classic Italian biscotti di Prato, *twice-cooked biscuits named for the small Tuscan city near Florence. The traditional recipe contains hazelnuts, flour, eggs, and sugar, but no butter or honey. These additions make my version sweeter and not quite as tough. There is no need to dip these in coffee to save your teeth.*

Don't be scared off by the size of this recipe. The biscotti keep so well, it's worth your while to make a large batch and freeze whatever you can't eat or give away.

This is a great hands-on recipe. Use your hands to mix the hazelnuts into the dough, and then to fashion the dough into long, even loaves. It's my kind of play dough.

YIELD: ABOUT 6 1/2 DOZEN

1¼ cups (2½ sticks) unsalted butter, at room temperature

4 cups sugar

²/₃ cup honey

3 large eggs

3 tablespoons Frangelico liqueur (optional)

1 teaspoon vanilla extract

7 cups all purpose flour

1 tablespoon plus 2 teaspoons baking powder

¼ teaspoon salt

4 cups hazelnuts, coarsely chopped

Preheat the oven to 450°F. Line a 12 by 17-inch baking sheet with parchment paper or silicone mats, or grease generously with butter or cooking spray. Using a mixer fitted with a paddle attachment, beat the butter and sugar together in a large bowl for 2 to 3 minutes or until light and white. Add the honey, eggs, Frangelico and vanilla extract; beat until combined. Add the flour, baking powder, and salt; mix at low speed until completely combined. The dough will be very stiff, but not sticky. Add the hazelnuts and use your hands to incorporate them evenly.

Spread a large piece of parchment paper or waxed paper over a flat work surface. Divide the dough in half. Shape each half into a roll about 17 inches long, 4½ inches wide. Use the waxed paper to roll and work the dough into shape. Set the rolls on a prepared baking sheet, leaving about 2 inches between them. Bake for 10 minutes, until the edges are golden brown and the insides are a light golden brown. The dough will spread and flatten slightly and will have shallow vertical cracks down the middle. Cool the baked dough completely on the baking sheet, about 1 hour at room temperature or 20 to 25 minutes in the refrigerator. (It will break apart if handled when hot.)

Lower the oven to 350°F. Cut each roll diagonally into ¼-inch-thick slices using a heavy knife with a 10-inch blade (a good clean chop works best). Place the slices on the baking sheet. The biscotti do not spread as they bake the second time, so they can be placed close enough to touch. Bake for about 20 to 25 minutes. The biscotti are done when they are golden brown. Initially, the biscotti will be slightly soft; they harden and become crisp as they cool. Let them rest for about 10 minutes before removing them from the baking sheet.

Biscotti keep for 2 weeks in an airtight container, or 1 month if wrapped and frozen. They make great Christmas presents.

Rather Sweet Variations

These simple cookies can be dolled up with any number of additions: try 2 cups of dried cranberries, dried cherries, or chocolate chips. (Add them along with the almonds.) To get four biscotti flavors from one batch, divide the dough into quarters before adding the almonds. Combine 1 cup of the almonds with ½ cup of any mix-in and add to one portion dough. Repeat with each mix-in.

Other variations include dipping one end of each fully baked and cooled biscotto into melted white or bittersweet chocolate, or substituting blanched slivered almonds for the hazelnuts. If you do so, substitute an equal amount of almond extract for the Frangelico.

LUNCHES AND
Light Dinners

RATHER SWEET'S longtime waitress Nancy Jones keeps a list of customers' favorite specials in her apron pocket. As soon as the dish appears on the luncheon board—usually by 10:30 A.M.—she calls to let them know. They invariably show up for lunch that day. She calls Mary Mustard when it's Wild Mushroom Soup day. Rhonda Cunningham, a local guidance counselor, appears on the list under Green Chile Crab Cakes. And the chicken pot pies, a standard Tuesday special, are so popular that regulars call early in the morning to reserve theirs for lunch.

The customers love Nancy, and she works hard to please them. "If they don't use a credit card, I may not know their names, but I know them, and I know what they eat," she says.

We serve lunch and dinner in our upstairs dining rooms, divided into two intimate eating spaces. The golden mustard-colored walls are decorated with colorful artwork and iron sconces that I had custom-made in Mexico. Swinging doors in shades of aqua and lilac separate the bar and the kitchen from the dining rooms. Two huge terra-cotta pots hold giant prickly cacti. On nice days—we get a lot of them here—customers can sit at metal tables on the deck overlooking our courtyard garden.

Our lunches are busy. The hairdressers from Precision Cut down the street come—six to eight at a time—several days a week and order salads with our popular balsamic vinaigrette. We make our salad dressings, salsas, chips, and mayonnaise from scratch.

The Apple-Almond Chicken Salad is a favorite among our regulars. Lynn MacWhithey, the owner of a local B and B, always orders it.

Uncle Albert, ninety-four, stops by almost every day decked out in his broad-brimmed straw hat, a kerchief at this neck and his white hair held back in low ponytail. A fourth-generation Fredericksburg native, he likes the special, whatever it is. "You wouldn't think someone his age would eat so hearty," says Nancy. He still drives a car, too.

On weekends we open for dinner, and our waitress Wanda Griffin is in charge. She always makes sure that fresh flowers fill the dining room, and she keeps a huge tray with samples of our desserts overflowing with tempting options. For large parties, customers order the Rather Sweet Bread and Cheese Board. We charge for it by the foot, and it comes with an assortment of breads, crackers, cheeses, and seasonal fruits gussied up with sprigs of fresh herbs from our back-door garden.

When I can, I escape from the kitchen and head up to the dining room for a meal-time stroll and chat with our customers, many of whom have become dear friends.

Beer Bread

Around here, beer bread recipes are as common as cowboy hats. I guess it's a Texas thing. I used to make beer bread frequently when I was in the catering business. I'm not sure where this recipe came from, but it is shockingly easy. It's great served with barbecue or chili, an unexpected but delicious substitute for the usual corn bread.

YIELD: 10 SERVINGS

3 cups all purpose flour

1 tablespoon baking powder

1 teaspoon salt

3 tablespoons sugar

1 (12-ounce) bottle good-quality beer or ale

1/2 cup (1 stick) unsalted butter, melted

Preheat the oven to 350°F. Generously grease a 9 by 5-inch loaf pan with butter or cooking spray. In a medium bowl, stir together the flour, baking powder, salt, and sugar. Pour in the beer and stir until just incorporated. (The dough will be sticky and heavy.) Pour half the melted butter into the bottom of the prepared loaf pan. Spoon in the bread dough and pour the remaining half of the butter on top. Bake for 50 to 60 minutes, until the bumpy top is golden brown. Remove from the pan and serve immediately.

This bread is best eaten warm, but I have had many takers once it has cooled. If there are any leftovers, wrap securely in plastic wrap and save for toasting the next day. The bread cuts most easily with a serrated knife. For more informal gatherings, it can be pulled apart like monkey bread.

Rather Sweet Variation

Beer bread lends itself to numerous mix-ins, including chopped chives, chile peppers such as jalapeños, green onions, or any grated cheese.

Rocket Rolls

These rolls have nothing to do with rocket propulsion, nor will they get you to the moon (though some of my particularly passionate customers might say they'll take you over the moon). Originally known as torpedo rolls, a bread baker's term describing the bread's shape, they owe their current name to a colleague's foggy memory. She arrived at the bakery one day and asked me if we were making "rocket rolls." I shot her a quizzical look and asked her what she was talking about.

"You know, those rocket rolls, the sweet white rolls with the fluffy insides." I chuckled when I realized her mistake. What a catchy name, I thought. We never called them torpedo rolls again.

I add a pinch of cinnamon to this challah-style dough, which gives the rolls a lovely scent and a delicious, mysterious flavor. Serve them warm with cold butter at dinner. Leftovers, if you have any, can be split in half lengthwise to make sandwiches for lunch the next day.

YIELD: 32 DINNER ROLLS, 16 SANDWICH ROLLS

3 (¼-ounce) packages active dry yeast, about 1 tablespoon

1 cup lukewarm water (105 to 115°F)

¼ cup light, flavorless vegetable oil, such as canola or safflower

1 large egg

¾ cup sugar

1½ cups water (more as needed)

6½ cups high-gluten flour or bread flour

1 tablespoon sea salt

Pinch of ground cinnamon

Extra-virgin olive oil, for brushing on the warm rolls

Dissolve the yeast in the 1 cup lukewarm water and let sit about 5 minutes, until foamy. Using a mixer fitted with a dough hook, combine the yeast mixture, oil, egg, and sugar in a large bowl. Add the 1½ cups water and mix until combined. Add the flour and mix on medium-low speed until the dough holds together, about 5 minutes. (If it does not form a cohesive ball, add water, 1 tablespoon at a time, until it does.) Let the dough rest in the bowl for 20 minutes. Add the salt and cinnamon and mix the dough on low speed for 1 minute. Transfer the dough to a large bowl that has been lightly greased with oil. Cover it with a clean tea towel and let rise in a warm, draft-free place until doubled in bulk, about 1½ hours.

Preheat the oven to 350°F. Line baking sheets with parchment paper or silicone mats, or grease with a light coating of olive oil or cooking spray. Punch down the dough to remove the air. If the dough seems too sticky to work with, coat your hands with a little flour. Pinch off pieces and roll them into golf ball–size rounds (for dinner rolls) or tennis ball–size rounds (for larger sandwich rolls). Arrange the dough rounds on the prepared baking sheets, spacing about 2 inches apart. Cover them with a clean tea towel and let rise in a warm, draft-free place about 20 minutes, until they become lighter and have the consistency of soft marshmallows. They will not double in bulk on the second rising.

Bake the rolls for 20 to 30 minutes, until golden brown. Remove them from the oven and brush with a light coating of olive oil. Serve immediately or at room temperature.

Nuevo Texas Waldorf Salad

Golden, fried strips of wonton wrappers arranged like pickup sticks atop this delicious salad add a glamorous touch. We offer it as a dinner appetizer in our upstairs dining room. Home-grown rosemary, available here year-round, and the fall harvest of local Texas pecans make this salad a hometown favorite. Don't confuse this recipe with the standard-issue Waldorf salad on hotel buffet tables, made with mealy Red Delicious apples, tough celery, and a slick of commercial mayonnaise.

YIELD: 4 SERVINGS

FRIED WONTON STRIPS

- 4 sheets packaged wonton or egg roll wrappers
- Olive oil, for frying

ROSEMARY VINAIGRETTE

- 1/3 cup fresh rosemary leaves
- 2 cloves garlic
- 1/4 medium-size red onion
- 1 tablespoon Dijon mustard
- 1/4 cup honey
- 1/2 cup white balsamic vinegar
- 1 1/2 teaspoons salt
- Freshly ground black pepper to taste
- 1/2 cup to 1 cup extra-virgin olive oil

SALAD

- 1/2 cup pecans
- 3 sweet-tart apples such as Braeburn, Medina, or Granny Smith
- 4 cups organic mixed greens
- 1/2 cup crumbled blue cheese, such as Stilton

To MAKE THE WONTON STRIPS: Use kitchen scissors to cut the wonton sheets into 3/4-inch-wide strips. Pour enough olive oil into a large, deep-frying pan to reach a depth of 1/2 inch and set over medium-high heat. When the oil is hot, pinch off a bit of 1 strip and set it in the oil. The oil is hot enough when the test strip sizzles and turns golden brown on one side in about 10 seconds. Use tongs to add the remaining strips several at a time, frying about 8 to 10 seconds on each side, until golden brown. Remove the strips from the pan and set them on paper towels to drain.

To MAKE THE VINAIGRETTE: Blend the rosemary, garlic, onion, mustard, honey, vinegar, salt, and pepper about 15 to 20 seconds in the bowl of a food processor fitted with a metal blade. Pour 1/2 cup olive oil through the feed tube in a slow stream and blend until the mixture emulsifies. (It won't take much longer than it takes to pour the oil in.) Taste and add more oil, if desired.

To MAKE THE SALAD: Preheat the oven to 350°F. Arrange the nuts on a baking sheet in a single layer and toast for 7 to 9 minutes, until golden brown and aromatic. Cool the nuts and then coarsely chop.

Core and slice the apples (but leave the peels on) and place them in a large bowl. Add the mixed greens, pecans, and blue cheese; toss gently. Pour half the salad dressing over the greens mixture and toss until all the ingredients are evenly coated. Add more salad dressing if desired, to taste. (Leftover salad dressing will keep in the refrigerator about 3 days.) Transfer the salad to individual serving plates, top with the fried wonton strips, and serve immediately.

Tip: Sliced apples turn brown if left out for too long. For years I used lemon juice to keep them fresh looking, but it always left a telltale flavor. Now I dip them in lemon-lime soda, which keeps them from browning and doesn't leave such a heavy taste-print. This trick works with any fruit that turns brown when exposed to oxygen, such as pears and bananas.

Rather Rich Corn Muffins

I serve these rich muffins in my upstairs café at dinnertime on weekends. A basket of muffins arrives at tables shortly after customers do, and these little gems inevitably disappear long before the salad course comes out.

YIELD: ABOUT 2 DOZEN

3/4 cup (1½ sticks) unsalted butter, melted

3 cups heavy whipping cream

3 large eggs

3½ cups all purpose flour

1½ cups coarse cornmeal plus extra to sprinkle over

1 cup sugar

2 tablespoons baking powder

½ teaspoon salt

1 cup fresh corn kernels or canned corn, drained (optional)

Preheat the oven to 350°F. Generously grease twenty-four standard muffin cups or line them with disposable muffin wrappers.

Pour the butter, cream, and eggs into the large bowl of a mixer fitted with a paddle attachment. Add the flour, cornmeal, sugar, baking powder, and salt on top. Mix at medium speed just until the ingredients are combined and not lumpy. Stir the corn into the batter.

Using a medium-size ice cream scoop, fill the muffin cups about two-thirds full with the batter. Sprinkle cornmeal over the tops of the muffins. Bake the muffins for 12 to 15 minutes, until lightly brown; they should spring back when you touch the tops lightly with your fingertips. They are best served warm, and are equally delicious toasted and, if you dare, buttered.

Tip: This batter can be refrigerated in a covered container for 3 days and baked just before serving. Be sure to add 3 to 5 minutes to the baking time to compensate for the temperature of the refrigerated muffin batter.

Apple-Almond Chicken Salad with Homemade Mayonnaise

We make this salad daily for the lunch rush. It's used in our best-selling sandwich. I like it best the way we serve it—on homemade focaccia bread. Add the toasted almonds just before serving; if they sit in the salad for more than an hour or so, they'll lose their crunch. Naturally, you can make this salad with store-bought mayo, but it won't be nearly as rich or tasty.

YIELD: 4 SERVINGS

HOMEMADE MAYONNAISE

- 2 large eggs
- 1 large egg yolk
- 1 teaspoon salt
- 1/2 teaspoon freshly ground white pepper
- 1 tablespoon Dijon mustard
- 2 tablespoons freshly squeezed lemon juice
- 1 cup vegetable oil, such as canola or safflower

CHICKEN SALAD

- 1 cup slivered blanched almonds
- 2 whole skinless, boneless chicken breasts
- 1 tart, crisp apple, such as Granny Smith, cored and diced
- 2 stalks celery, diced
- 1 green onion, thinly sliced
- 1/4 cup minced red onion
- 1/4 cup chopped fresh parsley
- 1/2 to 3/4 cup mayonnaise (above)
- Salt and freshly ground black pepper

To MAKE THE MAYONNAISE: Process the eggs, egg yolk, salt, pepper, mustard, and lemon juice in a blender on medium speed until thoroughly mixed. Switch the blender to low speed and add the vegetable oil in a slow, steady stream. The mayonnaise will thicken as you pour. The mayonnaise is ready when it takes on a thick, creamy consistency, just after all of the oil has been added. Pour it into a clean container, cover, and refrigerate immediately. This recipe makes about 1 1/2 cups mayonnaise, so you'll have some left over. It will keep in the refrigerator for up to 1 week.

Preheat the oven to 350°F.

To MAKE THE SALAD: Arrange the almonds on a baking sheet in a single layer and toast for 7 to 9 minutes, until golden brown and aromatic. Set aside to cool.

Fill a large sauté pan with water two-thirds of the way to the top. Bring the water to a simmer and add the chicken breasts (make sure they are completely covered with water). Cover the pan and simmer over low heat about 10 minutes, until the chicken is no longer pink when you cut through the middle with a knife. Remove the chicken from the pan and let it cool.

When the chicken is cool enough to handle, shred it into bite-size pieces with a fork or your hands and transfer it to a large bowl. Or if you prefer a more manicured look, dice it with a knife. Add the apple, celery, green onion, red onion, parsley, and ½ to ¾ cup of the mayonnaise; toss until all of the ingredients are combined. Season to taste with salt and pepper. The salad can be made up to this point and refrigerated for up to 1 week. Add the almonds just before serving.

Rather Sweet Variation

For a more exotically flavored chicken salad, try adding any one of these as you make the mayonnaise: 1 teaspoon curry powder, a pinch of saffron, 1 tablespoon chopped fresh chives, 1 clove raw garlic, or 1 teaspoon fresh herbs, such as rosemary or tarragon. Additions should be combined with the egg mixture before the oil is added. Note: the very young, the elderly, and anyone immunocompromised should avoid eating raw eggs.

Field Greens with Spiced Pecans, Goat Cheese, and Balsamic Vinaigrette

Customers routinely request the recipe for this balsamic vinaigrette, our house salad dressing. It goes on the small green salads we serve for lunch as well as on a fancier version we serve at dinner. I used to serve it with goat cheese rounds coated with crunchy panko (Japanese bread-crumbs), but last fall's arrival of succulent, freshly harvested Texas pecans inspired me to include some of the local bounty in my salad.

A word to the wise for cooks with nut-loving nibblers wandering loose around the house: double the spiced pecan recipe. A friend of mine made them and set them aside for the evening's salad, only to find an empty bowl at dinnertime. The spiced nuts can be frozen and are fabulous served alone as an accompaniment to cocktails.

YIELD: 4 SERVINGS

SPICED PECANS

1¹/₂ cups pecan halves

3 tablespoons unsalted butter

¹/₂ teaspoon ground cumin

¹/₄ teaspoon cayenne pepper

¹/₄ teaspoon salt

BALSAMIC VINAIGRETTE

2 cloves garlic, minced

1 teaspoon Dijon mustard

1 tablespoon honey

¹/₂ cup balsamic vinegar

¹/₄ cup red wine vinegar

1 tablespoon freshly squeezed lemon juice

1 teaspoon salt

¹/₂ cup to 2¹/₄ cups extra-virgin olive oil (see **Tip**)

SALAD

1 (6-ounce) goat cheese round, at room temperature

3 cups assorted baby greens, washed and dried

1 small bunch arugula, washed and dried

1 pint cherry tomatoes, preferably organic, quartered

To make the spiced pecans: Preheat the oven to 350°F. Place the pecans in a medium bowl. Melt the butter in a small saucepan over medium heat. Stir in the cumin, cayenne, and salt. Pour the butter mixture over the pecans and toss to coat well. Spread the spiced pecans in a single layer on a baking sheet and toast for 7 to 9 minutes, until golden brown and aromatic. Set aside to cool at least 15 minutes.

To MAKE THE VINAIGRETTE: Blend the garlic, mustard, honey, both vinegars, lemon juice, and salt about 15 to 20 seconds in a blender or food processor fitted with a metal blade. Pour ½ cup olive oil through the feed tube in a slow stream and blend until the mixture emulsifies (this won't take much longer than it takes to pour the oil in). Taste the dressing and add more oil as desired (see Tip).

To MAKE THE SALAD: Cut the goat cheese round into quarters and gently form each quarter into a disk. Coarsely grind ½ cup of the spiced pecan halves in a food processor fitted with a metal blade. Pour the ground pecans into a medium bowl. Roll the goat cheese rounds in the ground pecans to cover completely.

Just before serving, toss the baby greens, arugula, the remaining 1 cup spiced pecans, and balsamic vinagrette to taste in a large salad bowl. (Leftover dressing will keep in the refrigerator up to 3 days.) Serve salads on individual plates. Top each salad with some of the cherry tomatoes and a disk of pecan-coated goat cheese.

Tip: Traditional salad dressing recipes call for three parts oil to one part vinegar. I don't like so much oil, so I have given a range. Experiment on your own to decide how much oil works for you. Try the least amount of oil first, and increase the amount by ¼ to ½ cup each time you make the dressing. Once you've figured out how much oil you prefer, make a note of it on this recipe. I'm always sure I'll remember these things without notes, but I never do!

Chicken Satay with Yogurt-Cucumber Dipping Sauce

Chef Kris Panzica, a Chicago native, developed this multiethnic recipe for an Academy Awards party she hosted a few years ago. "I was also inspired by the flavors I've tasted on Devon Avenue in Chicago, where all the city's Middle Eastern places are located," she says. Now Kris prepares it regularly for dinner in our upstairs dining room, where it has become an instant hit.

Perfect for a buffet party, this dish must be mostly prepared and assembled ahead of time (the chicken needs to marinate for two hours, and the yogurt has to drain for a few hours as well). Once the advance preparation is done, pop the chicken skewers on the grill for a short turn, pile them on a beautiful platter, and serve.

Don't forget to soak the wooden skewers in water at least 30 minutes before threading the chicken. Otherwise, the skewers could burn up on the grill before the chicken is done. Figure one skinless, boneless chicken breast for two people as an appetizer and one breast per person as a main course.

YIELD: 6 MAIN-COURSE OR 12 APPETIZER SERVINGS

DIPPING SAUCE

- 1 (32-ounce) container full-fat or low-fat plain yogurt
- 1 cucumber, peeled, seeded, and finely diced
- 1 clove garlic, minced
- 1/4 cup finely chopped fresh parsley
- Zest and juice of 1 lemon, preferably organic
- 2 teaspoons salt
- Freshly ground black pepper
- 1/4 cup extra-virgin olive oil

CURRY PASTE

- 10 cloves garlic, minced or crushed
- 1 fresh jalapeño chile, seeded and diced
- 2 fresh serrano chiles, seeded and diced
- 3 tablespoons peeled, minced fresh ginger
- 1/2 small red onion, cut into small dice
- 3 tablespoons curry powder
- 2 tablespoons ground cumin
- 1 large stalk fresh lemongrass, crushed and cut into 2-inch lengths
- 1/4 cup chopped fresh cilantro
- Zest and juice of 2 limes, preferably organic
- 3/4 cup extra-virgin olive oil

CHICKEN SKEWERS

- 6 skinless, boneless chicken breasts

To MAKE THE DIPPING SAUCE: Line a colander with fine cheesecloth or coffee filters. Set the colander over a large bowl. Spoon the yogurt into the colander and drain at least 2 hours, or overnight in the refrigerator. The yogurt is ready when it is almost as thick as cream cheese.

Discard the liquid that has collected in the bottom of the bowl. In a large bowl, combine the yogurt, cucumber, garlic, parsley, lemon zest and juice, salt, and pepper to taste. Whisk in the olive oil until the mixture is smooth. Cover and refrigerate until ready to serve.

To MAKE THE CURRY PASTE: Combine the garlic, jalapeño, serranos, ginger, onion, curry powder, cumin, lemongrass, lime zest and juice, and olive oil in a large bowl.

To PREPARE THE CHICKEN: Cut the chicken into 1-inch strips. Stir the chicken strips into the curry paste, making sure the chicken is thoroughly coated. Cover and refrigerate about 2 hours. Submerge the wooden skewers in water and soak at least 30 minutes. Thread the chicken strips onto the skewers. At this point, you can cook the chicken immediately or cover and refrigerate overnight. Coat the grill with cooking spray and preheat to medium. Grill the skewers 3 to 5 minutes per side. Or preheat the broiler and broil the skewers about 4 inches away from the heat source for approximately the same length of time.

Serve the skewers hot or at room temperature, alongside bowls of the dipping sauce.

Caesar Salad Pizzas

My daughter Frances and I love salads, and we eat a lot of them. We also like pizzas, but we try not to eat too many of them. I invented this dish so we could feast on two of our favorite foods with half as much guilt.

YIELD: FOUR 8-INCH PIZZAS

CRUST

- 1½ cups lukewarm water (110° to 115°F)
- 2 (1-ounce) packages active dry yeast
- 2 tablespoons olive oil, plus additional for brushing on crusts
- 2 teaspoons honey
- 4 to 5 cups all purpose flour
- 3 tablespoons semolina flour (optional)
- 1 teaspoon sea salt
- ½ teaspoon crushed red pepper flakes (optional)
- ¼ cup coarse cornmeal
- 1 cup freshly shredded Parmesan cheese

DRESSING

- 2 cloves garlic, minced
- 1 anchovy fillet (optional)
- 2 large eggs, beaten, or ½ cup pasteurized egg product
- ½ cup freshly squeezed lemon juice
- 2 teaspoons Worcestershire sauce
- 2 teaspoons Dijon mustard
- 1 cup extra-virgin olive oil
- 1½ cups freshly grated Parmesan cheese
- Salt and freshly ground black pepper

SALAD

- 1 large head romaine lettuce, washed and cut into 1½-inch slices
- 1 pint organic cherry tomatoes, halved (optional)

- Freshly shaved Parmesan cheese, for garnish (optional)

To make the crust: Combine the lukewarm water, yeast, olive oil, and honey in the bowl of a mixer fitted with a dough hook. Add 3 cups of the all purpose flour, the semolina flour, salt, and crushed red pepper; mix on low speed. With the machine running, add 1 cup of the all purpose flour to make a soft dough. Mix the dough on low speed about 5 minutes longer, until smooth. Add up to 1 more cup of the all purpose flour as necessary to keep the dough from sticking to the bowl.

Turn the dough out onto a floured surface and knead until smooth and elastic, about 10 to 15 turns. Place in a large oiled bowl. Cover and let rest at room temperature for 30 to 40 minutes.

Generously coat 2 baking sheets with olive oil. Sprinkle the sheets with cornmeal. Preheat the oven to 450°F. (If you have a pizza stone, use it instead of the baking sheets, preheating it along with the oven. No need to grease the stone, just sprinkle it with cornmeal just before you bake the pizzas.)

Divide the dough into quarters. Roll each piece into a ball, place the dough balls on a baking sheet, cover with a damp towel, and

(continued)

let rest for 10 to 15 minutes longer. Use immediately, or cover with plastic wrap and refrigerate up to 3 hours.

Using a floured rolling pin, flatten each dough ball into an 8-inch circle. Brush each dough round with olive oil and sprinkle each with ¼ cup Parmesan cheese. Transfer the crusts onto the prepared baking sheets and bake for 10 to 15 minutes, until browned and crisp.

To MAKE THE DRESSING: Press the garlic and anchovy into a paste in a mortar with a pestle. Scrape the paste into a medium bowl. Whisk in the eggs, lemon juice, Worcestershire sauce, and mustard, then slowly add the olive oil in a thin, steady stream, whisking until thoroughly incorporated. Stir in the Parmesan cheese and season to taste with salt and pepper.

To make the dressing in a food processor, place the garlic, anchovy, eggs, lemon juice, Worcestershire sauce and mustard in the bowl of a food processor fitted with a metal blade. Process until smooth. With the processor running, add the olive oil through the feed tube in a thin, steady stream. Pour the dressing into a bowl, stir in the Parmesan cheese, and season to taste with salt and pepper.

To MAKE THE SALAD: Toss the lettuce and tomatoes with the dressing. Place a generous amount of salad on top of each warm pizza crust. Garnish with shaved Parmesan cheese. Serve flat like a tostada.

Dainty souls and those who like to mound lots of salad on their pizza will cut it with a knife and fork. Others may want to take their chances with dripping dressing, folding the pizza taco style and eating it out of hand.

Wild Rice and Chickpea Salad

When I need a break from kitchen chaos, I love to sneak away to see my friend Paula Dis-browe, the cowgirl chef at Hart & Hind Fitness Ranch, which is deep in the Texas Hill Coun-try. When I first met her she was a city girl—as in New York City. A food writer and chef, she came to Rather Sweet to research a Christmas article for Food & Wine. *It wasn't too long afterward that she and her fiancé, an accomplished bread baker, left the Big Apple for jobs at Hart & Hind, about two and a half hours from my bakery. The ranch is owned by Kit and Carl Detering from Houston, and has become my favorite getaway. Paula and I cook together, and sometimes I fill in for her at the ranch.*

This is Paula's recipe, which first appeared in an issue of Food & Wine. *If you have a hard time finding wild rice, you can substitute Uncle Ben's Wild Rice mix in a box; just don't use the seasoning packet. I sometimes substitute dried cranberries for the golden raisins.*

YIELD: 6 SERVINGS

1½ cups wild rice, preferably organic

1 tablespoon kosher salt

2½ tablespoons freshly squeezed lemon juice

2 tablespoons red wine vinegar

2 tablespoons Dijon mustard

1 tablespoon honey

1 teaspoon curry powder

1 tablespoon ground cumin

Pinch of cayenne pepper

¼ cup extra-virgin olive oil

1 (15-ounce) can chickpeas (garbanzo beans), drained and rinsed

½ pound smoked ham, diced

8 small green onions, (white and light green parts only), thinly sliced

¼ cup golden raisins

Salt and freshly ground black pepper

Hot pepper sauce, such as Tabasco

Fill a large saucepan three-quarters full with water and bring to a boil. Add the wild rice and salt and simmer over medium heat until the rice is tender but still firm to the bite, about 45 minutes. Drain and rinse the rice under cold water.

Meanwhile, in a large bowl, whisk together the lemon juice, vinegar, mustard, honey, curry powder, cumin, and cayenne. Add the olive oil and whisk until combined. Toss in the chickpeas, ham, green onions, raisins, and wild rice. Season the salad to taste with salt, pepper, and hot pepper sauce. Serve at room temperature.

The salad can be refrigerated overnight. Bring it to room temperature and toss before serving.

Wild Mushroom Soup

My friend Lynn Connolly serves this soup at her restaurant, Pasqual, in Wichita Falls. She spent a week working with me at my bakery, and we swapped recipes. A soul-warming soup on a crisp fall evening, it's always a big hit served with warm corn muffins.

YIELD: 4 SERVINGS

1/4 cup (1/2 stick) unsalted butter

1 medium onion, finely chopped

1/2 pound cremini or white button mushrooms, sliced

1/2 pound shiitake mushrooms, sliced

3 tablespoons all purpose flour

4 cups chicken or beef broth, preferably handmade

1/4 teaspoon freshly ground white pepper

1/4 teaspoon ground nutmeg

1 tablespoon freshly squeezed lemon juice

1/4 cup dry sherry (optional)

1/4 cup heavy whipping cream

Pinch of cayenne pepper

Salt

Chopped fresh chives, for garnish

Melt the butter over medium heat in a large sauté pan. Add the onion and cook until soft and transparent. Add all the mushrooms and cook on medium heat about 10 minutes, until they give up their liquid and then absorb it. Remove the saucepan from the heat and stir in the flour, 1 tablespoon at a time. Return the pan to low heat and gradually pour in the broth, stirring constantly. Add the white pepper, nutmeg, lemon juice, and sherry. Simmer the soup over medium-low heat for 10 minutes. Add the cream and stir until the soup is hot. Add the cayenne. Season with salt, if needed. Transfer to serving bowls and garnish with chives.

Tip: Nut-brown-colored cremini mushrooms are similar in size to their cultivated white cousins, but they pack a bigger flavor punch. Many supermarkets carry them, often right next to the white button mushrooms. Cremini mushrooms are actually baby portobello mushrooms picked before they reach their full size.

Curried Butternut Squash Soup

This soup is thick, hearty, and rich—even without the addition of the optional cream, which I put in or leave out depending on my mood and whether I plan on hitting the gym that day. I am continually surprised at the universal popularity of this soup, despite its bold doses of curry, cinnamon, and ginger. (Feel free to cut down on the spices, especially the ginger, which gives the soup a heady kick.) Great the first day it's made, the soup is even better a day later, after the flavors of the vegetables and spices have had time to mingle and mellow. Anna Wynne-Smith, a friend and a wonderful cook, shared this recipe with me before she returned to her native South Africa. I think of her whenever I make it.

YIELD: 4 TO 6 SERVINGS

2 tablespoons unsalted butter

1/2 medium-size yellow onion, chopped

1 medium-size carrot, peeled and sliced

1 1/2 pounds butternut squash, peeled, seeded, and cubed

1 medium-size russet potato, peeled and cubed

1 teaspoon ground ginger

1 teaspoon ground cinnamon

1 1/2 tablespoons curry powder

1/2 teaspoon salt

2 cups chicken stock, preferably homemade

1/2 cup milk (low-fat is okay)

1/2 cup heavy whipping cream (optional)

1/2 teaspoon honey

1/2 teaspoon Hungarian sweet paprika

Freshly ground black pepper

Sour cream, for garnish

Melt the butter in a large, heavy-bottomed stockpot set over medium-high heat. Add the onion and carrot; sauté over medium heat about 3 minutes, until the onions begin to soften. Add the squash, potato, ginger, cinnamon, curry powder, and salt and sauté for 2 minutes. Add the stock, milk, cream, honey, and paprika and bring the soup to a boil. Cover the pot, decrease the heat, and simmer the soup over low heat about 45 minutes, until the vegetables are soft.

Purée the soup in a blender in batches until smooth. Add black pepper to taste. If the soup seems too thick, add more milk or cream. Serve hot with a dollop of sour cream on top.

Tip: Peeling and dicing butternut squash may not be your idea of a good time. Look in the freezer case for frozen, cubed butternut squash. I've even seen organic versions in some grocery stores.

Texas Tortilla Soup

We make tortilla soup every week for our luncheon soup special. No one ever seems to get tired of it. Ours is a more brothy version than the typical tortilla soup. I love the clean, clear flavor of the broth, which is infused with the lightly smoky taste of ancho chiles.

Wrinkly ancho chiles are actually red (fully ripened) poblano chiles that have been dried. They often come in cellophane packages and can be found in most grocery stores in the Mexican food section.

Cook the chicken for this soup according to the instructions in the recipe for Apple-Almond Chicken Salad with Homemade Mayonnaise (page 158).

YIELD: 8 SERVINGS

SOUP

8 plum tomatoes

4 tablespoons olive oil

1 medium-size yellow onion, diced

6 cloves garlic, minced

1 red bell pepper, diced

2 teaspoons chili powder

2 teaspoons ground cumin

4 cups chicken stock, preferably homemade

1 dried ancho chile pepper

1 (15-ounce) can peeled tomatoes

Salt and freshly ground black pepper

3 cooked, shredded chicken breasts (see page 158)

3 ears fresh corn or 1 (8-ounce) package frozen corn (optional)

GARNISHES

2 ripe avocados, peeled and sliced

Tortilla chips or strips

2 plum tomatoes, diced

1/4 cup chopped fresh cilantro

1 cup shredded Monterey Jack cheese

Sour cream (optional)

To MAKE THE SOUP: Preheat the oven to 350°F. Slice the tomatoes in half. Spread 1 tablespoon of the olive oil on a baking sheet or pizza pan and arrange the tomatoes on top, skin side up. Drizzle the tomatoes with another 1 tablespoon of the olive oil. Roast the tomatoes for 25 to 35 minutes, until the skins wrinkle and the tomatoes are slightly brown around the edges.

Heat the remaining 2 tablespoons oil in a heavy-bottomed, 4-quart soup pot over medium heat. Add the onion, garlic, and bell pepper and sauté about 5 minutes, until the vegetables become soft. Stir in the chili powder and cumin and cook for 1 minute. Add the chicken stock and ancho chile. Bring to a boil over medium-high heat, then cover, decrease the heat, and simmer about 15 minutes, until the ancho chile softens. Remove the chile from the soup and pull off and discard the stem. Cut the chile in half and discard the seeds, if desired. (Leaving the seeds in makes for a spicier soup.) Place the softened chile, the

(continued)

canned tomatoes with their juices, and the roasted tomatoes (including as much of the juices and browned tomato bits as possible) in the bowl of a food processor fitted with a metal blade. Purée the chile-tomato mixture about 1 minute. Transfer the chile-tomato mixture to the soup and continue simmering, covered, about 1 hour. Add salt and pepper to taste, along with the cooked chicken. If using fresh corn, cut the kernels from the cobs, add the corn to the soup, and simmer for 5 minutes.

To GARNISH THE SOUP: Ladle the soup into medium bowls. Lean 3 to 4 slices of avocado against the edge of each bowl, partially sticking out of the soup. Arrange the tortilla chips or strips in a similar way. Sprinkle each bowl with a handful of diced tomatoes, some cilantro, and 2 tablespoons of shredded cheese. Top with a spoonful of sour cream. Serve immediately.

Gulf Coast Shrimp Quesadillas

My popular Friday lunchtime special quesadillas could easily work as a fast weeknight dinner. I have one customer who comes in every Friday to eat it, but she always requests it on our soft, untoasted focaccia bread, mango salsa and all. I'm sticking with the tortilla version.

YIELD: 4 SERVINGS

MANGO SALSA

2 mangoes, diced

1 fresh jalapeño chile, stemmed, seeded, and finely diced

1/2 medium-size red onion, diced

1 tablespoon freshly squeezed lime juice

1/4 teaspoon salt

1/4 cup bottled Thai-style chili sauce

2 cloves garlic, minced

2 tablespoons chopped fresh cilantro

QUESADILLAS

1 pound uncooked large shrimp, peeled and deveined

1 teaspoon salt

1/4 teaspoon cayenne pepper

2 tablespoons olive oil

1 medium-size yellow onion, sliced

Dash of Worcestershire sauce

Dash of hot pepper sauce, such as Tabasco

1 red bell pepper, cut into 1/2-inch slices

Salt and freshly ground black pepper

8 (8-inch-diameter) flour tortillas

2 cups shredded Monterey Jack cheese

To MAKE THE SALSA: Combine the mango, jalapeño, onion, lime juice, salt, chili sauce, garlic, and cilantro in a medium bowl. Cover and refrigerate for up to 2 days or until ready to serve

To MAKE THE QUESADILLAS: Rub the shrimp evenly with salt and cayenne. In a large sauté pan set over medium-high heat, sauté the shrimp 1 to 3 minutes, until they curl and turn pink. Remove the shrimp from the heat and set aside in a large bowl.

In a separate sauté pan, heat the oil over medium heat. Add the onion, Worcestershire sauce, and hot sauce and sauté about 5 minutes. Add the bell pepper and continue cooking about 5 minutes longer, until the onions are brown and caramelized. Remove the onion mixture from the heat and stir in salt and pepper to taste.

Coat a griddle or large sauté pan with cooking spray or a thin layer of olive oil and place it over medium-high heat. Once the griddle is hot, arrange 2 tortillas in a single layer. Sprinkle ½ cup cheese evenly over each. In another large sauté pan or if there is room on the griddle, arrange 2 more tortillas and divide the shrimp mixture evenly among them. Once the cheese has melted, flip the cheese tortillas over onto the shrimp tortillas, making 2 quesadillas. If you don't have enough room on the griddle or on the stovetop to work with 2 pans simultaneously, wait until the cheese has melted on the first 2 tortillas, top the cheese with the shrimp mixture, and then cover with the other two tortillas. Cook them, flipping occasionally, until they are golden brown and crispy on both sides, about 5 minutes total. Repeat for the remaining tortillas and filling. Cut the quesadillas into quarters and transfer them to serving plates. Serve immediately with the mango salsa.

Brie and Brisket Quesadillas

This recipe grew out of desperation and a last-minute need for a lunch special. I remembered I had a cooked brisket in the cooler and a wheel of Brie at its peak. I quickly warmed and sliced the brisket, grabbed a batch of flour tortillas, topped them with brisket, sliced Brie, shredded Monterey Jack, and a dollop of barbecue sauce, and threw them on the griddle. My desperation quesadilla has become a weekly luncheon staple.

Although it looks complicated, once the brisket is cooked, the dish goes together quickly and easily. Just remember to think ahead and cook the brisket. A cooked brisket will keep in the refrigerator for about three days. Once it's done, all that's left is assembly.

The barbecue sauce comes together quickly, but if time is a concern use your favorite bottled barbecue sauce. There are so many good ones out there—one of my favorites is Stubb's. Serve the quesadillas with pico de gallo *and* guacamole.

YIELD: ABOUT 4 SERVINGS

BRISKET

- 1 (3-pound) beef brisket
- Salt and freshly ground black pepper
- 1 teaspoon chili powder
- 2 cloves garlic, minced
- 1 (12-ounce) can cola drink

MANGO BARBECUE SAUCE

- 3 tablespoons olive oil
- 1 yellow onion
- 5 cloves garlic, minced
- 1 cup ketchup
- 1/4 cup freshly squeezed lemon juice
- 3 tablespoons Worchestershire sauce
- 2 teaspoons Dijon mustard
- 1 teaspoon salt
- 1/2 teaspoon freshly ground pepper
- 1/4 cup Fischer & Wieser Mango Ginger Habanero sauce or bottled mango chutney

QUESADILLAS

- 8 (8-inch-diameter) flour tortillas
- 8 ounces Brie cheese, thinly sliced, with rind left on
- 1 cup shredded Monterey Jack cheese

To MAKE THE BRISKET: Preheat the oven to 325°F. Rub the meat with the salt, pepper, chili powder, and garlic; set it in a large ovenproof casserole dish. Pour the cola over it, cover the dish, and bake about 2 to 2½ hours, until tender. Turn the brisket over once during cooking, after about 1½ hours.

To MAKE THE BARBECUE SAUCE: Heat the olive oil in a large sauté pan over medium heat. Sauté the onion for 5 minutes, add the garlic, and sauté 1 minute more. Stir in the ketchup, lemon juice, Worchestershire sauce, mustard, salt, pepper, and mango sauce or chutney. Cook the sauce until heated through and puree it in a blender or food processor fitted with a metal blade. Measure 1 cup of the sauce for use in the quesadillas; the remaining sauce can be refrigerated in a glass jar up to 1 week.

To MAKE THE QUESADILLAS: Remove the brisket from its cooking liquid and remove any visible fat. Slice about half of the brisket against the grain. (The remaining brisket can be wrapped and frozen; there will be enough left over to make a second meal for 4 people.) Set a large frying pan or griddle on medium-high heat. Coat with a thin layer of cooking spray.

Lay 2 tortillas on the griddle and cover each with 3 to 4 slices of brisket and the Brie, ¼ cup shredded Monterey Jack, and a spoonful of barbecue sauce. Top with 2 tortillas. Grill the quesadillas until the bottoms are crisp and golden brown. Turn with a spatula and grill until the second side is crisp and golden brown. Repeat for the remaining tortillas and filling. Transfer the quesadillas to a large serving plate and cut each into quarters. Serve hot.

Rather Sweet
Bread and Cheese Board

I happened upon several long, skinny bread boards a couple of years ago and immediately imagined them laden with an arrangement of breads, cheeses, and fruits. The longest board is four feet long. We charge by the foot—the longer the board, the greater the assortment. The idea took off, and it has become one of our biggest special-order items. A friend ordered the four-footer for a New Year's bash at her home. Decorated with seasonal fruits and fresh herb sprigs from my kitchen garden, it became the centerpiece of the party.

You can make your bread and cheese board as big or small as you like. If you don't have a suitable wooden board, try a long platter or a series of small ones. Pick your favorite breads, cheeses, and fruits for your creation, or consult with a knowledgeable cheesemonger at your local grocery store. I always include cheese from two of my favorite Texas cheese producers— Pure Luck Texas organic farm (www.purelucktexas.com) in nearby Dripping Springs and Paula Lambert's Mozzarella Company (www.mozzarellacompany.com) in Dallas. Below are some suggestions to get you started.

YIELD: UP TO YOU!

BREAD

Thinly sliced baguettes, brushed with olive oil, butter, salt, and pepper and baked in a 400°F oven about 3 minutes per side until crisp

Sliced raisin-nut bread

Focaccia squares

Assorted crackers

CHEESES, SPREADS, OLIVES

Aged manchego, a semifirm Spanish cheese made from sheep's milk

French Brie

Paula Lambert's bocconcini, hand-formed, bite-size fresh mozzarella balls

Pure Luck Chipotle-Smoked Jalapeño Chèvre, a soft goat cheese

Queso de Valdeon, a semisoft cheese from Spain

Roaring Forties Blue, a blue cheese from Australia's King Island Dairy

White Stilton

Vermont Cheddar

Small bowls of pestos, tapenades, or bruschetta toppings

Small bowls of assorted olives

HERBS, FRUITS, AND FLOWERS

Sprigs of fresh rosemary, thyme, or oregano

Edible flowers such as nasturtiums or pansies

Pomegranate seeds

Sliced pears

Grapes

Sliced apples

Persimmons

Quince paste

Green Chile Crab Cakes with Tomatillo Salsa

Crab cakes are only as good as the crabmeat they're made from, so be sure to use the freshest, sweetest lump crabmeat available in your area. We get delicious lump blue crabmeat from a Texas producer. Dungeness crab or king crab legs can be used, too. Panko, available at Asian markets, are light, unusually crispy breadcrumbs often used in tempura batters.

This recipe makes eight three-inch diameter crab cakes—enough to serve four people as a main course or eight as an appetizer.

YIELD: 8 CAKES

TOMATILLO SALSA

- 1 pound tomatillos, papery skins removed, halved
- 1 medium-size yellow onion, sliced
- 5 cloves garlic, peeled
- 2 tablespoons olive oil
- 1 teaspoon salt, or more to taste

CRAB CAKES

- 4 tablespoons butter
- 4 tablespoons olive oil
- 1/2 medium-size yellow onion, diced
- 1/4 cup diced red bell pepper
- 2 cloves garlic, minced
- 1 Roasted Chile (page 185), optional
- 1/3 jalapeño chile, seeded and finely diced
- 1 pound lump crabmeat, cleaned
- Juice of 1 lime
- 2 tablespoons chopped fresh cilantro
- 2 large eggs, lightly beaten
- 3 cups panko (Japanese breadcrumbs)
- 1/2 cup mayonnaise
- 1/2 teaspoon salt
- 1/4 teaspoon freshly ground black pepper

To make the salsa: Preheat the oven to 450°F. Place the tomatillos, onion, and garlic in a baking pan. Drizzle the olive oil over the vegetables and roast, stirring once, for 20 minutes, until the vegetables are brown around the edges. Cool the vegetables for 10 minutes. Spoon the vegetables into a blender or a food processor fitted with a metal blade and process until puréed. Transfer the purée to a glass jar and refrigerate until cold, about 45 minutes.

To make the crab cakes: Melt 2 tablespoons of the butter and 2 tablespoons of the olive oil in a large skillet set over medium heat. Add the onion, bell pepper, garlic, and both chiles; sauté for 5 minutes. Transfer the vegetable mixture to a medium bowl and cool for 5 minutes. Wipe out the skillet with a paper towel (it will be used again to sauté the crab cakes).

In a large bowl, combine the crabmeat, lime juice, cilantro, eggs, 2 cups of the breadcrumbs, the mayonnaise, salt, and pepper. Stir in the vegetable mixture and form into eight 3-inch-diameter patties.

Pour the remaining 1 cup breadcrumbs into a medium bowl. Coat the patties in crumbs. Melt the remaining 2 tablespoons butter and 2 tablespoons olive oil in the same large skillet over medium heat. Add the crab cakes and cook for 3 to 4 minutes on each side, until they are golden brown and crispy on the outside. Serve immediately with the tomatillo salsa.

Leftover crab cakes can be wrapped tightly and refrigerated for 2 days. Set the oven rack in the middle of the oven and reheat the crab cakes under the broiler for 2 minutes.

Tip: Island Crab Company, located in Rockport, Texas, harvests 25,000 to 30,000 pounds of crabmeat monthly from the nearby bays off the coast of the Gulf of Mexico. Island Crab's lump crabmeat is sweet, succulent, and remarkably free of shell and cartilage. That's because it is inspected under black lights, which make the shell and cartilage glow. The bulk of the company's crabmeat goes to seafood suppliers and restaurants on the East Coast, but the company gladly accepts orders from individuals. Prices vary: Crab harvested in the spring tends to cost a little less because of relatively greater supply. The fall run costs more because difficult weather conditions often translate into smaller harvests. There is a two-pound minimum for orders, but company officials say the meat will keep in the refrigerator up to ten days if stored in a bowl of ice and can be frozen up to three months without any loss of flavor or quality. Orders can be shipped by next-day airmail, or same-day deliveries can be picked up at the airport closest to your home. The company has no website or answering machines, so if you call after hours, the phone will ring endlessly and then you'll hear the screaming beep of the fax. Fax orders are accepted. Call 361-729-9929 for more information.

All-Sold-Out Chicken Pot Pies

I cannot make enough chicken pot pies. Regulars call on Tuesday mornings to reserve a pie, forcing me to erase them from the Tuesday specials board before we open for lunch. I keep doubling the number I make, but the demand grows to meet the expanded supply. I'm about to have a line out the door waiting for pot pies.

YIELD: 6 SERVINGS

FILLING

3 tablespoons unsalted butter

1 medium-size yellow onion, chopped

1 large russet potato, peeled and diced

3 cloves garlic, minced

1 red bell pepper, diced

8 ounces button mushrooms, sliced

1/2 teaspoon crushed red pepper flakes

Salt and freshly ground black pepper

1 purchased cooked rotisserie chicken or
   1 whole stewed chicken, cooled (see
   page 180)

8 ounces fresh green beans, cut into
   1-inch pieces (optional)

1 (8-ounce) package frozen peas
   (optional)

CREAM SAUCE

1/2 cup (1 stick) unsalted butter

1 cup all purpose flour

2 1/2 cups chicken stock, preferably
   homemade

1/2 cup heavy whipping cream (optional)

Dash of hot pepper sauce, such as
   Tabasco

Salt and freshly ground white pepper

CRUST

1 cup (2 sticks) chilled unsalted butter

3 cups all purpose flour

10 ounces chilled cream cheese

1 teaspoon salt

1/4 teaspoon freshly ground white pepper

1 large egg

To make the filling: Melt the butter in a large sauté pan set over medium heat. Add the onion and potato; sauté for 5 minutes. Add the garlic, bell pepper, and mushrooms and sauté about 15 minutes, until the potatoes are tender. Stir in the crushed red pepper and add salt and pepper to taste.

While the vegetables are sautéing, skin the chicken, pull the meat off the bones, and shred the meat or cut into bite-size pieces. Place the green beans in a microwave-safe bowl and add enough water to cover. Cover the dish and microwave on high power about 10 minutes, until the beans are tender. Drain thoroughly. Stir the beans, peas, and chicken into the vegetable mixture. Set the filling aside.

(continued)

Chicken Pot
Pies
SOLD OUT

To MAKE THE CREAM SAUCE: Melt the butter over medium heat in a large saucepan. Add the flour and whisk until smooth. Whisk in the chicken stock and cook the sauce over medium heat until it thickens to the consistency of a cream soup. Add the cream, hot pepper sauce, and salt and white pepper to taste. Pour the cream sauce over the chicken filling and stir to combine. Fill individual 1¼-cup capacity oven-safe bowls three-quarters of the way to the top with the creamed chicken filling.

To MAKE THE CRUST: Preheat the oven to 375°F. Cut the butter into 16 pieces. In the bowl of a food processor fitted with a metal blade, pulse the butter and flour until crumbly. Add the cream cheese, salt, and white pepper. Continue pulsing just until the dough forms a ball.

Set the dough on a flat surface dusted with flour. Use a floured rolling pin to roll the dough out to ¼-inch thickness. Measure the diameter of the pot pie bowls—mine are about 4 inches across—and cut out dough rounds that are 1½ inches larger in diameter. Whisk the egg in a small bowl. Lay the dough rounds on top of the pot pies, making sure the dough hangs evenly over each bowl. Brush the dough lightly with the beaten egg. Bake the pies for 20 to 25 minutes, until golden brown. Serve immediately.

Rather Sweet Variation

Pot pies lend themselves to all manner of vegetable additions, such as diced carrots, fresh corn kernels, diced turnips, sliced celery, cut-up asparagus spears, or sliced wild mushrooms. Just add them to the sauté mix and enjoy.

Tip: My friend Suzie Humphreys Mayo is often on the road for work and likes to make sure her husband eats well while she's away. She double wraps the pot pies in plastic wrap and pops them in the freezer. Her husband bakes them at 350°F for about 30 minutes and dinner is ready. (The pies will keep frozen for 2 to 3 weeks.) Miss Emily, the eighty-seven-year-old mother of another good friend, loves to have a stock of frozen pot pies in her freezer. I never put green beans in hers; she prefers peas.

Prosciutto Tostadas with Shrimp and Parsley

My dear friend David Garrido is one of the most talented chefs in Texas. The son of a Mexican diplomat, he was born in Canada, grew up in Mexico, Puerto Rico, and Costa Rica, and attended school in Switzerland.

As the executive chef at Jeffrey's in Austin, he delivers extraordinary food that showcases his natural intuition about flavors. That, coupled with his charisma and charm, makes it no wonder that Jeffrey's shows up annually on lists of Austin's best restaurants.

YIELD: 4 SERVINGS

5 tablespoons extra-virgin olive oil

8 jumbo shrimp, peeled, deveined, and cut into small chunks

2 green onions, chopped

2 cloves garlic, minced

2 tablespoons freshly squeezed lemon juice

2 tablespoons champagne vinegar

1/4 cup chopped fresh Italian parsley

Sea salt and freshly ground black pepper

4 (8-inch-diameter) flour tortillas

8 thin slices prosciutto

2 cups mixed baby greens

1 yellow bell pepper, roasted, peeled, stemmed, and julienned (see chile roasting, page 185)

Preheat the oven to 375°F. In a sauté pan, heat the olive oil over medium heat. Add the shrimp pieces, green onions, and garlic. Cook for 1 minute, or until the shrimp is cooked through. Remove the pan from the heat and add the lemon juice, vinegar, and parsley. Season with salt and pepper and set aside.

Place the tortillas in the oven for 3 to 6 minutes, until lightly toasted and crunchy. Remove them from the oven and transfer to individual serving plates. Arrange the prosciutto on top of the tortillas. Toss the mixed greens with shrimp mixture and place on top of the prosciutto. Garnish with the roasted yellow pepper strips and serve immediately.

King Ranch Casserole

Here's another Texas classic that shows up everywhere, from recipe websites to greasy-spoon menus. Neiman Marcus's three-pound version—advertised on its website as alternating layers of corn tortillas and chunks of chicken breast with green chiles smothered in a delectable ranchera sauce—is ready to heat and eat as soon as it is delivered to your door.

I haven't a clue how Neiman's makes it, but I have yet to see a published recipe that doesn't include a can of cream of mushroom soup and a can of cream of chicken soup. I have devised a fresher version that doesn't rely on canned soups. The result is rich and satisfying, but inevitably more labor-intensive than the original. Purists may want to make their own chicken broth from a fresh, whole stewing chicken and then use the meat in the casserole. If speed is an issue, feel free to rely on store-bought chicken broth and a roasted chicken. (Leftover chicken or turkey works well, too.)

The 150-year-old King Ranch, by the way, is arguably the best-known ranch in Texas, and possibly the world. A national historic landmark, it covers more area than the state of Rhode Island and is credited with being the birthplace of two major American cattle breeds. Ironically, King Ranch officials seem much slower to claim credit for this enduring casserole. As public-relations honcho Martin Clement commented to Texas Monthly in 1989, "Kind of strange, a King Ranch casserole made with chicken."

YIELD: 10 TO 12 SERVINGS

CHICKEN AND STOCK

- 1 whole stewing chicken
- 2 carrots, unpeeled, cut into 3-inch pieces
- 2 stalks celery, cut into 3-inch pieces
- 10 whole peppercorns
- 5 quarts water

ROASTED CHILES

- 3 New Mexican green chiles

CREAM SAUCE

- 1/2 cup (1 stick) unsalted butter
- 1 medium-size yellow onion, chopped
- 1 red bell pepper, chopped
- 8 ounces button mushrooms, sliced
- 4 cloves garlic, minced
- 1/2 teaspoon chili powder
- 1/4 teaspoon cayenne pepper
- 1 teaspoon salt
- 1 teaspoon freshly ground black pepper
- 1 cup all purpose flour
- 3 cups chicken stock (above)
- 1/2 cup heavy whipping cream
- 1 (10-ounce) can Rotel tomatoes
- Roasted, diced New Mexican green chiles (above)

CASSEROLE

- 18 corn tortillas
- 1 cup shredded Monterey Jack cheese
- 1 cup shredded sharp Cheddar cheese

To PREPARE THE CHICKEN AND STOCK: Place the chicken, carrots, celery, and peppercorns in a large stockpot and add the water. Bring to a boil over high heat. Decrease the heat to medium-low and simmer the stock for 1 hour, uncovered. (The liquid level should drop by about 1 inch.) Turn the heat as low as possible and simmer uncovered for at least 2 hours.

Remove the chicken from the warm stock and refrigerate it. Use a large strainer to strain the chicken broth into a large container. Discard the vegetables and refrigerate the stock. When the chicken is cool enough to handle, discard the skin and pull the meat off the bones. Cut or shred it and set aside. Measure 3½ cups of the stock for use in the recipe; save the remainder for another use.

To ROAST THE CHILES: Preheat the broiler. Broil the chiles about 2 minutes per side, until blackened and blistered on all sides. Remove from the broiler using tongs or oven mitts and enclose in a paper bag to sweat for 5 minutes. Remove the chiles from the bag and peel. Slice in half, and remove and discard the stems and seeds. (If you like your foods hot and spicy, keep some of the seeds.) Dice the chiles.

To MAKE THE CREAM SAUCE: Melt the butter in a large sauté pan over medium heat. Add the onion, bell pepper, mushrooms, and garlic. Sauté on medium-low heat about 7 minutes. Stir in the chili powder, cayenne, salt, and pepper and cook for 1 minute longer. Sprinkle the flour in the pan, ½ cup at a time, and stir until the white of the flour is no longer visible. Whisk in 3 cups of the chicken stock, 1 cup at a time, whisking until smooth after each addition. Whisk in

the cream and stir in the diced roasted chiles. Add the tomatoes. The cream sauce should be thick.

To MAKE THE CASSEROLE: Preheat the oven to 350°F. Grease a 9 by 13-inch baking dish with butter or cooking spray. Place ½ cup of the stock in a bowl large enough to hold an unfolded tortilla. Stack the tortillas in the bowl, 6 at a time, until ready to layer in the baking pan. Make sure all of the tortillas are amply covered in stock. Line the bottom of the prepared pan with a layer of 6 tortillas, making sure each tortilla overlaps the previous one by about one-third. (A thick layer of tortillas will make it easier to cut the casserole once it's cooked.) Cover the tortillas with half of the cream sauce. Add half of the chicken and sprinkle with one-third of each kind of cheese. Add a second layer of 6 soaked tortillas, the remaining cream sauce and chicken, and another third of each kind of cheese. Top with the remaining 6 tortillas and the rest of the cheese.

Bake the casserole for 45 minutes to 1 hour, until hot, bubbling, and lightly browned on top. Remove the casserole from the oven and let sit about 10 minutes. Cut into squares and serve. The cooked casserole can be refrigerated up to 3 days or frozen up to 3 weeks.

Tip: The unique flavor of New Mexican green chiles gives them a very loyal following, but they are not always easy to find. More readily available poblano chiles can be substituted.

Ground Beef Gorditas

Gorditas, or "little fat ones," are fried tortilla cakes made from masa harina—*flour made from corn that has been treated with lime (calcium oxide)—and lard. I make mine with butter in deference to the general American distaste for foods made with lard. Roughly speaking, gorditas are the Mexican equivalent to the American hamburger bun, and as such are filled with varying meat mixtures. This ground beef mixture is my favorite filling.*

Use fresh masa dough if you are lucky enough to have a source for it, usually Mexican grocery stores or tortilla factories. If not, buy dry masa mix and follow the directions for reconstituting it with water. Queso fresco, also known as queso blanco, *is a white, fresh Mexican cheese available in Latin markets and, depending where you live, in many grocery stores. If you can't find it substitute shredded Monterey Jack.*

YIELD: 8 SERVINGS

GORDITA DOUGH

- 4 cups corn masa mix, or 12 ounces fresh masa dough
- 1 teaspoon salt, if necessary (more as needed)
- ½ cup (1 stick) unsalted butter, at room temperature
- Safflower oil, for frying

BEEF FILLING

- 1 pound lean ground beef
- 1 tablespoon finely chopped yellow onion
- 3 cloves garlic, minced
- ½ teaspoon salt
- ½ teaspoon ground cumin
- ½ teaspoon freshly ground black pepper
- 1 tablespoon hot pepper sauce, such as Tabasco
- 1 (8-ounce) can plain tomato sauce

- ½ head iceberg lettuce, shredded
- ½ cup chopped tomatoes
- 1 cup queso fresco, crumbled
- Sliced black olives (optional)
- ½ cup sour cream, Mexican crema, or crème fraîche

To make the dough: If using masa mix, combine water with the masa mix in a large bowl according to the package directions. Beat the masa mix, water, and 1 teaspoon salt in an electric mixer fitted with a paddle attachment until the dough forms a ball. If using fresh masa dough, just add the butter and mix until the dough again forms a ball. Taste the dough and add more salt if necessary. Using your hands, shape the masa dough into eight 4-inch-diameter circles, each about ½ inch thick. Grease a griddle or large skillet with a light coating of oil or cooking spray and set it over medium-high heat. Cook the gorditas for 5 to 10 minutes on each side, until lightly browned.

Fill a large skillet with enough safflower oil to reach ½ inch in depth. Heat the oil over medium heat until the hot oil bubbles when a pinch of dough is dropped in. Use a spatula to lower the gorditas into the hot oil. (They should bubble lustily.) Fry the gorditas about 5 minutes on each side, until

golden brown and crisp. Transfer the gorditas to paper towels to drain.

To MAKE THE BEEF FILLING: In a large skillet, sauté the beef and onion over medium-high heat for 8 to 10 minutes, until the meat is brown. Drain off the fat. Add the garlic, salt, cumin, pepper, hot pepper sauce, and tomato sauce. Cook 5 minutes longer.

To assemble, split the gorditas in half and set them on individual dinner plates. Spoon the beef filling atop the bottom halves and scatter lettuce on top. Sprinkle each with 1 tablespoon chopped tomatoes, 2 tablespoons cheese, and a few olive slices. Drizzle with 1 tablespoon sour cream and lean the top half of the gordita at an angle atop the beef mixture. Or set the accompa-niments in separate bowls and let diners assemble their own. Serve immediately.

Tip: I use safflower oil for frying at high temperatures because it has a high smoking point—in other words, it can with-stand relatively high heat before it starts smoking and burning. Both canola oil and olive oil have lower smoking points than safflower oil.

Savory Crab and Shrimp Cheesecake

Tony Vallone wanted a seafood cheesecake, and I was elected to create it. My onetime boss, the owner of several Houston restaurants, had recently tasted one, and he wanted to add it to the menu of his namesake restaurant, Tony's. I remembered seeing a mascarpone cheesecake somewhere and decided to use the rich Italian cream cheese as a base for a shrimp and crab dish.

Pair this savory cheesecake with a green salad for a lunch or simple dinner, or cut it into small squares and serve as an appetizer.

YIELD: ABOUT 8 MAIN-COURSE SERVINGS

CRUST

60 saltine crackers (about 2 sleeves)

1 cup (2 sticks) unsalted butter, melted

1 teaspoon freshly ground white pepper

1½ teaspoons salt

MASCARPONE FILLING

1 pound uncooked shrimp, fresh or frozen

1½ teaspoons salt

¼ teaspoon cayenne pepper

1 tablespoon unsalted butter

12 ounces cream cheese, at room temperature

1½ pounds mascarpone cheese

5 large eggs

½ cup all purpose flour

½ pound lump crabmeat, cleaned

2 green onion tops, thinly sliced

To MAKE THE CRUST: Grease a 9 by 13-inch baking pan or a 10-inch springform pan with butter or cooking spray. Place the saltines in a heavy-duty plastic bag, seal it, and crush the crackers finely, using your hands or a rolling pin. Don't worry if some pieces are large, and others small, it adds to the rustic look. (This can be done in a food processor as well.) Stir the crackers together with the butter, white pepper, and salt. Press evenly into the pan.

To MAKE THE FILLING: Preheat the oven to 350°F. Defrost, peel, and devein the shrimp, if necessary. Rub the shrimp evenly with the salt and cayenne. Heat the butter in a sauté pan over medium heat and cook the shrimp 1 to 3 minutes, until they curl and turn pink. Transfer the shrimp to a small bowl and refrigerate while preparing the cheese mixture.

Using a mixer fitted with a paddle attachment, beat the cream cheese on medium-high speed until fluffy. Add the mascarpone and beat on medium speed for 1 minute (do not overbeat the mascarpone at this stage, or the mixture might curdle). Add the eggs, one at a time, beating about 30 seconds on medium-high speed after each addition. Add the flour and beat on medium speed until the mixture is creamy and thickens slightly, about 1 minute. Coarsely chop the cooled shrimp and fold it into the cheese mixture along with the crab and green onions. Spread the cheese mixture evenly over the saltine crust. Bake the cheesecake for 30 to 40 minutes, until it is brown on top and set. (Nudge the pan, and if the cheese-cake jiggles, continue to bake until firm.) If using a 10-inch springform pan, bake the cake for 50 to 60 minutes. Cool the cheese-cake at least 30 minutes when using the 9 x 13-inch pan and 60 minutes for the 10-inch. Cut it into squares or wedges and serving. Serve warm or at room temperature.

TREATS
Kids Love

IT'S A GREAT COMBINATION: kids, kitchens, and bakeries. I love it when kids come in, especially my regulars. They call me Miss Rebecca, rush in, and give me great big hugs. I give them Pretty-in-Pink Shortbread Pigs. I'm definitely getting the better deal, but you couldn't convince them of that.

My five-year-old friend Lauren Mayes, with light brown hair and a sparkly smile that carries a hint of mischief, burst into tears the day I ran out of pig cookies. A few days later I asked her why. After all, I'd offered any number of delectable substitutes. Between careful bites of her now-headless pink pig, she answered, "Because I love them so much," as if this were self-evident. Her little friend, Olivia Allbritton, nodded solemnly as she munched away the last of her pig's legs.

I've always thought kids belonged in kitchens, probably because my daughter grew up in them. When she was tiny I kept her in a playpen under my pastry table. She spent part of her childhood coloring at the waitstaff station while I worked.

When she was in elementary school, we moved to upstate New York so I could study with noted bread baker Daniel Leader. Each day, she and I arrived at the bakery at

3:00 A.M.; I would get to work and she would snooze among stacks of flour. At 9:00 A.M. I'd take her to school. It certainly made her food-savvy. As a youngster, she'd head for the walk-in refrigerator and nab a big tablespoon of caviar straight from the tin. She developed a lifelong love for my Peanut Butter–Banana Cream Pie with Hot Fudge Sauce, which I've since named for her. Now that she's older, she has worked at the Rather Sweet counter, helped me schlep desserts to charity events, and, one summer, even developed a short-lived line of sorbets. And she's not the only young adult helping to keep the bakery going. Aaron Hierholzer, then a high school senior, was washing dishes for the previous tenant. We hired him as soon as we opened for business. "I came with the building," he says. Now that he's a sophomore at Trinity University in San Antonio, he works summers and over the Christmas and Thanksgiving holidays. Both his sister and his cousin have worked here in previous summers; it's becoming a family tradition. In fact, I'm currently angling to start training his two younger brothers. Aaron may have come with the building, but with college graduation just a few years away, who knows how long we'll be able to keep him. Given our steady supply of cookies and other goodies, it seems we always attract kids of all ages.

At Christmastime I make stacks of trays of Ginger People, cover the cookies in white royal icing, and invite local kids to hang them on our tree. Sturdy enough to make lasting ornaments as well as tasty enough to eat, not all of them survive the short trip from tray to tree.

It's a rare kid who doesn't fancy peanut butter cup candies, and I have found that few can resist the bakery's Peanut Butter-cups with Peanut-Penuche Icing. It's a peanut butter cupcake with a square of chocolate buried inside and topped with a blanket of rich peanut butter–brown sugar frosting. Decorated with Reese's Pieces, which were put on the culinary map by the kids' classic *E.T. The Extra Terrestrial*, they are sure to be a hit at children's birthday parties. For these, even E.T. might phone home.

Sticky-Fingers Bars

These gooey bars are sweet enough to qualify for honorary candyhood. Few can resist the combination of peanuts and chocolate; make them for your kids or for the kid in you. They freeze beautifully and can be served frozen. Don't be thrown off by the Lyle's Golden Syrup, a liquid cane sugar. It has a lot more flavor than corn syrup, which is cloyingly sweet but entirely lacking in character. Whenever a recipe calls for a large amount of corn syrup, I often substitute Lyle's. You'll have no trouble finding it in most large grocery stores.

Developing this recipe turned into a bigger challenge than I expected. Finally, after a frustrating round of trial and error, I knew I'd nailed it when I gave a sample of the final batch to my business partner, Dan. He shot me an ecstatic look and said, "I think I need a moment."

YIELD: ABOUT 2 DOZEN

CRUST

- 1 cups (2 sticks) unsalted butter, at room temperature
- 1 cup sugar
- 1 tablespoon vanilla extract
- 2 cups all purpose flour
- 1/2 cup salted peanuts, coarsely chopped
- 4 (2.07-ounce) Snickers bars

FILLING

- 3 large eggs
- 1 1/4 cups sugar
- 1/4 cup Lyle's Golden Syrup (see Tip on page 17) or light corn syrup
- 2 tablespoons unsalted butter, melted
- 1 tablespoon vanilla extract
- Pinch of salt

- 1 cup smooth peanut butter
- 1 cup salted peanuts, coarsely chopped
- 3 ounces bittersweet chocolate, coarsely chopped

To MAKE THE CRUST: Preheat the oven to 375°F. Line a 9 by 13-inch baking pan with aluminum foil, leaving several inches hanging over the short ends of the pan. Grease the foil with butter or cooking spray.

Using a mixer fitted with a paddle attachment, beat the butter, sugar, and vanilla in a large bowl on medium speed about 1 minute, until creamy. Add the flour and peanuts and mix on medium-low speed just until incorporated. Press the dough evenly into the prepared pan. Bake for 12 to 15 minutes, until the crust is golden brown. Set aside to cool about 10 minutes. Decrease the oven temperature to 350°F. Cut the Snickers bars into 1/4-inch-thick pieces. Cover the top of the crust with an even layer of Snickers slices, leaving about 1/4 inch between slices.

To MAKE THE FILLING: Whisk the eggs, sugar, syrup, butter, vanilla, and salt in a large bowl until combined. Pour the mixture over the crust and bake for 25 to 30 minutes, or until set (it should not wiggle when you remove the pan from the oven). Cool for 20 to 30 minutes.

(continued)

Spread the peanut butter in an even layer on top of the filling. Add the chopped peanuts in an even layer. Melt the chocolate in a small bowl in a microwave on medium high. Check every 30 seconds to ensure the chocolate does not burn. Stir until smooth. Use a spoon to drizzle the chocolate over the chopped peanuts.

Refrigerate for at least 1 hour. Grab the foil edges and lift the bars out of the pan and cut into bars.

Well-wrapped bars will keep about 5 days at room temperature and about 3 weeks frozen.

Tip: A great peanut butter divide pits those who love sweetened, commercial peanut butters such as Skippy and Jif against those who swear by the natural, unsweetened stuff that separates at room temperature. Luckily, either one works in this recipe. Both will spread more easily after spending 30 to 60 seconds on high in a microwave oven.

Ginger People

Nancy Jackson, a good friend and a good customer, gave me this recipe. I was gearing up to start production on the mandatory hordes of Christmastime ginger men and women and longed for fresh inspiration. Nancy boasted that she had the best recipe around.

I said, "Prove it." She brought her recipe into the bakery the next day. I haven't used my old recipe since.

The recipe makes sturdy dough, perfect for rolling out and cutting into holiday shapes. If you feel ambitious, decorate the cookies with royal icing.

To hang the cookies on a Christmas tree, use the large end of a chopstick to punch a hole near the top edge of each cookie before baking. Once the cookies have been baked, cooled, and decorated, thread a ribbon through each hole, tie a knot at the top, and hang.

Be sure to allow enough time for the dough to chill so it will handle properly. (This is not one of those recipes you can whip up for a school function on one night's notice.)

YIELD: ABOUT 4 DOZEN

COOKIES

- 1 cup sugar
- 1/2 cup dark molasses
- 1/2 cup water
- 1 tablespoon ground ginger

- 2 teaspoons ground cinnamon
- 1 teaspoon ground cloves
- 1 cup (2 sticks) unsalted butter
- 4 cups all-purpose flour
- 1 1/2 teaspoons baking soda
- 1/4 teaspoon salt

ROYAL ICING

3 large egg whites

4 cups sifted powdered sugar

1 teaspoon lemon juice

To MAKE THE COOKIES: In a large saucepan, stir together the sugar, molasses, water, ginger, cinnamon, and cloves. Bring to a boil, stirring until the sugar dissolves. Remove the pan from the heat and add the butter, stirring occasionally until melted. Cool for 15 minutes. In a large bowl, stir together the flour, baking soda, and salt. Add the flour mixture to the ingredients in the saucepan. Mix with a wooden spoon until completely blended. Spoon the dough into a gallon-size, resealable freezer bag, flatten the dough to an even thickness, and seal. Refrigerate the dough at least 6 hours or overnight.

Preheat the oven to 375°F. Remove the dough from the refrigerator and cut into 4 portions. Roll out 1 portion at a time, storing the remainder of the dough in the refrigerator. On a flat, smooth, lightly floured surface, roll out the chilled dough to ¼-inch thickness. Cut out the cookies with cookie cutters. Use a spatula to move the cookies onto ungreased baking sheets, leaving about 1 inch between thm. Combine the dough scraps and reroll the dough to cut out more cookies. Roll any subsequent scraps into a thick log, wrap it in plastic wrap, and freeze for 10 minutes. Cut ¼-inch-thick rounds off the log to make round cookies. (Reroll the dough scraps only once, or the cookies will become tough from overhandling.)

Bake the cookies for 10 to 12 minutes, until firm. Cool the cookies on the baking sheets about 5 minutes before transferring to racks to cool completely.

To MAKE THE ICING: Whisk the egg whites until frothy. Whisk in the powdered sugar and lemon juice until smooth and incorporated. Stored in a closed container in the refrigerator the icing will keep for up to 3 days. (For those who are concerned about consuming raw egg products, use pasteurized egg whites, available at most grocery stores.)

Spoon the icing into a pastry bag fitted with a plain round tip (Or, spoon it into a plastic sandwich bag, snip off a corner, and squeeze out the icing.) Decorate the cookies as whimsy dictates. I like to decorate them with faces, hair, hats, aprons, coats, dresses, and shoes.

Set the iced cookies on racks for the icing to harden, about 30 minutes. When the icing is completely set, store the cookies gently stacked in an airtight container. They will keep for up to 2 weeks at room temperature.

Franny's Fave Peanut Butter-Banana Cream Pie with Hot Fudge Sauce

This is my teenage daughter's favorite dessert, and it has been since she was in third grade. I used to bring pieces home from work when she was in elementary school, and we'd eat them together. This dessert reminds me of a hot fudge banana split in pie form. I always serve it with lightly sweetened whipped cream.

YIELD: 8 SERVINGS

CRUST

2 cups all purpose flour

1/2 teaspoon salt

2 tablespoons sugar

2/3 cup (11 tablespoons) chilled unsalted butter

4 to 5 tablespoons ice water

FILLING

1/4 cup banana liqueur, such as crème de banane

1 envelope plus 1/2 teaspoon unflavored gelatin

1 vanilla bean

2 3/4 cups milk

4 large egg yolks

3/4 cup sugar

3 tablespoons cornstarch

3 to 4 ounces bittersweet chocolate

2 ripe bananas

Lemon-lime soda (see Tip on page 157)

1/4 cup creamy peanut butter, at room temperature

HOT FUDGE SAUCE

2 cups heavy whipping cream

1/2 cup firmly packed golden brown sugar

1/4 cup (1/2 stick) butter

2 cups semisweet chocolate chips

12 ounces bittersweet chocolate, coarsely chopped

1/4 teaspoon salt

3 to 4 tablespoons Jack Daniel's whiskey, (optional)

WHIPPED CREAM TOPPING

2 cups chilled heavy whipping cream

1/2 cup powdered sugar

3/4 cup roasted peanuts, coarsely chopped

To MAKE THE CRUST: Preheat the oven to 425°F. Using a mixer fitted with a whisk attachment, combine the flour, salt, and sugar on low speed for about 30 seconds. Cut the chilled butter into 1/2-inch cubes. Add the butter to the flour mixture and combine on slow speed for 1 to 1 1/2 minutes, until the mixture looks crumbly, with bits of dough the size of dried currants. Add 4 tablespoons ice water, 1 tablespoon at a time, mixing on low speed for 10 seconds after each addition. After the last addition, the dough should begin to clump together in a ball. If not, continue mixing about 10 more seconds. (If it still looks too dry, add an additional tablespoon of ice water.) Gently mold the dough into a disk, wrap it in plastic wrap, and refrigerate at least 1 hour.

Unwrap the dough and transfer to a lightly floured flat surface. Roll it into a ⅛-inch-thick circle large enough to cover the bottom and sides of a 9-inch deep-dish pie plate. (To keep the dough from sticking, gently pick up the dough periodically as you roll it out and rotate it in place, adding more flour underneath if necessary.) Wrap the dough lightly over the rolling pin and set it in the ungreased 9-inch pie plate. Press it into place and crimp the outside edges with your fingers or a fork. Use a fork to prick the bottom of the unbaked crust. Cover the bottom and sides of the crust with a sheet of parchment paper and fill with pie weights or dried beans. (I use the cheapest red beans I can find.)

Bake for 10 minutes. Remove the parchment and weights. If the crust is not golden brown, return it to the oven for 1 to 3 minutes. Cool on a rack until the custard filling is ready.

To MAKE THE FILLING: Pour the banana liqueur into a small metal bowl, sprinkle the gelatin on top, and let it soften for 5 minutes. Set the bowl over a small saucepan with 2 inches of simmering water and warm the gelatin until it has completely dissolved

and looks clear. Cut the vanilla bean pod in half lengthwise. Combine the milk and vanilla bean pod in a medium saucepan and bring to a boil. Turn off the heat, cover the saucepan, and let the vanilla steep in the milk while preparing the yolk mixture.

In a large bowl, whisk the egg yolks. Add the sugar gradually, whisking constantly until the mixture lightens in color to a lemony hue, about 15 minutes total. Whisk in the cornstarch. Pour the milk through a strainer into a glass measuring cup or pitcher with a spout. Gradually pour the milk into the yolk mixture, whisking constantly. Pour the mixture into a clean saucepan set over medium heat and whisk constantly until it begins to thicken and coats the back of a spoon. Reduce the heat and whisk for 2 minutes. Remove from the heat and whisk in the gelatin, mixture, being sure to incorporate it thoroughly. Let the filling cool completely, about 30 minutes.

In the meantime, melt the chocolate in a small bowl in a microwave on medium-high. Check every 30 seconds to ensure the chocolate does not burn. Using a pastry brush, evenly coat the bottom and sides of the crust with bittersweet chocolate. Refrigerate the pie crust while the chocolate hardens and sets, 10 to 15 minutes.

Slice the bananas diagonally and brush them with lemon-lime soda to prevent discoloration (see the Tip on page 198 for more information). Spread the peanut butter evenly over the bottom of the baked crust. Layer on half the banana slices, all of the filling, and the remaining banana slices.

(continued)

Cover the pie with plastic wrap. Make sure the plastic comes in direct contact with any custard not covered by bananas to totally seal it and prevent a skin from developing on the surface. Refrigerate the pie overnight before serving.

To MAKE THE FUDGE SAUCE: Heat the cream and brown sugar in a heavy saucepan over medium heat. When the sugar is dissolved, add the butter, chocolate chips, and bittersweet chocolate and stir over medium-low heat until the chocolate is melted and the mixture is smooth. Stir in the salt. Remove the fudge sauce from the heat and stir in the Jack Daniel's. Keep warm until ready to slice and serve the pie, or cover and store in the refrigerator up to 1 month. The sauce can be reheated in the microwave or in a saucepan on the stovetop over low heat as often as necessary.

To MAKE THE TOPPING: Using a mixer fitted with a whisk attachment, whip the cream in a medium bowl on high speed until thick, with medium-soft peaks forming when you lift the mixer out of the bowl (this takes $1\frac{1}{2}$ minutes with a handheld mixer, and even less time with a standard mixer). Be careful not to overwhip the cream, or it will separate. Whip in the powdered sugar.

To serve the pie, cut it in wedges, add a dollop of whipped cream and a sprinkle of chopped peanuts, and top with a generous pour of hot fudge sauce.

Peanut Buttercups with Peanut-Penuche Icing

These cakelike muffins were a favorite of my grandmother's, and I have her handwritten recipe to prove it. The icing takes its name from penuche, a fudgelike candy made by boiling brown sugar, milk, and butter. I added the bittersweet chocolate in the cupcake's middle, thereby converting it into an inside-out peanut butter cup.

YIELD: 12 CUPCAKES

CUPCAKES

1³/₄ cups all purpose flour

1 tablespoon baking powder

¹/₄ teaspoon salt

1¹/₄ cups firmly packed dark brown sugar

6 tablespoons unsalted butter, at room temperature

¹/₃ cup peanut butter, smooth or chunky

1 cup milk

1 teaspoon vanilla extract

2 large eggs

3.5-ounce bar bittersweet chocolate, cut into 12 squares

PEANUT-PENUCHE ICING

¹/₄ cup (¹/₂ stick) unsalted butter

¹/₄ cup peanut butter, smooth or chunky

¹/₄ cup milk

1 cup firmly packed dark brown sugar

¹/₈ teaspoon salt

1 teaspoon vanilla extract

¹/₂ cup powdered sugar

To MAKE THE CUPCAKES: Preheat the oven to 350°F. Lightly coat 6 Texas-size muffin cups with nonstick cooking spray or Baker's Joy. Using a mixer fitted with a paddle attachment, combine the flour, baking powder, salt, and sugar in a large bowl on medium speed for about 30 seconds. (Don't worry if there are a few sugar lumps.) Add the butter, peanut butter, milk, and vanilla. Mix for 1 minute on medium-low speed. Add the eggs and beat for 1¹/₂ minutes on medium-high speed. Fill the prepared muffin cups with batter halfway to the top. Place 2 squares of chocolate in the middle of the batter and add more batter to fill the muffin cups three-quarters of the way to the top.

Bake for 30 to 35 minutes, until the tops of the muffins are light brown and a toothpick stuck into the middle comes out with no crumbs clinging to it. (A bit of melted chocolate from the center may show, but that doesn't count.)

Cool the muffins for 10 minutes before removing them from the pan. Let them cool on racks at least 5 minutes longer before frosting.

To MAKE THE ICING: Combine the butter, peanut butter, milk, brown sugar, and salt in a medium saucepan over medium heat. Bring the mixture to a low boil and cook for 1½ minutes without stirring. Take the pan off the burner and cool about 30 minutes (do not let it sit longer than 30 minutes or the icing will not mix smoothly). Add the vanilla and powdered sugar. Using a mixer fitted with a paddle attachment, beat on medium speed until the icing is creamy and of spreading consistency, about 1 minute. Ice the cooled cupcakes immediately.

Tightly wrapped, the cupcakes will keep for 2 days at room temperature and up to 3 weeks frozen.

Tip: Dealing with peanut butter or other sticky ingredients such as honey or corn syrup can be a royal pain, especially when moving them from measuring cup to batter. A light coating of cooking spray on the inside of the measuring cup will allow peanut butter or any other sticky ingredient to slide out much more easily.

PB&J Cookies with Honey-Roasted Peanuts

One day when I was making my usual plain peanut butter cookies, I started daydreaming about the peanut butter and jelly sandwiches I used to eat as a kid. On a whim I added jelly to the centers, and these PB&J cookies were born. I make giant ones at my bakery. Kids and adults snap them up as soon as they emerge from my ovens. Use a thick jam so it is less likely to melt into the cookie. Any flavor you like is fine.

YIELD: 6 1/2 DOZEN

1½ cups (3 sticks) unsalted butter, at room temperature

1½ cups smooth peanut butter

1½ cups granulated sugar

1½ cups firmly packed dark brown sugar

3 large eggs

1 tablespoon vanilla extract

3 cups all purpose flour

1½ teaspoons baking soda

1½ teaspoons salt

1 cup honey-roasted peanuts, coarsely chopped

¾ cup jam, jelly, or fruit spread

Preheat the oven to 375°F. Line baking sheets with parchment paper or silicone mats, or grease generously with butter or cooking spray. Using a mixer fitted with a paddle attachment, beat the butter and peanut butter in a large bowl on medium speed about 1 minute, until fluffy. Add both sugars and beat about 30 seconds, until combined. Add the eggs and vanilla and beat until smooth. Stir in the flour, baking soda, and salt on low speed until thoroughly combined. Stir in the peanuts. (The dough will be soft.)

Using a 1¾-inch scoop, drop the dough onto the prepared baking sheets, leaving at least 2 inches between cookies (they will puff and spread as they bake). Make a small indentation in the middle of each cookie with the end of a wooden spoon. Put ¼ teaspoon of jam in each indentation. Bake for 10 to 12 minutes, until the cookies are golden around the edges (for a crispier cookie, remove from the oven once they are golden brown all over). Let the cookies cool on the baking sheets about 10 minutes, then transfer them to racks to cool completely.

Store the cookies in an airtight container at room temperature up to 1 week. They'll keep for 1 month in the freezer if tightly wrapped in foil or plastic wrap.

Rather Sweet Variation

For plain peanut butter cookies, omit the jam and decorate the cookies by dipping a fork into water and then into a small bowl of

(continued)

granulated sugar. Scoop the cookie dough onto the baking sheet and press the fork horizontally into the dough to leave a pattern on each cookie.

Tip: I always keep a little dough in the bank—cookie dough, that is. That way, I can have freshly baked cookies fast. Almost any cookie dough can be stored in a tightly closed container and refrigerated at least 2 weeks (for longer storage, use the freezer.) You can scoop the dough onto baking sheets straight out of the refrigerator and pop them in the oven. Since the dough goes into the oven cold, you'll have to bake the cookies a few minutes longer than the recipe recommends. Set the timer for the regular baking time and check the cookies for doneness every minute thereafter. If you want to make giant cookies like the ones we sell at Rather Sweet, use a scoop with a 2½-inch diameter. I use a professional No.10 scoop with a 7-tablespoon capacity. Use a small scoop or tablesoon to make an indentation and fill it with about 1 tablespoon of jam per cookie. Bake the cookies 3 to 4 minutes longer than recommended for the standard size. You'll end up with about 4 dozen cookies.

Mars Pies

I've always been fascinated by the planet Mars, so I created these in honor of the first unmanned landing on the planet. The recipe is a takeoff on an old Southern favorite, moon pies.

YIELD: 6 PIES

COOKIES

- 1 cup (2 sticks) unsalted butter, at room temperature
- ½ cup powdered sugar
- 1 cup all purpose flour
- 1 cup whole-grain graham flour
- ¼ teaspoon salt
- ½ teaspoon baking powder
- 1 teaspoon vanilla extract

CHOCOLATE-CARAMEL GANACHE

- 10 ounces bittersweet chocolate, finely chopped
- 1 cup heavy whipping cream
- 10 caramel candies, unwrapped

CHOCOLATE-MARSHMALLOW FILLING

- 1½ envelopes unflavored gelatin
- 1 cup cold water
- 1½ cups sugar
- 1 cup light corn syrup
- ⅛ teaspoon salt
- 6 tablespoons unsweetened cocoa powder

CHOCOLATE COATING

- 8 ounces bittersweet chocolate (between and 55 and 62 percent cacao), coarsely chopped

TO MAKE THE COOKIES: Preheat the oven to 350°F. Line a baking sheet with parchment paper or silicone mats, or grease generously with butter or cooking spray. Using a mixer fitted with a paddle attachment, cream the butter and sugar in a large bowl on medium speed until fluffy. Add both flours, the salt, baking powder, and vanilla. Beat on medium speed until thoroughly incorporated. On a flat, lightly floured surface, roll the dough out to ¼-inch thickness. Using a round 3½-inch-diameter cookie cutter, cut out 6 cookies (you'll have just enough dough). Transfer to the prepared baking sheet and bake 10 to 12 minutes, until golden brown. Cool the cookies completely on racks before covering with ganache.

TO MAKE THE GANACHE: Place the chocolate in a medium bowl. Heat the cream and caramels over medium-low heat, stirring occasionally, until the caramels have melted completely. Pour the hot mixture over the chocolate and stir until melted.

TO MAKE THE FILLING: Using a mixer fitted with a whisk attachment, whip the gelatin into ½ cup of the cold water. In a medium saucepan, heat the sugar, corn syrup, the remaining ½ cup water, and the salt without stirring until it reaches the soft-ball stage, registering 234° to 240°F on a candy thermometer. Add the warm sugar mixture to the gelatin mixture in a slow, thin stream, stirring continuously on low speed. Increase to high speed and beat about 5 minutes, until the mixture has thickened and cooled. Reduce the speed to low, add the cocoa powder 1 tablespoon at a time, and beat until incorporated.

TO MAKE THE CHOCOLATE COATING: Microwave the chocolate in a bowl for 1 minute on a medium-high. Stir, and if it has not completely melted, keep microwaving for 30-second intervals. Stir until smooth.

To assemble the pies, place the cookies on a baking sheet covered with waxed paper, leaving about 2 inches between the cookies. Spread a ¼-inch-thick layer of ganache on top of each cookie and refrigerate about 10 minutes, until set. Spread a layer of marshmallow filling (about 2 tablespoonfuls) over the ganache; it will flow over the edges of the cookie. Spoon about 2 to 3 tablespoons of the melted chocolate to cover each cookie completely. Refrigerate the cookies about 10 minutes, until the chocolate layer has hardened. Store the cookies in an airtight container with waxed paper between layers.

Tip: A time-consuming recipe, this one is more manageable when broken down into stages. Try making the cookies the first day and finishing the rest the next. They are worth the effort.

Pretty-in-Pink
Shortbread Pigs

When The Ladies' Home Journal *asked me to submit some of my favorite Christmas cookie recipes, I had to send them one of my oldest, dearest favorites. I can never get enough of these simple, buttery classics. At the bakery we use this basic shortbread recipe for just about every holiday and season imaginable—hearts for Valentine's Day, bunnies for Easter, and jungle animals for summertime.* The Ladies' Home Journal *cut them into doves and iced them with blue and white frosting. I like them best cut into pig shapes and iced with pink-tinted frosting in honor of Priscilla, my pet, a real live pygmy pig.*

YIELD: 20 COOKIES

SHORTBREAD

- 2 cups (4 sticks) unsalted butter, at room temperature
- 1¹/₂ cups powdered sugar
- 2 tablespoons vanilla extract
- 4 cups all purpose flour
- 2 teaspoons baking powder

POWDERED SUGAR ICING

- 2 cups powdered sugar, sifted
- ¹/₄ cup milk
- 1 teaspoon vanilla or almond extract (optional)
- Pink food coloring

To MAKE THE SHORTBREAD: Preheat the oven to 350°F. Line baking sheets with parchment paper or silicone mats, or grease generously with butter or cooking spray. Using a mixer fitted with a paddle attachment, beat the butter and sugar in a large bowl on medium-high speed until fluffy. Add the vanilla and beat until combined. In a separate bowl, stir together the flour and baking powder. Add the flour mixture slowly to the butter mixture, stirring on low speed. Stop beating as soon as the flour mixture is completely incorporated. (Overbeating will produce a tough cookie.)

Form the dough into a ball, cover in plastic wrap and refrigerate for 30 minutes before rolling it out. On a flat, smooth floured surface, roll the chilled dough out to ¹/₄-inch thickness. Cut out the cookies with a 4-inch pig cookie cutter. Use a spatula to transfer the cookies to the prepared baking sheets, placing them ¹/₂ inch apart. Combine the dough scraps and reroll the dough to cut out more cookies. (Reroll the dough scraps only once, or the cookies will become tough from overhandling. Roll any subsequent scraps into a thick log, wrap it in plastic wrap, and freeze for 10 minutes. Cut ¹/₄-inch-thick rounds off the log to make round cookies.)

Bake the cookies for 10 to 12 minutes, until light brown around the edges. Cool the cookies for 10 minutes on the baking sheet.

(continued)

Remove with a spatula and cool completely on racks about 5 minutes before icing.

To MAKE THE ICING: Whisk together the powdered sugar, milk, and extract. Divide the icing into 2 parts, with most of it going into a medium bowl. Use food coloring to tint the larger batch of icing. Leave the remaining frosting untinted. When the cookies are cool, dip them face down in the pink icing, being sure to cover the whole cookie. Set the cookies, icing side up, on parchment paper and let the icing harden before continuing to decorate. If you do not have a pastry bag, cut a tiny tip off a corner of a plastic sandwich bag. Spoon the white icing into the bag and squeeze a dot out of the corner hole to make an eye, and a set of round beads around the each pig's neck to make a string of pearls.

Store the cookies in an airtight container at room temperature up to 1 week or tightly wrapped in aluminum foil or plastic wrap for 1 month in the freezer.

Tip: This recipe makes a lot of dough. If you want to avoid a marathon baking session, divide the dough in half or quarters, wrap each segment separately, and freeze one or more for later use. The dough will keep at least a week in the refrigerator and at least 1 month in the freezer. (Let the frozen dough sit at room temperature for 10 to 15 minutes before rolling it out.)

Maple-Glazed Oatmeal Cookies

My oatmeal cookie recipe reflects a lifelong aversion to raisins—thanks to an incident involving my big brother and a rotten box of the shriveled fruit. I substitute dried cranberries and add a touch of maple syrup to both the cookie dough and the icing.

YIELD: ABOUT 4 DOZEN

COOKIES

- 1/2 cup (1 stick) unsalted butter, at room temperature
- 1/4 cup pure maple syrup
- 1/2 cup granulated sugar
- 3/4 cup firmly packed golden brown sugar
- 2 large eggs
- 1 1/2 cups all purpose flour
- 1/4 teaspoon salt
- 2 teaspoons baking soda
- 3 cups old-fashioned rolled oats
- 1 1/2 cups dried cranberries

MAPLE GLAZE

- 1 cup powdered sugar, sifted
- 3 tablespoons pure maple syrup
- 4 to 5 tablespoons heavy whipping cream or milk
- Pinch of salt

To MAKE THE COOKIES: Preheat the oven to 350°F. Line baking sheets with parchment paper or silicone mats, or grease generously with butter or cooking spray. Using a mixer fitted with a paddle attachment, cream the butter, syrup, and both sugars in a large bowl on medium-high speed. Add the eggs and beat on medium-high until thoroughly combined. Add the flour, salt, baking soda, oats, and cranberries and mix on medium-low speed until combined.

Using a 1 3/4-inch scoop, drop golf ball–size mounds of dough onto the prepared baking sheets, spacing them about 1 inch apart. Lightly press the dough down to flatten each cookie slightly. Bake for 7 to 10 minutes, until the cookies are golden brown. Cool on baking sheets for 10 minutes, then transfer to racks to cool completely.

To MAKE THE GLAZE: Combine the sugar, maple syrup, 4 tablespoons cream, and salt in a medium bowl. Whisk until smooth. If it looks too thick, add another tablespoon of cream. Dip the tops of the cooled cookies into the glaze and set them on waxed paper. The glaze will harden in approximately 30 minutes.

♕ Tip: Do not mistake inexpensive pancake syrup for the real thing. Real maple syrup is made from the sap of maple trees. It takes a whole lot of raw sap to make just a little maple syrup, which makes it relatively expensive. Accept no substitutes; your taste buds are worth it.

Jubilation Granola Chews

The long list of ingredients may make these look daunting, but measuring and assembling them is the most time-consuming part of this recipe. Once that's done, just stir everything together, press it into a pan. These are softer and chewier than most commercial granola bars.

YIELD: ABOUT 16 BARS

3/4 cup firmly packed golden brown sugar

3/4 cup honey

1/3 cup maple syrup

1/4 cup water

1/4 cup (1/2 stick) unsalted butter

1/3 cup peanut butter

1/2 teaspoon kosher salt

2 teaspoons vanilla extract

4 cups old-fashioned rolled oats

1 cup almonds, sliced or slivered

1 cup sweetened shredded coconut

1 cup sweetened dried cranberries or golden raisins

1/2 cup sunflower seeds

2 tablespoons sesame seeds

1/4 cup golden flax seeds

Preheat the oven to 350°F. Generously grease a 9 by 13-inch baking pan with butter or cooking spray. Combine the brown sugar, honey, maple syrup, and water in a medium saucepan set over medium-high heat. When the mixture comes to a boil, reduce the heat to medium and simmer about 8 to 10 minutes until it reaches the soft-ball stage, registering 234° to 240°F on a candy thermometer.

Stir in the butter, peanut butter, salt, and vanilla. Spread the oatmeal, almonds, coconut, sunflower and sesame seeds evenly on 2 baking sheets. Bake for 7 to 10 minutes, stirring once, until lightly browned. Combine the oats, almonds, coconut, cranberries, and sunflower, sesame, and flax seeds in a large bowl. Pour in the honey mixture and stir to combine. Cool for about 30 minutes. Pour the mixture into the prepared pan. Evenly press the granola into the pan using a sheet of waxed paper or plastic wrap to keep your hands from sticking. Cool for another 30 minutes before cutting into bars. Cut the bars in half the long way and in eighths the short way to make 4½ by 1½-inch bars.

Rather Sweet Variation

These bars can accommodate almost any mix-in you can dream up. Substitute any dried fruit, nut, or seed you fancy, or substitute any type of nut butter for the peanut butter. For vegans, omit the butter altogether and add an equal amount of nut butter.

Tip: Flaxseed has become the darling of the health food set, and I'm partial to it, too. It has a wonderful nutty flavor and is high in omega 3-fatty acids, which experts have dubbed a "good" fat.

Pumpkin Yumkins

I found this recipe with my grandmother's things, but can't remember ever making it. The unusual name caught my imagination and I decided to try it. The yumkins turned out to a cross between a muffin and a cupcake, all dressed up with orange-flavored cream cheese frosting. I serve them around Christmas and Thanksgiving, but they are great anytime, especially for brunch.

YIELD: 1 DOZEN

YUMKINS

- 1 cup pecans
- 1/2 cup (1 stick) unsalted butter, at room temperature
- 1 cup firmly packed dark brown sugar
- 1 large egg
- 1 (15-ounce) can pure pumpkin
- 1 teaspoon vanilla extract
- 2 cups all purpose flour
- 1 teaspoon baking soda
- 1 teaspoon baking powder
- 1/4 teaspoon salt
- 1 cup chopped dates

CREAM CHEESE FROSTING

- 1 (3-ounce) package cream cheese, at room temperature
- 1 teaspoon freshly squeezed orange juice
- 2 cups powdered sugar
- Zest of 1 orange, preferably organic

To MAKE THE YUMKINS: Preheat the oven to 350°F. Arrange the nuts on a baking sheet in a single layer and toast for 7 to 9 minutes, until golden brown and aromatic. Cool the nuts, and then coarsely chop.

Grease 12 standard-size muffin cups with butter or cooking spray. Using a mixer fitted with a paddle attachment, cream the butter and sugar in a large bowl on medium speed about 1 minute. Add the egg and beat on medium speed for 1 minute. Add the pumpkin and vanilla and beat until combined. Stir in the flour, baking soda, baking powder, and salt. Stir in the dates and pecans. The batter will be thick.

Spoon the batter into muffin cups just to the top. Bake about 20 minutes, until the muffins are firm to the touch or a toothpick inserted into the middle comes out clean. Cool the muffins in the pan for 5 minutes, then invert them onto racks to cool for 30 minutes before frosting.

To MAKE THE FROSTING: Using a mixer fitted with the paddle attachment, beat the cream cheese and orange juice on medium speed about 20 seconds. Add the powdered sugar 1/2 cup at a time, beating until incorporated after each addition. Stir in the orange zest.

Coat the tops of the cooled yumkins with frosting. Do not wrap until the frosting has set, about 45 minutes. Well-wrapped yumkins will keep about 3 days at room temperature.

DRINKS

FREDRICKSBURG IS A SMALL TOWN. We don't even have a movie theater. So a lot of entertaining takes place at private parties—in restaurants and in people's homes. I love to entertain, and I love to try new drink ideas on friends.

When entertaining at home, I offer one or two festive drinks rather than stocking up on an all-purpose array of alcohol. In this chapter, I've included recipe ideas from two Rather Sweet chefs and one from my mother, who loved to throw parties.

We host numerous private parties in the upstairs dining room, and since we serve beer and wine only, sangria is often our drink of choice.

Last spring my friend DeAnn Sears called to see if we could host an impromptu high school graduation party for her son. It was 11:00 P.M. "My whole family was in town, they were starving, and Rebecca says, 'Come on over,'" DeAnn says. "She got out all kinds of great food, turned on the music, and had a beautiful party."

As it happened, we'd had a big private event earlier in the day, and there was a lot of extra food. As soon as DeAnn called, I started hauling it out. Then I made a couple of pitchers of Watermelon Lemonade. It turned out to be a great night for everybody.

Watermelon Lemonade

A cold glass of lemonade is a surefire antidote to Fredericksburg's inevitable summertime heat spells. I keep a five-gallon glass jar stocked with this lemonade on the bakery's front counter all summer long. It looks especially appealing with diced fruit floating on the top. It will also look great in your glass pitcher.

YIELD: 12 SERVINGS

SUGAR SYRUP

2 cups water

2 cups sugar

LEMONADE

2 cups water

2 cups freshly squeezed lemon juice

1 cup freshly squeezed lime juice

4 cups ice cubes

2 cups diced watermelon

Mixed diced fruit of your choice (such as apples, pears, or strawberries)

1 orange, preferably organic, sliced into rounds

1 lemon, preferably organic, sliced into rounds

1 lime, preferably organic, sliced into rounds

To MAKE THE SUGAR SYRUP: Combine the water and sugar in a medium saucepan. Turn the heat to medium-high and boil for 10 minutes. If you are planning to make the lemonade immediately, place 2 cups of the sugar water in the freezer or refrigerator while you do the rest of the prep work. (The recipe makes about 2 cups syrup. When stored in a tightly sealed glass jar, sugar syrup keeps indefinitely in the refrigerator.)

To MAKE THE LEMONADE: Mix the 2 cups chilled sugar syrup, water, lemon juice, and lime juice in a big bowl or pitcher. Add the ice cubes and diced watermelon and other fruit. Add the orange, lemon, and lime rounds. Stir well and chill until icy cold.

Frothy Vanilla Milk

So simple. So absolutely perfect for drinking with holiday cookies while gathered around a crackling fire. I love the richness of this drink when made with whole milk, but it works fine using reduced-fat, low-fat, or even skim milk.

4 cups whole milk

2 tablespoons granulated sugar

2 tablespoons golden brown sugar

1½ whole vanilla beans, split in half lengthwise

Sweetened whipped cream, for garnish (optional; see page 196)

Ground nutmeg, for dusting (optional)

In a large saucepan, combine the milk and both sugars. Scrape the vanilla seeds from the middle of the beans into the saucepan and also add the split beans. Bring the milk to a simmer; cover, remove from the heat, and let stand for 30 minutes to allow the vanilla to flavor the milk. Discard the vanilla beans and rewarm the milk over moderate heat, whisking vigorously, until frothy and warm. Serve in mugs with a dollop of sweetened whipped cream and a sprinkle of nutmeg.

Tommye Wood's Milk (Sure Packs a) Punch

My mother was always ready for a party. For anyone who wasn't, her punch provided a sure-fire cure. This recipe came from a book she created for me before she died. "For Becca," she wrote. "Some things you like me to cook for you! Love, Mother."

The directions for making the punch were even shorter than her inscription: "Mix and chill and have a party." This is strong stuff, so feel free to reduce the amount of alcohol to suit your taste.

YIELD: ABOUT 25 SERVINGS

1½ gallons premium-quality vanilla ice cream

4 cups whole milk

2 cups bourbon

1 cup rum

¼ cup brandy

Ground nutmeg, for dusting

Remove the ice cream from the freezer and let it sit at room temperature until it begins to soften, about 15 minutes. Stir together the milk, bourbon, rum, and brandy in a large punch bowl. Spoon the ice cream into the punch bowl and stir lightly, so that some of the ice cream mixes with the rest of the ingredients and some floats on top. Dust with nutmeg and serve immediately.

Rather Sweet Sangria

Sweet and sour at the same time, pomegranate molasses is a staple of Middle Eastern cooking that is beginning to gain notice in the United States. It's made by boiling down pomegranate juice until it reaches a molasses-like consistency. I sometimes include it in salad dressings, using it in much the same way as balsamic vinegar. Here it adds a piquant kick to the sangria we serve in our upstairs dining room. I favor the Indo-European brand, available in specialty food stores.

YIELD: 8 SERVINGS

SIMPLE SYRUP

- 4 cups water
- 3¹/2 cups sugar
- 2 fresh limes, preferably organic, halved
- 2 fresh lemons, preferably organic, halved

SANGRIA

- 1 (750 ml) bottle fruity red Spanish wine, such as a Rioja
- 2 cups (475 ml) brandy
- 1 tablespoon pomegranate molasses
- Juice of 1 lime
- 2 (16.9-ounce) bottles chilled sparkling water, such as San Pellegrino
- 1 fresh lime, preferably organic, sliced
- Seeds of 1 pomegranate

TO MAKE THE SIMPLE SYRUP: Combine the water, sugar, limes, and lemons in a large saucepan over medium-high heat. Simmer for 30 minutes, until syrupy. Remove the saucepan from the heat and cool the syrup about 30 minutes. Squeeze the juice from the lime and lemon halves into the syrup. Pour the syrup into a clean glass jar, cover, and refrigerate until needed. It will keep at least 1 month in the refrigerator.

TO MAKE THE SANGRIA: Combine the wine, 2 cups of the simple syrup, brandy, pomegranate molasses, and lime juice in a large bowl. Chill until ready to serve. Add the sparkling water, lime slices, and pomegranate seeds just before serving. Ladle into ice-filled glasses.

The sangria will keep, covered, for 1 week in the refrigerator. It may get sweeter as it sits. Taste it before serving and add an additional 1 cup chilled wine and 1 bottle of chilled sparkling water if necessary.

Hill Country Guanabana Margaritas

My friend Steve Howard, local chef and caterer, gave me this recipe. Fresh guanabana (or soursop), a tropical fruit with white pulpy insides, is rarely seen outside of its native Latin America. But guanabana nectar, with its sweet-acid taste, is readily available in this country and can be found in Latin American markets under the Goya label.

YIELD: 4 SERVINGS

¹/₄ cup freshly squeezed lime juice

¹/₄ cup freshly squeezed lemon juice

³/₄ cups **Cuervo Gold tequila**

3 tablespoons **Grand Marnier**

1 tablespoon powdered sugar

¹/₄ cup guanabana nectar

1 cup crushed ice

Coarse sugar, for coating the rims of the glasses

1 lime wedge

Mix the lime juice, lemon juice, tequila, Grand Marnier, sugar, and guanabana nectar in a large cocktail shaker. Add the crushed ice and shake until cold. Pour coarse sugar onto a small plate. Rub the edge of 4 cocktail glasses with the lime wedge and dip in the coarse sugar. Use a cocktail strainer to pour the drinks into the glasses. Serve immediately.

No Bull Bloody Marys

This recipe is an attempt to re-create a drink one of my chefs admired at Chicago's Mad Bar, which I'm told has closed. The combination of Guinness, vodka, and tomato juice may sound strange to the uninitiated, but it is delicious. (Midwestern red beer drinkers should feel right at home with this heady concoction.)

Don't forget to use our local favorite, Tito's Handmade Vodka (www.titos-vodka.com), made in Austin at a micro-distillery. The winner of several national awards, Tito's beat out several of the vodka biggies, companies that spend millions on advertising annually. Owner Tito Beveridge, who calls himself a fifth-generation Texan, apparently endured endless ribbing about his last name while growing up in San Antonio. Who knew he'd get the last laugh?

YIELD: 4 SERVINGS

4 cups tomato juice

Juice of 2 limes

4 shots high-quality vodka

2 teaspoons fresh or prepared horseradish

2 teaspoons Worcestershire sauce

1 teaspoon celery salt

Hot pepper sauce, such as Tabasco

Salt and freshly ground black pepper

Coarse salt, for coating the rims of the mugs

1 (12-ounce) ice-cold can Draft Guinness

Pimiento-filled green olives, for garnish (optional)

Combine the tomato juice, lime juice, vodka, horseradish, Worcestershire sauce, celery salt, hot pepper sauce, and salt and pepper to taste in a large pitcher filled with ice. Dampen the rims of 4 beer mugs with water and dip them in a bowl of coarse salt. Divide the tomato juice mixture evenly among the mugs. Float 3 ounces of Guinness on top of each and serve immediately. Garnish with green olives speared on colorful toothpicks.

Index

A

Acute Catering, 135
Albert, Uncle, 59, 151
Allbritton, Olivia, 191
All-Sold-Out Chicken Pot Pies, 180–82
Almonds
    Almond Bliss German Chocolate
      Cake, 112–14
    Almond Tuiles, 118–19
    Apple-Almond Chicken Salad with
      Homemade Mayonnaise, 158–59
    Chock-Full-of-Nuts Cookies, 132
    Custard Icing, 112, 113
    Dulce de Leche–Arborio Rice
      Pudding, 106–7
    Dulce de Leche Macaroons, 142
    Jonnie's Breakfast Granola, 13
    Jubilation Granola Chews, 210
    Mrs. Chisholm's Divinity, 79
    Muchas Leches Cake with Sugared
      Almonds, 109–11
    Ruby-Flecked Florentines, 141
    Texas Big Hairs Lemon-Lime
      Meringue Tarts, 32–34
American Beauty Cake, 84–85
Angel Food Cake, 92–93
Anthony's, 42
Apples
    Apple-Almond Chicken Salad with
      Homemade Mayonnaise, 158–59
    Apple Crostatas, 62
    Chef Mark's Southern Comfort
      Apple Pie, 53–54
    Mini Apple-Cinnamon Loaves with
      Calvados Glaze, 99–100
    Nuevo Texas Waldorf Salad, 156–57
    preventing browning of, 157
Apple-Smoked Bacon and Cheddar
    Scones, 24–26
Ashley (friend of Frances), 31
Aunt Mollie's Coconut Cream Pie,
    50–51

B

Bacon
    Apple-Smoked Bacon and Cheddar
      Scones, 24–26
    Individual Baked Omelets, 19
    Savory Fried Pies, 48
Baker's Joy, 67
Balsamic Vinaigrette, 160–61
Bananas
    Banana Bran Muffins, 21
    Banana Pancakes, 18
    Bananas Foster Shortcakes, 90–91
    Banana Syrup, 90–91
    Chocolate-Banana Pancakes, 18
    Franny's Fave Peanut
      Butter–Banana Cream Pie with
      Hot Fudge Sauce, 196–98
    freezing overripe, 21
    preventing browning of, 198
Bars
    Blackberry Pie Bars, 146
    Chocolate–Pecan Pie Bars, 145
    cutting, into diamonds, 145
    Jubilation Granola Chews, 210
    Lemon-Champagne Bars with
      Strawberry Brûlée, 147–48
    Oatmeal Crisps, 77
    Sticky-Fingers Bars, 193–94
    Texas Pecan Pie Bars, 145
Basic Pie Crust, 50–51
Beef
    Brie and Brisket Quesadillas, 174–75
    Ground Beef Gorditas, 186–87
Beer
    Beer Bread, 153
    No Bull Bloody Marys, 219
Beveridge, Tito, 219
Bill (customer), 83
Biscotti, Bunches of, 148–49
Black-and-White Cranberry Tarts,
    43–44
Blackberries
    Blackberry Pie Bars, 146
    defrosting, 146
Blair House, 11
Bloody Marys, No Bull, 219
Blueberries
    Fourth of July Fried Pies, 47–48
    Frangelico-Hazelnut Fruit Tart,
      42–43
Bob (customer), 7
Bourbon
    Bourbon Pumpkin Tart with
      Streusel Topping, 38–39
    Tommye Wood's Milk (Sure
      Packs a) Punch, 216
Bran Muffins, Banana, 21

Bread
  Beer Bread, 153
  Crème Brûlée French Toast, 20
  Eddie's Autumn Pumpkin Bread
    with Pecan Streusel Topping,
    12–13
  Fresh Ginger-Pear Quick Bread, 11
  Mini Apple-Cinnamon Loaves
    with Calvados Glaze, 99–100
  Rather Sweet Bread and Cheese
    Board, 177
Bread Alone, 4, 12, 24
Brie and Brisket Quesadillas, 174–75
Brownies
  Caramel-Filled Brownies, 135–36
  Plain, Old-Fashioned Brownies, 136
  Toffee Bar Brownie Torte, 102–3
  Turbo-Charged Brownies with
    Praline Topping, 137–38
Bruce (customer), 7
Bunches of Biscotti, 148–49
Buttermilk Pecan Pie, 45

C
Caesar Salad Pizzas, 163–64
Café Annie, 120
Café Chocolate-Cherry Bites, 133
Cakes. See also Cheesecakes; Cupcakes
  Almond Bliss German Chocolate
    Cake, 112–14
  American Beauty Cake, 84–85
  Angel Food Cake, 92–93
    dividing batter for, 136
  Glazed Lemon-Cranberry Loaf
    Cake, 76–77
  Mahogany Cake, 70–71
  Mexican Chocolate Fudge–Pecan
    Cake, 67–69
  Muchas Leches Cake with Sugared
    Almonds, 109–11
  Orange-Date Bundt Cake, 72–73
  Peach Queen Cake with Dulce de
    Leche Buttercream Frosting,
    94–95
  Seventh Heaven Chocolate Truffle
    Cake, 114–16
  Strawberry Ricotta Cake, 92–93
  Totally Rummy Pound Cake, 74–75
  Tropical Carrot Cake with Coconut–
    Cream Cheese Frosting, 122–23
  Tuxedo Cake, 86–88
  White-on-White Buttermilk Cake
    with Jack Daniel's Buttercream,
    120–21

Calvados Glaze, 99, 100
Cappuccino Cheesecakes, 78
Caramel-Filled Brownies, 135–36
Caramel Sauce, 97, 98–99
Carrot Cake, Tropical, with Coconut–
  Cream Cheese Frosting, 122–23
Central Market, 66
Cheese
  All-Sold-Out Chicken Pot Pies,
    180–82
  Apple-Smoked Bacon and
    Cheddar Scones, 24–26
  Brie and Brisket Quesadillas, 174–75
  Caesar Salad Pizzas, 163–64
  Cappuccino Cheesecakes, 78
  Cheese-Filled Kolaches, 16
  Cream Cheese Frosting, 211
  Cream-Filled Pumpkin Roll, 97–99
  Field Greens with Spiced Pecans,
    Goat Cheese, and Balsamic
    Vinaigrette, 160–61
  Fredericksburg Peach Cream
    Cheese Tart, 40–41
  Ground Beef Gorditas, 186–87
  Gulf Coast Shrimp Quesadillas,
    172–73
  King Ranch Casserole, 184–85
  Larger-than-Life Praline Cheese-
    cake, 89–90
  Nuevo Texas Waldorf Salad, 156–57
  "Pizza" Fried Pies, 48
  Rather Sweet Bread and Cheese
    Board, 177
  Savory Crab and Shrimp Cheese-
    cake, 188–89
  Savory Fried Pies, 48
  Strawberry Ricotta Cake, 92–93
  Tiramisù with Homemade
    Ladyfingers, 104–5
  Toffee Bar Brownie Torte, 102–3
  Tropical Carrot Cake with Coconut–
    Cream Cheese Frosting, 122–23
Cheesecakes
  Cappuccino Cheesecakes, 78
  Larger-than-Life Praline Cheese-
    cake, 89–90
  Savory Crab and Shrimp Cheese-
    cake, 188–89
Chef Mark's Southern Comfort Apple
  Pie, 53–54
Cherries, dried
  Café Chocolate-Cherry Bites, 133
  Jonnie's Breakfast Granola, 13
  Mrs. Chisholm's Divinity, 79

Cherries, fresh
  Black-and-White Cherry Tarts, 44
  Fourth of July Fried Pies, 47–48
  pitting, 48
Chicken
  All-Sold-Out Chicken Pot Pies,
    180–82
  Apple-Almond Chicken Salad with
    Homemade Mayonnaise, 158–59
  Chicken Satay with Yogurt-
    Cucumber Dipping Sauce,
    162–63
  King Ranch Casserole, 184–85
  Texas Tortilla Soup, 170–72
Chickpea and Wild Rice Salad, 167
Chiles
  Curry Paste, 162, 163
  Green Chile Crab Cakes with
    Tomatillo Salsa, 178–79
  King Ranch Casserole, 184–85
  roasting, 185
  Texas Tortilla Soup, 170–72
Chisholm, Mrs., 79
Chock-Full-of-Nuts Cookies, 132
Chocolate
  Almond Bliss German Chocolate
    Cake, 112–14
  American Beauty Cake, 84–85
  Black-and-White Cranberry Tarts,
    43–44
  Café Chocolate-Cherry Bites, 133
  Cappuccino Cheesecakes, 78
  Caramel-Filled Brownies, 135–36
  Chocolate-Banana Pancakes, 18
  Chocolate-Caramel Ganache, 204,
    205
  Chocolate Chip Scones, 23
  Chocolate-Dipped Macaroons,
    142–43
  Chocolate-Flavored Buttercream,
    121
  Chocolate Glaze, 86, 88
  Chocolate-Pecan Glaze, 67, 69
  Chocolate–Pecan Pie Bars, 145
  Dark Chocolate Glaze, 84, 85
  Dulce de Leche Macaroons, 142
  Franny's Fave Peanut
    Butter–Banana Cream Pie with
    Hot Fudge Sauce, 196–98
  Ganache, 36–37, 78
  Ganache Frosting, 114–15
  Grasshopper Parfaits, 57
  Grasshopper Pie, 56–57
  Mahogany Cake, 70–71

Chocolate, *continued*
  Mahogany Icing, 70–71
  Mars Pies, 204–5
  Mexican Chocolate Fudge–Pecan
    Cake, 67–69
  Milk Chocolate Mousse, 84, 85
  My Favorite Chocolate Chip
    Cookies, 127
  Peanut Buttercups with Peanut-
    Penuche Icing, 200–201
  Plain, Old-Fashioned Brownies, 136
  Seventh Heaven Chocolate Truffle
    Cake, 114–16
  Silken Chocolate-Walnut Tart, 55
  Sticky-Fingers Bars, 193–94
  Texas Big Hairs Chocolate-Hazel-
    nut Meringue Tarts, 36–37
  Toffee Bar Brownie Torte, 102–3
  Triple-Threat Chocolate Chip
    Cookies, 128–30
  Triple-Threat Rocky Road Cookies,
    130
  Turbo-Charged Brownies with
    Praline Topping, 137–38
  Tuxedo Cake, 86–88
Cinnamon Rolls, Jailhouse Potato-,
  8–10
Clement, Martin, 184
Cobblers
  Hill Country Peach Cobbler, 65
  Individual Pear-Maple Cobblers, 66
Cocoa powder, 69
Coconut
  Almond Bliss German Chocolate
    Cake, 112–14
  Aunt Mollie's Coconut Cream Pie,
    50–51
  Chocolate-Dipped Macaroons,
    142–43
  Chocolate–Pecan Pie Bars, 145
  Coconut Cream Flan, 80
  Custard Icing, 112, 113
  Dulce de Leche Macaroons, 142
  Jonnie's Breakfast Granola, 13
  Jubilation Granola Chews, 210
  Muchas Leches Cake with Sugared
    Almonds, 109–11
  Oatmeal Crisps, 77
  Texas Pecan Pie Bars, 145
  Tropical Carrot Cake with
    Coconut– Cream Cheese Frost-
    ing, 122–23
Coffee
  Café Chocolate-Cherry Bites, 133

Cappuccino Cheesecakes, 78
Espresso Crème Brûlée, 100–101
Mahogany Cake, 70–71
Mahogany Icing, 70–71
Tiramisù with Homemade
  Ladyfingers, 104–5
Toffee Bar Brownie Torte, 102–3
Turbo-Charged Brownies with
  Praline Topping, 137–38
Commander's Palace, 90
Connolly, Lynn, 168
Cookies. *See also* Bars; Brownies
  Almond Tuiles, 118–19
  Bunches of Biscotti, 148–49
  Café Chocolate-Cherry Bites, 133
  checking doneness of, 133
  Chock-Full-of-Nuts Cookies, 132
  Chocolate-Dipped Macaroons,
    142–43
  crème-filled chocolate, 44
  dividing batter for, 136
  Double-Ginger Chews, 140
  Dulce de Leche Macaroons, 142
  freezing dough for, 204
  Ginger People, 194–95
  Maple-Glazed Oatmeal Cookies, 209
  My Favorite Chocolate Chip
    Cookies, 127
  PB&J Cookies with Honey-Roasted
    Peanuts, 203–4
  Plain Peanut Butter Cookies, 203–4
  Pretty-in-Pink Shortbread Pigs,
    206–8
  scooping dough for, 125–26
  Snow-Tipped Sand Tarts, 143
  Sugar Saucers, 130–31
  Triple-Threat Chocolate Chip
    Cookies, 128–30
  Triple-Threat Rocky Road Cookies,
    130
Corn Muffins, Rather Rich, 157
Cox, Mark, 53, 118
Crab
  Green Chile Crab Cakes with
    Tomatillo Salsa, 178–79
  Savory Crab and Shrimp Cheese-
    cake, 188–89
Cranberries, dried
  Jonnie's Breakfast Granola, 13
  Jubilation Granola Chews, 210
  Maple-Glazed Oatmeal Cookies, 209
  Mrs. Chisholm's Divinity, 79
  Ruby-Flecked Florentines, 141

Cranberries, fresh
  Black-and-White Cranberry Tarts,
    43–44
  Glazed Lemon-Cranberry Loaf
    Cake, 76–77
Cream, whipping, 111
Cream-Filled Pumpkin Roll, 97–99
Cream Sauce, 180, 182, 184, 185
Crème brûlée
  Crème Brûlée French Toast, 20
  Espresso Crème Brûlée, 100–101
Crostatas
  Apple Crostatas, 62
  Emergency Fruit Crostatas, 61–62
Cucumber-Yogurt Dipping Sauce,
  162–63
Cunningham, Rhonda, 151
Cupcakes
  Mexican Chocolate Fudge–Pecan
    Cake, 67–69
  Peanut Buttercups with Peanut-
    Penuche Icing, 200–201
  Pumpkin Yumkins, 211
Curried Butternut Squash Soup, 169
Curry Paste, 162, 163
Custard Icing, 112, 113

D
Dark Chocolate Glaze, 84, 85
David (friend), 47
Detering, Kit and Carl, 167
Disbrowe, Paula, 167
Divinity, Mrs. Chisholm's, 79
Double-Ginger Chews, 140
Drinks
  Frothy Vanilla Milk, 215
  Hill Country Guanabana
    Margaritas, 218
  No Bull Bloody Marys, 219
  Rather Sweet Sangria, 217
  Tommye Wood's Milk (Sure
    Packs a) Punch, 216
  Watermelon Lemonade, 214
Dulce de leche
  Dulce de Leche–Arborio Rice
    Pudding, 106–7
  Dulce de Leche Buttercream
    Frosting, 94–95
  Dulce de Leche Macaroons, 142

E
Eddie's Autumn Pumpkin Bread with
  Pecan Streusel Topping, 12–13
Eggs. *See also* Meringue
  Egg Kolaches, 17

Homemade Mayonnaise, 158
Individual Baked Omelets, 19
separating, 85
whites, beating, 85
whites, leftover, 114
Emergency Fruit Crostatas, 61–62
Emily (customer), 7
Emily, Miss, 182
Espresso Crème Brûlée, 100–101
Essence of Orange Muffins, 27

F
A Fare Extraordinaire, 40, 76
Field Greens with Spiced Pecans,
    Goat Cheese, and Balsamic
    Vinaigrette, 160–61
Flan, Coconut Cream, 80
Flaxseed, 210
Fourth of July Fried Pies, 47–48
Frances (daughter), 4, 31, 135, 165,
    191, 196
Frangelico-Hazelnut Fruit Tart, 42–43
Franny's Fave Peanut Butter–Banana
    Cream Pie with Hot Fudge
    Sauce, 196–98
Fredericksburg Peach Cream Cheese
    Tart, 40–41
French Toast, Crème Brûlée, 20
Fresh Ginger-Pear Quick Bread, 11
Fried Wonton Strips, 156
Frostings. See Icings and frostings
Frothy Vanilla Milk, 215
Fruit, dried. See also individual fruits
    Jonnie's Breakfast Granola, 13
    Mrs. Chisholm's Divinity, 79
    Ruby-Flecked Florentines, 141
Fruit, fresh. See also individual fruits
    Emergency Fruit Crostatas, 61–62
    Frangelico-Hazelnut Fruit Tart,
        42–43
    Petite Pavlovas with Lemon Cream
        and Fresh Fruit, 64–65
    preventing browning of, 198
    Rather Sweet Bread and Cheese
        Board, 177
    Watermelon Lemonade, 214

G
Ganache, 36–37, 78
    Chocolate-Caramel Ganache, 204,
        205
    Ganache Frosting, 114–15
Garrido, David, 183
Ginger
    Double-Ginger Chews, 140

Fresh Ginger-Pear Quick Bread, 11
Ginger Crust, 89
Ginger People, 194–95
Glazed Lemon-Cranberry Loaf Cake,
    76–77
Glazes
    Calvados Glaze, 99, 100
    Chocolate Glaze, 86, 88
    Chocolate-Pecan Glaze, 67, 69
    Dark Chocolate Glaze, 84, 85
    Lemon Glaze, 28–29, 76, 77
    Maple Glaze, 209
    Orange Glaze, 27
Gorditas, Ground Beef, 186–87
Granola
    Jonnie's Breakfast Granola, 13
    Jubilation Granola Chews, 210
Grasshopper Parfaits, 57
Grasshopper Pie, 56–57
Green Chile Crab Cakes with
    Tomatillo Salsa, 178–79
Greens
    Field Greens with Spiced Pecans,
        Goat Cheese, and Balsamic
        Vinaigrette, 160–61
    Prosciutto Tostadas with Shrimp
        and Parsley, 183
Griffin, Wanda, 151
Ground Beef Gorditas, 186–87
Guanabana Margaritas, Hill Country,
    218
Gulf Coast Shrimp Quesadillas, 172–73

H
Hall, Gloria and Ken, 31
Hart & Hind Fitness Ranch, 167
Hazelnuts
    Bunches of Biscotti, 148–49
    Frangelico-Hazelnut Fruit Tart,
        42–43
    Texas Big Hairs Chocolate-
        Hazelnut Meringue Tarts, 36–37
Hemwattakit, Jeannie, 120
Hierholzer, Aaron, 191–92
Hill Country Guanabana Margaritas,
    218
Hill Country Peach Cobbler, 65
Homemade Mayonnaise, 158
Hot Fudge Sauce, 196, 198
Howard, Steve, 218

I
Ice cream
    Bananas Foster Shortcakes, 90–91
    sandwiches, 140

Tommye Wood's Milk (Sure
    Packs a) Punch, 216
Icings and frostings. See also Glazes
    Chocolate-Caramel Ganache, 204,
        205
    Chocolate-Flavored Buttercream,
        121
    Coconut–Cream Cheese Frosting,
        122, 123
    Cream Cheese Frosting, 211
    Custard Icing, 112, 113
    Dulce de Leche Buttercream
        Frosting, 94–95
    Ganache, 36–37, 78
    Ganache Frosting, 114–15
    Jack Daniel's Buttercream, 120, 121
    Mahogany Icing, 70–71
    Peanut-Penuche Icing, 200, 201
    Powdered Sugar Icing, 206, 208
    Royal Icing, 195
    Whipped Cream Frosting, 86, 88,
        92, 93
Individual Baked Omelets, 19
Individual Pear-Maple Cobblers, 66
Island Crab Company, 179

J
Jack Daniel's Buttercream, 120, 121
Jackson, Nancy, 194
Jailhouse Potato-Cinnamon Rolls,
    8–10
Jeffrey's, 183
Jim (customer), 7
Joanie (customer), 7
Jones, Nancy, 151
Jonnie's Breakfast Granola, 13
Jubilation Granola Chews, 210

K
Kamp, Dan, 31
Kaplan, Doreen and Richard, 135
King Ranch Casserole, 184–85
Kolaches, 15–17

L
Ladyfingers, Homemade, Tiramisù
    with, 104–5
Lambert, Paula, 177
Lane, Mariana, 4
Larger-than-Life Praline Cheese-
    cake, 89–90
Leader, Daniel, 24, 191
Lemons
    Glazed Lemon-Cranberry Loaf
        Cake, 76–77

Lemons, *continued*
    Lemon-Champagne Bars with
        Strawberry Brûlée, 147–48
    Lemon Glaze, 28–29, 76, 77
    Lemon-Lime Curd, 32, 34
    Lemon Zest Tart Crust, 40–41
    Petite Pavlovas with Lemon Cream
        and Fresh Fruit, 64–65
    Texas Big Hairs Lemon-Lime
        Meringue Tarts, 32–34
    Watermelon Lemonade, 214
    Whole Lemon Muffins, 28–29
    zesting, 34
Lerner, Karen, 40, 76
Limes
    Lemon-Lime Curd, 32, 34
    No Bull Bloody Marys, 219
    Rather Sweet Sangria, 217
    Texas Big Hairs Lemon-Lime
        Meringue Tarts, 32–34
    zesting, 34
Lyle's Golden Syrup, 17, 193

M
Macadamia nuts
    Chock-Full-of-Nuts Cookies, 132
    Tropical Carrot Cake with
        Coconut–Cream Cheese
        Frosting, 122–23
Macaroons
    Chocolate-Dipped Macaroons,
        142–43
    Dulce de Leche Macaroons, 142
MacWhithey, Lynn, 151
Mad Bar, 219
Mahogany Cake, 70–71
Mahogany Icing, 70–71
Maple syrup, 209
    Individual Pear-Maple Cobblers, 66
    Maple-Glazed Oatmeal Cookies, 209
Margaritas, Hill Country Guanabana,
    218
Mark's, 53
Marshmallows
    Grasshopper Pie, 56–57
    Mars Pies, 204–5
    Triple-Threat Rocky Road Cookies,
        130
Mars Pies, 204–5
Mary (customer), 83
Mayes, Lauren, 191
Mayo, Suzie Humphreys, 182
Mayonnaise, Homemade, 158
Meagan (customer), 7

Meringue
    Aunt Mollie's Coconut Cream Pie,
        50–51
    Petite Pavlovas with Lemon Cream
        and Fresh Fruit, 64–65
    Texas Big Hairs Chocolate-
        Hazelnut Meringue Tarts, 36–37
    Texas Big Hairs Lemon-Lime
        Meringue Tarts, 32–34
Mexican Chocolate Fudge–Pecan
    Cake, 67–69
Microplane, 34, 105
Milk Chocolate Mousse, 84, 85
Mini Apple-Cinnamon Loaves with
    Calvados Glaze, 99–100
Mitchell, Brenda Greene, 45
Mitchell, Mollie Wright, 50
Mother's Day Pancakes, 18
Mousse
    Milk Chocolate Mousse, 84, 85
    White Chocolate–Snickers Mousse,
        118–19
Mozzarella Company, 177
Mrs. Chisholm's Divinity, 79
Muchas Leches Cake with Sugared
    Almonds, 109–11
Muffins
    Banana Bran Muffins, 21
    Eddie's Autumn Pumpkin Bread with
        Pecan Streusel Topping, 12–13
    Essence of Orange Muffins, 27
    filling tins for, 29
    Pumpkin Yumkins, 211
    Rather Rich Corn Muffins, 157
    Whole Lemon Muffins, 28–29
Mushrooms
    cremini, 168
    King Ranch Casserole, 184–85
    Wild Mushroom Soup, 168
Mustard, Mary, 151
My Favorite Chocolate Chip Cookies,
    127

N
No Bull Bloody Marys, 219
Nuevo Texas Waldorf Salad, 156–57
Nuts. *See also individual nuts*
    Chock-Full-of-Nuts Cookies, 132
    Mrs. Chisholm's Divinity, 79
    toasting, 132

O
Oats
    Jonnie's Breakfast Granola, 13
    Jubilation Granola Chews, 210

Maple-Glazed Oatmeal Cookies, 209
    Oatmeal Crisps, 77
    types of, 77
Omelets, Individual Baked, 19
Oranges
    Essence of Orange Muffins, 27
    Orange-Date Bundt Cake, 72–73
    Orange Glaze, 27
    Orange-Potato Rolls, 10
    zesting, 34
Oxford, Kay, 18

P
Pam (customer), 7
Pancakes
    Banana Pancakes, 18
    Chocolate-Banana Pancakes, 18
    Mother's Day Pancakes, 18
Panzica, Kris, 162
Parfaits, Grasshopper, 57
Parrish, Don, 128
Pasqual, 168
Pavlovas, Petite, with Lemon Cream
    and Fresh Fruit, 64–65
PB&J Cookies with Honey-Roasted
    Peanuts, 203–4
Peaches
    Fourth of July Fried Pies, 47–48
    Fredericksburg Peach Cream
        Cheese Tart, 40–41
    Hill Country Peach Cobbler, 65
    Peach-Filled Kolaches, 16–17
    Peach Jam Scones, 22
    Peach Queen Cake with Dulce de
        Leche Buttercream Frosting,
        94–95
Peanuts and peanut butter
    Franny's Fave Peanut
        Butter–Banana Cream Pie with
        Hot Fudge Sauce, 196–98
    Jubilation Granola Chews, 210
    PB&J Cookies with Honey-Roasted
        Peanuts, 203–4
    Peanut Buttercups with Peanut-
        Penuche Icing, 200–201
    Plain Peanut Butter Cookies, 203–4
    Sticky-Fingers Bars, 193–94
Pears
    Frangelico-Hazelnut Fruit Tart,
        42–43
    Fresh Ginger-Pear Quick Bread, 11
    Individual Pear-Maple Cobblers, 66
Pecans
    Buttermilk Pecan Pie, 45

Café Chocolate-Cherry Bites, 133
Caramel-Filled Brownies, 135–36
Chef Mark's Southern Comfort
    Apple Pie, 53–54
Chock-Full-of-Nuts Cookies, 132
Chocolate Chip Scones, 23
Chocolate-Pecan Glaze, 67, 69
Chocolate–Pecan Pie Bars, 145
Cream-Filled Pumpkin Roll, 97–99
Eddie's Autumn Pumpkin Bread
    with Pecan Streusel Topping,
    12–13
Jailhouse Potato-Cinnamon Rolls,
    8–10
Larger-than-Life Praline Cheese-
    cake, 89–90
Mexican Chocolate Fudge–Pecan
    Cake, 67–69
Mini Apple-Cinnamon Loaves
    with Calvados Glaze, 99–100
Mrs. Chisholm's Divinity, 79
My Favorite Chocolate Chip
    Cookies, 127
Nuevo Texas Waldorf Salad, 156–57
Orange-Date Bundt Cake, 72–73
Peach Queen Cake with Dulce de
    Leche Buttercream Frosting,
    94–95
Plain, Old-Fashioned Brownies,
    136
Pumpkin Yumkins, 211
Spiced Pecans, 160
Texas Big Hairs Lemon-Lime
    Meringue Tarts, 32–34
Texas Pecan Pie Bars, 145
Texas Pralines, 81
Totally Rummy Pound Cake, 74–75
Triple-Threat Chocolate Chip
    Cookies, 128–30
Triple-Threat Rocky Road Cookies,
    130
Turbo-Charged Brownies with
    Praline Topping, 137–38
Whole Lemon Muffins, 28–29
Petite Pavlovas with Lemon Cream
    and Fresh Fruit, 64–65
Pies
    All-Sold-Out Chicken Pot Pies,
        180–82
    Aunt Mollie's Coconut Cream Pie,
        50–51
    baking dough scraps from, 51
    Basic Pie Crust, 50–51
    Buttermilk Pecan Pie, 45

Chef Mark's Southern Comfort
    Apple Pie, 53–54
Fourth of July Fried Pies, 47–48
Franny's Fave Peanut
    Butter–Banana Cream Pie with
    Hot Fudge Sauce, 196–98
Grasshopper Pie, 56–57
"Pizza" Fried Pies, 48
Savory Fried Pies, 48
"Pizza" Fried Pies, 48
Pizzas, Caesar Salad, 163–64
Plain, Old-Fashioned Brownies, 136
Plain Peanut Butter Cookies, 203–4
Pomegranate molasses, 217
Potatoes
    Individual Baked Omelets, 19
    Jailhouse Potato-Cinnamon Rolls,
        8–10
    Orange-Potato Rolls, 10
Pot Pies, All-Sold-Out Chicken,
    180–82
Pound Cake, Totally Rummy, 74–75
Powdered Sugar Icing, 206, 208
Pralines, Texas, 81
Pretty-in-Pink Shortbread Pigs,
    206–8
Prosciutto Tostadas with Shrimp and
    Parsley, 183
Pudding, Dulce de Leche–Arborio
    Rice, 106–7
Pumpkin
    Bourbon Pumpkin Tart with
        Streusel Topping, 38–39
    Cream-Filled Pumpkin Roll, 97–99
    Eddie's Autumn Pumpkin Bread
        with Pecan Streusel Topping,
        12–13
    Larger-than-Life Praline Cheese-
        cake, 89–90
    Pumpkin Yumkins, 211
Punch, Tommye Wood's Milk (Sure
    Packs a), 216
Pure Luck Texas, 177

Q
Quesadillas
    Brie and Brisket Quesadillas, 174–75
    Gulf Coast Shrimp Quesadillas,
        172–73

R
Rand (customer), 7
Raspberry Tarts, Black-and-White, 44
Rather Rich Corn Muffins, 157

Rather Sweet Bread and Cheese
    Board, 177
Rather Sweet Sangria, 217
Reedy, Jill, 109
Rice Pudding, Dulce de Leche–
    Arborio, 106–7
Ricotta Cake, Strawberry, 92–93
Robertson, Kim, 60
Rocket Rolls, 154–55
Rolls
    Cream-Filled Pumpkin Roll, 97–99
    Jailhouse Potato-Cinnamon Rolls,
        8–10
    Orange-Potato Rolls, 10
    Rocket Rolls, 154–55
Rosemary Vinaigrette, 156
Royal Icing, 195
Ruby-Flecked Florentines, 141
Rum
    Banana Syrup, 90–91
    Coconut Cream Flan, 80
    Tiramisù with Homemade
        Ladyfingers, 104–5
    Tommye Wood's Milk (Sure
        Packs a) Punch, 216
    Totally Rummy Pound Cake, 74–75

S
Safflower oil, 187
Salads
    Apple-Almond Chicken Salad with
        Homemade Mayonnaise, 158–59
    Caesar Salad Pizzas, 163–64
    Field Greens with Spiced Pecans,
        Goat Cheese, and Balsamic
        Vinaigrette, 160–61
    Nuevo Texas Waldorf Salad, 156–57
    Wild Rice and Chickpea Salad, 167
Salsas
    Mango Salsa, 172–73
    Tomatillo Salsa, 178
Sangria, Rather Sweet, 217
Satay, Chicken, with Yogurt-Cucum-
    ber Dipping Sauce, 162–63
Sauces
    Caramel Sauce, 97, 98–99
    Cream Sauce, 180, 182, 184, 185
    Hot Fudge Sauce, 196, 198
    Mango Barbecue Sauce, 174–75
    Yogurt-Cucumber Dipping Sauce,
        162–63
Sausage
    "Pizza" Fried Pies, 48
    Sausage Kolaches, 16

Sausage, *continued*
Savory Crab and Shrimp Cheesecake, 188–89
Savory Fried Pies, 48
Schlotzsky's, 4, 12
Scones
  Apple-Smoked Bacon and Cheddar Scones, 24–26
  Chocolate Chip Scones, 23
  Peach Jam Scones, 22
Sears, DeAnn, 213
Seventh Heaven Chocolate Truffle Cake, 114–16
Shortbread Pigs, Pretty-in-Pink, 206–8
Shortcakes, Bananas Foster, 90–91
Shrimp
  Gulf Coast Shrimp Quesadillas, 172–73
  Prosciutto Tostadas with Shrimp and Parsley, 183
  Savory Crab and Shrimp Cheesecake, 188–89
Silicone baking mats, 126
Silken Chocolate-Walnut Tart, 55
Simple Syrup, 217
Snow-Tipped Sand Tarts, 143
Soups
  Curried Butternut Squash Soup, 169
  Texas Tortilla Soup, 170–72
  Wild Mushroom Soup, 168
Southern Comfort Apple Pie, Chef Mark's, 53–54
Spiced Pecans, 160
Squash Soup, Curried Butternut, 169
Stansbury, Jonnie, 11, 13, 92
Star Canyon, 109
Stenicka, Charlie, 15
Steve (colleague), 12
Sticky-Fingers Bars, 193–94
Stowe, Madeleine, 86
Strawberries
  Lemon-Champagne Bars with Strawberry Brûlée, 147–48
  Strawberry Ricotta Cake, 92–93
Sugar Saucers, 130–31
Sugar Syrup, 214
Syrups
  Banana Syrup, 90–91
  Lyle's Golden Syrup, 17, 193
  Simple Syrup, 217
  Sugar Syrup, 214

T
Tarts
  Black-and-White Cranberry Tarts, 43–44
  Bourbon Pumpkin Tart with Streusel Topping, 38–39
  Frangelico-Hazelnut Fruit Tart, 42–43
  Fredericksburg Peach Cream Cheese Tart, 40–41
  Lemon Zest Tart Crust, 40–41
  Silken Chocolate-Walnut Tart, 55
  Texas Big Hairs Chocolate-Hazelnut Meringue Tarts, 36–37
  Texas Big Hairs Lemon-Lime Meringue Tarts, 32–34
Texas Pecan Pie Bars, 145
Texas Pralines, 81
Texas Tortilla Soup, 170–72
Tiramisù with Homemade Ladyfingers, 104–5
Tito's Handmade Vodka, 219
Toffee Bar Brownie Torte, 102–3
Tomatillo Salsa, 178
Tommye Wood's Milk (Sure Packs a) Punch, 216
Tony's, 5, 53, 92, 188
Torte, Toffee Bar Brownie, 102–3
Tostadas, Prosciutto, with Shrimp and Parsley, 183
Totally Rummy Pound Cake, 74–75
Triple-Threat Chocolate Chip Cookies, 128–30
Triple-Threat Rocky Road Cookies, 130
Tropical Carrot Cake with Coconut–Cream Cheese Frosting, 122–23
Tuiles, Almond, 118–19
Turbo-Charged Brownies with Praline Topping, 137–38
Tuxedo Cake, 86–88

V
VelAnne Howle (customer), 3
Vallone, Tony, 4, 5, 118, 188
Vanilla
  bean paste, 101
  Frothy Vanilla Milk, 215
Vinaigrettes
  Balsamic Vinaigrette, 160–61
  Rosemary Vinaigrette, 156

W
Waldorf Salad, Nuevo Texas, 156–57
Walnuts
  Chock-Full-of-Nuts Cookies, 132
  Mrs. Chisholm's Divinity, 79
  My Favorite Chocolate Chip Cookies, 127
  Silken Chocolate-Walnut Tart, 55
  Triple-Threat Chocolate Chip Cookies, 128–30
  Triple-Threat Rocky Road Cookies, 130
  Whole Lemon Muffins, 28–29
Watermelon Lemonade, 214
Whipped Cream Frosting, 86, 88, 92, 93
Whisks, 38–39
White, Mark, 43
White chocolate
  Black-and-White Cranberry Tarts, 43–44
  high-quality, 119
  Snow-Tipped Sand Tarts, 143
  White Chocolate–Snickers Mousse, 118–19
  White-on-White Buttermilk Cake with Jack Daniel's Buttercream, 120–21
Whole Lemon Muffins, 28–29
Wild Mushroom Soup, 168
Wild Rice and Chickpea Salad, 167
Winchester, Dee, 56
Wine
  Lemon-Champagne Bars with Strawberry Brûlée, 147–48
  Rather Sweet Sangria, 217
Wonton Strips, Fried, 156
Wood, Peggy, 80
Wood, Virginia, 1, 130
Wunsche Bros. Cafe, 45
Wynne-Smith, Anna, 169

Y
Yeast, proofing, 10
Yogurt-Cucumber Dipping Sauce, 162–63

Z
Zesting, 34